European Unification in the Sixties

*Published volumes in the series*
*"The Atlantic Policy Studies"*

HENRY A. KISSINGER
The Troubled Partnership:
A Reappraisal of the Atlantic Alliance

ZBIGNIEW BRZEZINSKI
Alternative to Partition: For a
Broader Conception of America's Role in Europe

JOHN O. COPPOCK
Atlantic Agricultural Unity:
Is It Possible?

HAROLD VAN B. CLEVELAND
The Atlantic Idea and Its European Rivals

MIRIAM CAMPS
European Unification in the Sixties:
From the Veto to the Crisis

# European Unification in the Sixties

## *From the Veto to the Crisis*

MIRIAM CAMPS

*A Volume in the series*
*"The Atlantic Policy Studies"*

*Published for the Council on Foreign Relations by*

McGRAW-HILL BOOK COMPANY

*New York Toronto London Sydney*

EUROPEAN UNIFICATION IN THE SIXTIES


Printed in the United States of America.


Library of Congress Catalog Card Number: 66-28829
First Edition
09697

# *Preface*

In October 1964 I finished a Chatham House essay called *What Kind of Europe?* in which I looked at the way the European Economic Community had been developing since General de Gaulle's veto on British membership and speculated a little about the future. That essay was, in a sense, the first instalment of this book, for under a joint arrangement between the Council on Foreign Relations and the Royal Institute of International Affairs in London I had rashly agreed to follow up the Chatham House book with one for the Atlantic Policy Series to be finished a year later. By October 1965, however, the European Community was in the midst of the worst crisis in its history, and it was agreed that I should not complete the book until the outlines of a settlement were clear. Perhaps it was as well that I was committed to finishing the book as soon as the end of the Community crisis was in sight, for the French decision to withdraw from the NATO integrated system, which was announced soon after their return to Brussels at the end of January, would otherwise have provided an unusually good excuse for further delay.

The Six are trying very hard to keep the backwash of the NATO crisis from swamping the Community. They seem likely to succeed, once again, in keeping their differences over political and defense questions from disastrously affecting the Common Market. Nevertheless, the new pattern of defense arrangements that emerges from the current discussion in the NATO will obviously affect the future development of the Community; possibly it may have important short-term effects as well, on the problem of the British relationship with the Six.

The descriptive and analytical parts of this book continue the chronicle of European developments that I began in *Britain and the European Community 1955–1963* and continued in the Chatham House essay, mentioned above. There is inevitably a little duplication between that essay and this book but not, I think, enough to trouble anyone with sufficient curiosity about these developments to read both books.

Any book about a developing phenomenon like the Community can only be a snapshot taken at a particular time in history. The descriptive part of this book focuses on an exceptionally turbulent period: it begins with General de Gaulle's veto on British membership in January 1963 and ends in the spring of 1966. There is an unplanned neatness about this period. It coincides with the second stage of the transition period laid down in the Treaty of Rome, it is bounded by the two most serious crises in the Community's short history, and it embraces an almost complete cycle in the development of British policy toward Europe. I have added to this picture—and what I think I can see in it—some speculation about the future of the process of European integration. Like the picture itself, the forecast is inevitably strongly affected by the atmosphere of the time in which it is written, the spring of 1966.

In a final chapter I have also indicated why I believe that the process of unification that has been occurring in Europe since the war has been in the interest of the United States and why it is in our interest that the process should continue, even though at times the process will create problems for ourselves and for other third countries. I have tried to look at this question as an American and from an American standpoint, for the consideration of American policy is the purpose of this series. Perhaps I should add that it has not been altogether easy for me to do so, for I now live in England and the arguments for British membership in the

Community seem to me, as a resident of that country, to be quite compelling.

Throughout this book I have used the expression "Europeans" and "Gaullists" much more frequently and rather more loosely than I should have liked. It is very difficult to avoid doing so without becoming unreadably verbose. The terms, when put in quotation marks, are, of course, shorthand descriptions for particular views and attitudes. Each term covers a range of opinion. And on some questions the views of the groups characterized by these terms overlap.

Broadly, the differences between them seem to me to be as follows. Those I have called "Gaullist" follow General de Gaulle in rejecting the concept of "integration" at the European level and of "interdependence" with the United States at the Atlantic level. They accept General de Gaulle's thesis that the nation-state is the only valid entity in international affairs, and that the European countries, linked in some loose coalition, should become a "third force" deliberately rejecting any very close tie with the United States. In contrast, those I have referred to as "Europeans" want to see an integrated Western Europe built on the Community model. Some of them believe that the process should be pushed as quickly as possible to a full federation; others are not yet sure of the ultimate form a united Europe should take but accept the Community method and its extension to other fields. Some of those I call "Europeans" attach importance to seeing the relationship with the United States become closer and more nearly equal at the same time that the European construction is being built; others tend to feel that "Europe" must be "built" before the relationship with the United States can be put on a satisfactory basis. But "Europeans," generally, and in contrast to the "Gaullists," accept the need for a close relationship with the United States and find a satisfactory model for the Atlantic relationship in the "two-pillar" concept.

When one is writing about questions that are the subject of daily discussion all about one it is more than usually difficult to know which thoughts are one's own and which thoughts one owes to others. It is impossible to list all those who have contributed to my understanding of European developments, and it is rather invidious to list only a few. In the writing of this book, I have, however, been particularly conscious of absorbing ideas from Richard Mayne, François Duchêne, John Pinder, Max Kohnstamm, and Robert Marjolin, and from my colleagues at both Chatham House and the Council on Foreign Relations, especially from Kenneth Younger and Andrew Shonfield at the former, and H. van B. Cleveland and William Diebold at the latter. I am very grateful to these friends, and also to the far wider group of Americans and Europeans (of both the Six and the Seven), in and out of the service of many governments and the European institutions, from whom I have learned a great deal over the years.

I should also like to add a special word of thanks to Susan Boyde, the deputy press librarian at Chatham House, for always being able to find the half-remembered reference, and to my secretary, Margaret Youdle, for indispensable help at all stages in the preparation of the manuscript.

M.C.

*May 1966.*

# *The Atlantic Policy Studies*

The Atlantic Policy Studies, a series of major works on the future of the Atlantic Community, was undertaken by the Council on Foreign Relations on the basis of a grant from the Ford Foundation. Miriam Camps' study of the European Community and the prospects for European unification is the fifth of these studies to be published.

Undertaken out of a conviction that a re-examination of United States relations with and policies toward Western Europe is urgently needed, the Atlantic Policy Studies are an attempt to come to grips with basic questions about the future of America's Atlantic relations.

The studies are policy-oriented, seeking not only to describe and forecast but also to prescribe. Each of the eleven studies is the responsibility of its author, but will consider its special problems in the light of the general aim of the program as a whole. The program is under the guidance of a Steering Committee, of which Charles M. Spofford is chairman.

The Atlantic Policy Studies are divided into four broad categories, dealing respectively with the broad strategic problems of the Atlantic Alliance, with Atlantic political relations; with the external environment of the West; and with economic relations among the Atlantic countries and between them and less developed countries.

Mrs. Camps' book is one of three studies of political relations among the Atlantic nations. Stanley Hoffmann of Harvard University gave a series of lectures at the Council in the spring of 1965, which reviewed the principal constraints, particularly the domestic constraints, on United States action in Atlantic affairs. His lectures will be published as a volume in the Atlantic Policy Series. A third political volume, by the Director of the Atlantic Policy Studies, will be addressed to the question of the future shape of political relations among the Atlantic countries.

Two studies have been made of the Atlantic world's external environment. *Alternative to Partition,* by Zbigniew K. Brzezinski of Columbia University, was published by McGraw-Hill in May of 1965. A second study, by Theodore Geiger of the National Planning Association, will examine the nature of the great transition now going on throughout Asia, Africa, and Latin America, and its implications for the future of relations with the Western world.

Atlantic military problems are considered in their political context in Henry A. Kissinger's *The Troubled Partnership: A Reappraisal of the Atlantic Alliance,* which McGraw-Hill published in April, 1965.

Economic problems of the Atlantic nations are the subject of four studies. John O. Coppock's book *Atlantic Agricultural Unity: Is It Possible?* examines agricultural policy in the Atlantic Community and offers a detailed international program for reorganizing Atlantic agriculture gradually into a more sensible economic pattern. A second book, by Richard N. Cooper of Yale University, will examine international financial arrangements and monetary institutions among the Atlantic nations, and prescribe policies for the future in this area. Trade arrangements and economic integration within the Atlantic Community and among the industrial countries are the subject of a third economic study, by Bela Balassa of Yale University, in collaboration with a group of economists from the United States, Europe, Canada and Japan. John Pincus of the RAND Corporation has undertaken a study of economic relations, trade and aid, between the industrial nations and the less developed countries.

*Harold van B. Cleveland*
Director, Atlantic Policy Studies
Council on Foreign Relations

# *Contents*

# European Unification in the Sixties

## CHAPTER ONE

# *Developments in the European Community from the Veto to the Crisis*

When the Treaty of Rome came into effect in 1958 anyone looking ahead and speculating about the way the Common Market was likely to develop would probably have forecast that the biggest difficulties would come in the first stage and in the third stage of the transition period, and that the second stage—the period from January 1, 1962, to January 1, 1966—would be, by contrast, relatively quiet. The uncertainties of embarking on a new experiment would be over, the difficulties of taking the final steps in the formation of a real common market still to come. In fact, the second stage was a time of great uncertainty and of near-mortal crisis, a period during which the hopes and expectations of the "Europeans" fluctuated wildly between extreme optimism and black despair.

In 1962, at the beginning of the second stage, the Community was at the high point in its short history: the process of forming a customs union was well ahead of schedule; the basic decisions on the common agricultural policy had, under French pressure, just been taken; the negotiations with the British were under way. General de Gaulle had, it is true, repeatedly ridiculed the ideas of the "Europeans," but, contrary to their fears, he had not attacked the EEC. Instead, under his leadership, the franc had been devalued and there had been no need for France to have recourse to the generous safeguard clauses written into the Treaty at the insistence of the French negotiators.

In its Action Program for the Second Stage,[1] published in October 1962, the Commission reflected the prevailing confidence that the customs union would be completed by January 1, 1967, three years ahead of schedule. In the Commission's view the time had come to turn to the more interesting, and more difficult, task of creating not simply a customs union but an economic union. The Treaty had defined the procedure and the timetable for the customs union, but the nature of the economic union had been only lightly sketched. It was, perhaps, mildly curious that this blueprint for the next few years had been formulated without any consultation with the British who were then expected soon to become members of the Community. But this was symptomatic of the prevailing view that the British were likely to be the slowest member of the caravan. Quite clearly, one purpose of the Action Program was to guard against a loss of momentum by charting the course for the next few years before the British joined.

A few months later, however, the Community experienced its first real crisis, not because the laggard had been let in but because the door had been slammed in its face. And less than three years later the Community was in a state of near paralysis. Between the two crises, the Six had apparently taken a giant step toward economic union by agreeing on the common prices for wheat and other cereals which would be applied throughout the Community in 1967. What lessons about the process of integration and what conclusions about the future of the Community can be drawn from this very turbulent phase of the Community's life which began with General de

[1] See European Economic Community, Commission, *Memorandum of the Commission on the Action Programme of the Community for the Second Stage,* Brussels, October 24, 1962.

Gaulle's dramatic veto early in 1963 and which ends, artificially enough, when this book was finished a few weeks after the Luxembourg settlement? Before attempting to answer these questions it may be useful to take a brief look at the way the Community seemed to be developing after the veto but before the severe crisis in mid-1965, and then to examine in some detail the 1965 crisis—how it happened, why it happened, the nature of the settlement.

In a very real sense the crisis that began in 1963 when General de Gaulle brought the negotiations with the British to an abrupt halt was simply the first half of the more serious crisis that began with the French boycott of the Community in July 1965. Both times the essential points at issue concerned the kind of Europe that was being built, and both times the French leadership on the Continent seemed to be threatened. In 1963 the difference in the conception of Europe related to the external orientation of the Community: in General de Gaulle's eyes Britain was a Trojan horse which once inside would seek to ensure that the Community maintained an unhealthily close relationship with the United States. And the challenge to French leadership on the Continent came from the United Kingdom. In 1965 the crisis was far deeper for the difference in conception concerned the nature of the Community, and the challenge to French leadership came not from an outsider who could be denied entry but from the Community process itself.

In 1963 the French government sought to justify its action with arguments about the unwillingness of the British really to play a European role and did its best to portray the veto, as it had its opposition to the free trade area negotiations, as another valiant effort to "save Europe." The Nassau agreement lent a little color to this argument; some of the British reactions to the veto a little more. But no one, except the confirmed Gaullists, really felt that the two situations were comparable. The strongest "Europeans" had been ready enough to thank the French for killing the free trade area for, probably legitimately, they saw in the looser, wider free trade area a threat to their own tighter, more far-reaching construction. The British application to join the Community had, in a sense, vindicated the "European" action in opposing the free trade area, and had seemed to confirm the correctness of M. Monnet's prediction that if the Six made a success of the Common Market the British would "face the facts" and apply to join.

The manner of the veto undoubtedly worried many "Europeans" more than the fact that the British had been excluded. The abruptness of the French action, the unilateral nature of the decision, the lack of consultation on a matter which concerned the Six collectively, the unwillingness of the de Gaulle government to give any weight to the views of the other members, and the fact that the reasons for the action were largely extraneous to the points on which the negotiations had been proceeding were all in flat contradiction with the spirit of the Community. And even those who had been worried by the prospect of British membership saw in the way the veto was applied a challenge to the Community.[2]

Nevertheless, in 1963, despite the fact that there were obvious differences of view about the method to be followed and about the external orientation of the Community, there still seemed to be enough common ground, enough overlap between the views of the Gaullists and the views of the "Euro-

[2] "The manner in which one member Government took and communicated its decision to interrupt the negotiations is not in harmony with the duties imposed by the Community. The results of an interruption affect the Community as a whole, not just one Member State. The Treaty defines accession as a Community matter. The opening of the negotiations was decided unanimously by the six member Governments at a session of the Council. The negotiations had been going on for fifteen months. In these circumstances one might at the very least have expected that the question of the future of the negotiations, if it had to be raised, would have been discussed fully and frankly amongst the members of the Community. This did not happen, and our Community has been faced with its first real crisis. To say this is no exaggeration; not to say it would be playing the matter down. The crisis is one of confidence, and that is what makes it so serious." From Dr. Hallstein's speech to the European Parliament on February 5, 1963. Reprinted in the EEC *Bulletin,* February 1963, p. 16.

peans," to enable the process of integration to continue. As long as French policy appeared to be directed toward a "European Europe" the differences among the Six seemed to many people to be differences of degree rather than of kind; a basis for compromise and for progress still seemed to exist. In 1965 the crisis was of a different order. The French position may have been born of disenchantment with the "Europeanism" of its partners, but the French position was itself irreconcilable with the objective of a "European Europe." The process of integration was under attack and independence for France seemed to rank higher in General de Gaulle's scheme of things than a "European Europe."

Although the veto left a bad taste and a thick residue of mistrust, the period of acute crisis during which the Community seemed threatened with stagnation as a consequence of the French action in January 1963 was surprisingly short. Dr. Hallstein made it plain in his long speech to the European Parliament in February that the Commission thought it unwise to jeopardize, or even to slow down, the development of the Community as a means of bringing pressure on the French.[3] The five governments were rather longer in coming to feel that the basis existed for a further development of the Community, but, except, perhaps, for a few weeks immediately after the veto, there was never much doubt but that the governments, too, would, in the end, give priority to saving the Community.

By April 1, 1963, the worst of the crisis was clearly over. At a Council of Ministers' meeting on April 1 and 2, Dr. Schroeder, the German Foreign Minister, sketched out the elements of a "synchronized working program" which offered

[3] "Everyone is agreed that the existence of the Community must not be jeopardized. This would, however, be an idle phrase if the Community no longer functioned properly. And that is what would happen if it became the practice for the procedures of the Community institutions to be subordinated to the thrashing out of all the underlying conflicts which have come to light in connection with the adjournment of the negotiations before their aim had been achieved. The functioning of the Community must never be exposed to risk even in the most well-intentioned tactics." EEC *Bulletin*, February 1963, p. 16.

a way out of the stalemate by tying progress on matters the French were interested in—agriculture and the extension of the arrangements for the association of the African states with the Community—to progress on matters of interest to the rest—in particular the Kennedy Round and the establishment of some link with the United Kingdom. The Council, at this same session, also confirmed the decision that had been taken by the member governments in happier days to accelerate the formation of the customs union, and it agreed to go ahead on July 1 with the second 30 per cent alignment in external tariffs and the sixth 10 per cent cut in internal tariffs. According to the timetable in the Treaty of Rome, the next reduction in internal tariffs and the next alignment of external tariffs were not required until January 1966. The decision to respect the accelerated schedule was, therefore, a positive sign of returning interest in the progress of the Community and not simply evidence of an unwillingness to violate the Treaty.

During the autumn of 1963 the French interest in the completion of the common agricultural policy and the German (and American) interest in progress on the Kennedy Round were skilfully exploited by the Commission to restore momentum to the Community. At the end of the year, thanks partly to the ingenuity of the Commission and partly to the willingness of the Germans to make substantial concessions, the Council seemed to be returning to something like its pre-veto method of operation. After two weeks of difficult negotiation and the customary all-night sessions a number of the most difficult outstanding problems were settled by a "package deal" on the traditional pattern. No decision was taken on the ambitious Mansholt Plan [4] for unifying cereals prices which had been launched in November, but consideration of this proposal was amicably postponed until the spring. Agreement was reached on the general nature of the Common Market organization for dairy products, beef and veal, and rice. And an interim arrangement was accepted for the Agricultural

[4] See footnote 7, p. 8.

Fund so that it could begin functioning. These were the particular points on which the French were then pushing for agreement. The other side of the bargain was agreement on mandates giving the Commission enough leeway (just) so that the Kennedy Round negotiations could proceed.[5]

Although much of the 1963 package deal remained to be filled in by the experts later on, and some of the most important points, e.g., all the price questions, were dealt with by deciding on new deadlines for agreement, there was immense relief that a deadlock, or an explosion, had been avoided.

There had been great fear before this successful marathon Council session at the end of 1963 that the repairs made after the veto were too fragile to take the strain of hard bargaining. The pre-veto atmosphere of mutual confidence no longer existed and a warning issued by General de Gaulle in July that the Community would "disappear" if the deadlines for the settlement of the outstanding agricultural issues were not met had raised fresh doubts about the depth of his commitment to the success of the Common Market. This July 1963 pronouncement was much more oblique than the French ultimatum the following year. The optimists interpreted it as saying no more than the obvious: unless the Six could agree on their agricultural policy they could not bargain collectively in the Kennedy Round and once they failed to maintain a common line a process of disintegration would inevitably set in.[6]

[5] For further details see Miriam Camps, *What Kind of Europe?*, Chatham House essay, 1965, pp. 30–33.

[6] For full text see *L'Année politique, 1963*, pp. 413–419. The most relevant paragraph reads as follows: "En effet, le terme adopté pour l'achèvement des règlements qui demeurent en suspens est le 31 décembre; d'abord, parce que le déséquilibre entre les conditions des échanges industriels et celle des échanges agricoles ne saurait durer plus longtemps; ensuite, parce que c'est sous cette condition, que les Six ayant pris acte du fait que la Grand-Bretagne ne peut entrer actuellement dans l'organisation d'une Europe européenne, se sont mis d'accord pour utiliser l'U.E.O., déjà existante, afin d'échanger leurs vues avec celle des Britanniques sur les problèmes économiques mondiaux. Enfin, c'est pour cette raison que les négociations tarifaires entre les Etats-Unis et l'Europe vont s'ouvrir au printemps prochain et que devant les grands vents qui ne manqueront pas

Others, including M. Pisani, the French Minister of Agriculture, and M. Monnet, had been inclined to interpret it more ominously.

The relief and rejoicing in Community circles at the end of 1963 were to be paralleled at the end of 1964. Both times, the elation at the success in reaching agreement was intensified by the fear of failure. Both times, too, the optimistic anticipation in which the year ended was soon followed by disappointments, although the second time round the fears were stronger, the jubilation more pronounced, the optimism about the prospects of future progress rosier, and the succeeding disillusion much deeper.

The successful December 1963 Council meeting raised hopes that the Six might be ready to adopt the Mansholt Plan which the Commission had put forward in November.[7] These hopes did not last long, for it soon became apparent that the German government was not prepared to take the political risk of alienating the important farm vote on which the Christian Democratic Union depended for its majority by lowering prices before the federal elections in the autumn of 1965. It soon became plain that the most that was conceivable during the spring was a decision, in principle, on the level and effective date of an eventual common price with all, or most, of the adjustment in national prices deferred until after the elections. But even this proved to be too optimistic. Discussions in the

de se lever à cette occasion, il faudra alors que le Marché Commun soit debout, complet et assuré, ou bien qu'il disparaisse."

[7] The Mansholt Plan was a proposal for unifying the cereals prices of the member countries in one step rather than by successive approximations as had, until that time, been the intention. The price of 425 DM per ton was proposed for soft wheat (related prices for other cereals were also proposed), and it was suggested that the single Community prices be adopted in time to apply to the 1964 harvest. The price proposed for soft wheat was lower than that then prevailing in Germany, Luxembourg, and Italy, and the Commission therefore suggested that farmers in these countries should be compensated from Community funds for their loss of income. These special compensatory measures would be limited to the transition period and would be replaced by measures benefiting farmers in all the member states by 1970 at the latest.

Special Agricultural Committee and in the Council of Ministers revealed stronger German opposition to the plan and considerably less support for the plan from the other governments—particularly the French—than the Commission had anticipated when it had made its proposals the previous November. Despite many long and arduous discussions little progress was made,[8] and early in June the Council of Ministers abandoned the attempt to reach even a decision in principle on the eventual common prices and decided unanimously simply to fix the "forks" for the 1964 harvest at the levels of the previous year.[9]

Although the discussions on the cereals prices had proved disappointing, the Community record during the spring of 1964 was by no means all black. In particular the governments, with Commission encouragement, at last seemed to be ready to take some of the steps toward economic union that the Commission had outlined in 1962 in its Action Program for the second stage.

The first few years of the Common Market were characterized by strong economic expansion in all the six countries; the member countries were in balance-of-payments surplus, both individually and collectively, and except in France, prices were relatively stable. There was, therefore, little need for coordination of monetary, budgetary, or general economic policy among the Six. About the middle of 1962 the economic situation changed: the rate of growth slowed down, and wages

[8] Price was the central issue, but the Six were not agreed on several aspects of the plan, such as the principle and amount of compensation to be given to those farmers who would have to accept lower prices. For details of the discussions during the spring and a summary of the modifications the Commission made during the spring in its own original proposals see Camps, *What Kind of Europe?*, cited, pp. 48–52.

[9] In order to increase the pressure on governments to reach an agreement on the common cereals prices the Commission refused to make a separate proposal for the prices to be applied to the 1964 harvest. In setting the 1964 prices the Council was thus exercising its right to amend a Commission proposal unanimously. The Commission proposal at this time was that the Council should agree on the level of the common prices but that the common prices should not apply until 1966.

and prices began rising sharply, particularly in Italy but also in France and, somewhat later, in the Netherlands. During 1963 and the first part of 1964 both France and Italy had large trade deficits, Germany a large surplus, and the Community countries were badly out of balance on current account, not only with one another but also, despite the German surplus, with third countries. This change in the economic situation gave the member governments of the Community a strong interest in coordinating their policies. The Commission was quick to exploit this interest, but it did so carefully and cautiously.

In January 1964 M. Marjolin made an important speech to the European Parliament underlining the dangers of inflation within the Community. This attracted widespread and on the whole favorable comment. It was followed up by a Commission "recommendation" to the member states on the measures they should take to restore the internal and external balance of the Community. This recommendation was adopted, in a rather attenuated form, by the Council in April. And, at the same time, the Council gave its approval to the establishment of three new committees within the Community framework: a Committee of the Governors of the Central Banks of the member countries, a Committee on Budgetary Policy, and a Committee on Medium-Term Policy.

The Council also agreed to the Commission's proposal that there should be consultations in the Monetary Committee when member governments took decisions, or important positions, on questions in the field of international monetary relations, in particular on questions concerning the general functioning of the international monetary system, the recourse by a member state to resources "mobilized through international agreements," and the participation by the member states in arrangements to support the currencies of third countries. The Council also agreed that "to the extent that circumstances permit," these consultations should take place before decisions or positions were adopted. The ministers also made a "declaration" that the governments of the member states would consult one another before making any modifications in the rates of exchange of their currencies, according to procedures which would be determined after receiving the advice of the Monetary Committee.[10]

These April decisions were potentially of great importance in laying the groundwork for an economic union. It is worth noting, however, that the terms in which the three new committees were established were extremely cautious: the emphasis was on coordination of national policies, not the elaboration of common policies; the committees were advisory rather than executive in character; and the role of the Commission in the new bodies was deliberately modest. There are few precise commitments in the Treaty of Rome on general economic policy and the Commission's own powers in this area are very limited. The Commission was therefore bound to move cautiously; in addition M. Marjolin was clearly aware of Gaullist susceptibilities and careful to avoid jeopardizing the effective coordination of policy by trying for institutional arrangements which would certainly have attracted French opposition, and might have been resisted by some of the other governments as well.

Although M. Marjolin and his colleagues were having some success in constructing a potentially useful infrastructure, the Community's failure to deal with the Italian balance-of-payments crisis in the spring of 1964 rather overshadowed these achievements. The Community's fumbling contrasted sharply with the speedy response from the United States and international sources and showed that there was, as yet, no

[10] It should be noted that this declaration was made by the ministers in their capacity as representatives of governments, not as the Council of Ministers, since Article 107 of the Treaty of Rome clearly leaves responsibility for exchange rates with the national governments: "Each Member State shall treat its policy with regard to rates of exchange as a matter of common interest."

very effective Community machinery nor any very deep conviction in the Six governments that they shared a common responsibility for the difficulties of one of the members.

Thus by the early summer of 1964 the optimism with which the year had opened had begun to fade. No progress had been made in reaching agreement on unified cereals prices. No progress had been made on various proposals the Commission had put forward hoping to push the member countries to harmonize their policies on commercial questions. And the lack of agreement on a common policy (or even on the principle of trying to have a common policy) had been underlined by the conspicuous failure of the Six to speak with one voice at the UNCTAD meetings in the spring. No progress had been made in trying to work out a common transport policy. The sister Community, Euratom, was in difficulty because the Six were unable to agree on the research program for the second stage. The High Authority of the Coal and Steel Community had made great play with the energy protocol signed in April; this opened the way to "legalizing" the subsidies being given to the coal mines. But an agreement on a common energy policy among the Six still seemed as far away as ever. Even the agreement on the fusion of the executives of the three communities which early in the year (1964) had seemed on the point of settlement had dragged on for many months, for apparently trivial reasons.

To some extent this slowing down was simply part of the pronounced annual cycle that has always characterized the work of the Community and no particular cause for concern. But it also reflected the continuing basic differences between the French and the others about the kind of Europe they were creating. Moreover, by the summer of 1964, relations between the French and Germans were clearly deteriorating. The fundamental differences between the two governments over the organization of defense—and, in particular, the nature of the tie with the United States—were becoming increasingly difficult to play down. These differences, which tended to crystallize at this time around the MLF proposal,[11] threatened to put new strains on the none too robust Community.

By the early summer of 1964 it was clear that both the German and the American governments were hoping that an agreement on the MLF could be signed and ratified before the German election campaign began in earnest in mid-1965. This meant, effectively, that an agreement would have to be reached by the end of 1964 or early in 1965. Endorsement of the MLF, on conditions, was the most prominent feature of the declaration made by M. Monnet's Action Committee for the United States of Europe in June 1964.[12] As it became apparent that the MLF proposal might soon become the subject of formal negotiations, rather than simply exploratory talks, the French position, which had previously been one of aloof ridicule of the plan, hardened into outright opposition.

During General de Gaulle's visit to Bonn early in July (for one of the regular meetings of the heads of government called for by the Franco-German Treaty of Cooperation) he sought to persuade the Germans to enter into closer bilateral relations with the French. According to press reports, he specifically sought German financial support for the French *force de frappe,* without, however, offering the Germans any part in its control. At the same time, and perhaps as a part of a con-

[11] The American proposal for a mixed-manned, multilaterally owned and controlled fleet of surface ships armed with Polaris missiles. See further discussion below, pp. 135 ff.

[12] The Action Committee Resolution endorsed the MLF as a "transitional solution" in the present "confused and difficult" situation: it pinned its faith on the willingness of the United States to negotiate a treaty incorporating the principle of "equal partnership" between a united Europe and the United States when the unification of Europe had proceeded to the point where an "authority capable of controlling and administering the European contribution to joint defense becomes a practical reality." The resolution did not expressly call for the end of the American veto at such time as Europe was united enough to make a joint contribution instead of separate contributions to the MLF, but it was clear that the kind of joint treaty the declaration envisaged would be one that supplanted the veto with equal commitments on both sides, in short a treaty that reflected full acceptance on both sides of real "interdependence."

certed effort to force the government to give priority to the link with France and to think again about the MLF, Dr. Erhard and his Foreign Secretary, Dr. Schroeder, were subjected to vigorous attacks from Herr Strauss, the leader of the CSU, and from Dr. Adenauer and the so-called "Gaullists" in the CDU, for giving too much support to American policy, for being insufficiently concerned with reunification, and for "sacrificing" the alliance with France. Dr. Erhard resisted these pressures. Speaking at a CSU conference in Munich shortly after his discussions with General de Gaulle he made it clear that, important though the Franco-German relationship was, it could not be an end in itself but must be a catalyst for action on a wider basis. He also reaffirmed in very forthright terms his determination to work for a European union which would act in partnership with the United States.[13]

Dr. Erhard presumably had Herr Strauss and his other German critics uppermost in his mind when he made this strong speech at Munich, but comment from Paris was not long in coming. At his semi-annual press conference on July 23, General de Gaulle ridiculed again, as he had done so often before, those who wanted to build a federal Europe and accused them of rejecting, consciously or unconsciously, an independent "European Europe" in favor of continued subordination to the United States.[14] He was also openly critical of German policy. The Franco-German Treaty had not evolved as he had hoped and it had not, he said, led to a common line of conduct because the Germans did not yet believe that a common policy must be "European and independent." Although there "is not and there could not be any opposition, strictly speaking, between Bonn and Paris," there was, he said,

[13] See *Frankfurter Allgemeine,* July 13, 1964.

[14] "We have seen many people, quite often, what is more, worthy and sincere, advocate for Europe not an independent policy, which in reality they do not visualize, but an organization unsuited to have one, linked in this field as in that of defense and of economy, to an Atlantic system, in other words, American, and consequently subordinate to what the United States calls its leadership." From text issued by French Embassy, London.

no agreement on a long list of subjects: defense, relations with Eastern Europe, and the related questions of frontiers, relations with China, peace in Asia, aid to developing countries, the common agricultural policy, and "consequently the future of the Community of the Six." As usual, General de Gaulle coupled his criticism with a warning:

> If this state of things were to last, there would be the risk, in the long run, of doubts among the French people, of misgivings among the German people, and, among their four partners of the Treaty of Rome, an increased tendency to leave things as they are, while waiting, perhaps, to be split up.

France, he said, was strong enough to be patient and to wait for the force of events to bring others around to the French view of Europe. And "in waiting for the sky to clear, France is pursuing, by her own means, that which a European and independent policy can and should be." [15]

The reaction in Germany to these strictures was not to make General de Gaulle more popular but to weaken the position of those Germans who had been pressing the government to give a higher priority to the French relationship, for General de Gaulle was too clearly equating France with Europe, too easily assuming that Germany would simply follow French leadership, and too obviously intervening in Germany's domestic political struggles.

It did not become clear until the spring of 1965 that the French government or, probably more accurately, General de Gaulle had decided that, given the divergencies between his policies and those of his partners, particularly the Germans, he must find a way to put a brake on the process of *engrenage*—of enmeshment with his Common Market partners—that the development of the Community along the lines laid down in the Treaty of Rome inevitably involved. But from the summer of 1964 there were increasing signs that the French govern-

[15] All quotations are from the translation of the press conference issued by the French Embassy, Press and Information Service, London.

ment had decided that there was little prospect of weaning the Germans from their close ties with the United States and, therefore, little hope of constructing General de Gaulle's version of a "European Europe." As discussed further below, the French decision in 1965 to seek to loosen the structure of the Community and thus to regain "independence" was, from a Gaullist standpoint, the logical consequence of the French failure to shake the Germans on the defense issue during the summer and autumn of 1964.

During the autumn of 1964 the Germans were subjected to intense pressure from the French both to forsake the MLF and to agree on common cereals prices. The strong French pressure on the cereals prices question during the autumn contrasted with the rather equivocal French position in the spring. Calculations based on French self-interest doubtless played some part in the new French attitude. But by the autumn the issue had acquired strong political overtones as well, and acceptance of a single price, like abandonment of the MLF, had become, in French eyes, a test of the "Europeanism" of the Germans. When the Community institutions resumed their activities after the traditional August lull, events were once again building up to a crisis.

In October (1964), in response to a request from the Council of Ministers, the Commission submitted a new paper on the cereals prices question, setting forth the points which it felt needed to be settled by the end of the year and those which it felt could be left for later decision. The Commission's central proposals remained unchanged: the prices put forward in the spring for soft wheat, barley, and maize were still felt to be appropriate and the Commission still believed that these should be decided on, in principle, in 1964 and applied to the harvest of 1966.[16] The only new point in the Commission's

[16] The other principal points singled out by the Commission as needing an immediate decision, and on which it reaffirmed its earlier proposals, were: the compensation to be paid to farmers in Germany, Luxembourg, and Italy who stood to lose from the reduction in price; the amendment of the Financial Regulations so that the cost of agriculture surpluses would be

résumé was the statement, designed to reassure the German government, that in its view there would be no case for a *downward* revision of the agreed cereals prices if the decisions taken in 1964 were reviewed before the prices went into effect.

When the Commission's paper was discussed by the agricultural ministers, M. Pisani, the French Minister of Agriculture, strongly supported the Commission's proposals and made it quite clear that the French government now placed a very high priority on the decision on the cereals prices being taken by the end of the year. The Germans, however, showed no signs of altering their position that it was impossible and unnecessary to take a decision before the German elections.

Immediately after this unproductive discussion by the ministers of agriculture, General de Gaulle issued another warning. According to the announcement made by M. Peyrefitte, the French Minister of Information, General de Gaulle had said that France would "cease to participate" in the European Economic Community if the common market for agriculture "was not organized as it had been agreed that it would be organized." [17] The threat was ominous but obscure. How would France "cease to participate"? By leaving the Community or simply by refusing to agree to any new decisions until it got its way on agriculture? And what were the new deadlines? The Treaty of Rome did not require the Six to have a common agricultural policy before 1970. Although German unwillingness to see any reduction in its internal prices had been largely, although not solely, to blame for keeping the Six from reaching agreement on the cereals prices, the German government had been formally within its rights. The only firm commitment the Council of Ministers had made was to decide one way or another on the Mansholt Plan by December 15: there had never been any agreement to decide on the unified cereals

---

borne in full by the Agricultural Fund from the time the single prices went into effect; the arrangements for fixing regional price differentials.

[17] See *Le Monde*, October 22, 1964.

prices by this date, although the French consistently implied that such a commitment had been made.

A few days later M. Couve de Murville in a long speech to the National Assembly shed a little more light on French intentions:

. . . we shall see how the Brussels talks develop, not only with regard to cereals but also with regard to dairy produce, meat, the financial ruling, and the rules on products which have yet to be established. In the meantime, it is fitting that France act in terms of the risks of dispersal which the behavior of some compel us to envisage and which cannot fail to continue to weigh upon us until the completion of the common agricultural policy. This means that we can only regard the coming period as one of waiting, only at the end of which, if our hopes are realized, could the European Community find itself fully confirmed.[18]

The French Foreign Minister also indicated that, in the circumstances, it was out of the question for the French to consider measures that were not *stricto sensu* provided by the Treaty. The specific allusion here was to the Commission's *Initiative 1964* suggesting a further acceleration in the timetable for the formation of the customs union,[19] but unwillingness to consider measures other than those strictly required by the Treaty characterized the French attitude until the outbreak of the crisis. It is again the rule today. M. Couve de Murville also made it abundantly plain that the settlement of the cereals prices and agreement among the Six on defense objectives were French preconditions for any progress toward a political union of the Six. And he pointedly questioned whether there would be any scope for a political union among the

[18] Statement made by the Minister of Foreign Affairs in the National Assembly, November 3, 1964. English translation issued by the French Embassy, London.

[19] The Commission appears to have put forward its *Initiative 1964* in an attempt to give some momentum to the Common Market. In the past, of course, the acceleration of the timetable for forming a customs union has had this effect. It is rather curious that the Commission thought this tactic would work in 1964, for the causes of the malaise were clearly political.

Six if the MLF were to be established. About a week later M. Pompidou was even more outspoken about the French opposition to the MLF.

In their efforts to persuade the Germans to yield on the cereals prices and to shelve the MLF the French at various times during the autumn called into question the continuation of the Common Market, of the NATO, and of the Franco-German treaty. These threats were very much resented by the Germans, and it seems probable that one result of the French tactics in the autumn of 1964 was to make the Germans readier to stand up to the French challenge the following year. The French government also played on German hopes and fears about German reunification and relations with East Germany and the USSR. On the one hand, a stream of representatives from Eastern European countries were welcomed in Paris, seven-year credits were extended to the Soviet Union in the context of the new trade agreement, and the twentieth anniversary of the Franco-Soviet pact was made the occasion for a strikingly warm message from General de Gaulle—all of which aroused speculation about a reversal of alliances. On the other hand, there were hints that the only path to German reunification lay through the Federal Republic's cutting its connections with the United States and following General de Gaulle in the creation of a "European Europe" which would eventually make possible the "rapprochement of all Europe." [20]

For a time during the autumn it seemed highly unlikely that an explosion of some sort could be avoided, for the United States appeared to be determined to get an agreement on the MLF (or an improved version of the British counter-proposal for an ANF [21]) and the French appeared to be equally determined that such a strong link with the United States should not be constructed. The hope in Community cir-

[20] This was one of the themes in General de Gaulle's speech at Strasbourg on November 22, 1964.

[21] The British proposal for an Atlantic Nuclear Force (ANF) is described below, pp. 147 ff.

cles was that the Common Market crisis and the MLF crisis could be taken separately. The Germans were therefore under strong "European" pressure—as well as strong Gaullist pressure—to agree to the cereals prices on December 15. Once the cereals prices decision had been taken, it was generally felt that the Community would be strong enough to weather the expected French fury if, in the new year, an agreement in principle was reached on some MLF/ANF compromise. It was widely assumed—perhaps optimistically—that the French would then have so much to lose on the agricultural side that they would be unlikely to wreck the Common Market.

Although the link between the cereals prices and the MLF was probably uppermost in most people's calculations during the autumn, the argument over cereals prices was still entangled as well with Kennedy Round tactics. In the spring the United States had threatened to delay depositing its list of exceptions until agreement had been reached on the ground rules for the agricultural side of the negotiations. During the summer and early autumn little progress was made in reaching agreement, and there was considerable uncertainty whether the United States would, in fact, deposit its exceptions list on the agreed date of November 16.

It had been clear from the outset that the French were anything but enthusiastic about the Kennedy Round: they were unlikely to be troubled by a United States' refusal to table its exceptions list because of the lack of agreement over the negotiating rules for agriculture. Had this happened, the French would simply have pointed to the Germans and blamed the stalemate in the Kennedy Round on German intransigence on the cereals prices. To prevent this situation from developing, the United States quietly loosened the connection it had previously made between the agreement on the ground rules for the agricultural side of the negotiation and the deposit of its exceptions list, and announced that it would be depositing its list on November 16, the agreed deadline. The American action, in turn, increased the pressure on the Community to reach agreement on its own list of exceptions. And on this question the discussions among the Six had been proceeding very slowly. The French were insisting on a long list of exceptions. For a time they also argued that they must be free to submit a national exceptions list as well as a Community list. Given the plethora of threats that had been emanating from Paris, this aroused suspicion that they were deliberately trying to make it impossible for the Six to agree among themselves and were trying to wreck the Kennedy Round as a part of a planned assault on all European-Atlantic arrangements and commitments.

The argument over the Community list was long and arduous, but in the end the Belgians and Italians proved as hard to satisfy as the French. For at the crucial meeting of the Council of Ministers—a session that lasted uninterruptedly for twenty hours just before the November 16 deadline—M. Couve de Murville unexpectedly eased the task of the Six by withdrawing a substantial number of the French requests.

The fact that the Six had shown themselves able to reach a compromise, and had demonstrated, once again, that the traditional method of the marathon still worked, improved the atmosphere in the Community and increased the confidence that the MLF-cereals prices crisis that had seemed unavoidable might somehow be defused. The French garnered the usual rather excessive gratitude from the others for having proved less obstructive than they had threatened to be. By making possible an acceptable settlement of the exceptions question, the French also, of course, stepped up the pressure on the Germans for agreement on the cereals prices, for this was now the key issue apparently blocking progress in the Kennedy Round.

Soon after the settlement of the exceptions list there were signs that the Germans would, in fact, give way on the cereals prices.[22] Dr. Schmuecker (the Minister of Economic Affairs)

[22] See *The Times,* November 27, 1964.

and Dr. Schwarz (the Minister of Agriculture) outlined the German position on the Commission's revised proposals at a meeting of the Council of Ministers on December 1, and the next day Dr. Erhard announced in the Bundestag that he had authorized the German delegation to accept the principle of the alignment of prices on July 1, 1967. That aspect of the crisis was clearly on the way to solution.

Early in December President Johnson decided that the United States should cease pressing the MLF upon its allies, thereby removing the other and more serious threat to the Community. There was no formal repudiation of the MLF; if asked, administration spokesmen still indicated support for the plan, but all American pressure for an early agreement was ostentatiously removed.[23]

By the time this change came, however, the Germans had already decided to make the concession on the cereals prices. It is a very open question whether they would have done so had not the pressure from all quarters been raised during the autumn and the conviction taken root that the Community would only survive the expected storm over the MLF/ANF if the principal outstanding agricultural issues had first been settled to French satisfaction.

Although the connection with the MLF controversy was important and probably the main reason for the German concession, it was not, of course, the only reason for the German concession. The link with the Kennedy Round was also very important. The fact that the French were now making the settlement of the common agricultural policy a *préalable* for resuming discussions among the Six on political union, which had been in suspense since April 1962, was also a factor. Dr. Erhard attached importance to these discussions, mainly, perhaps, because he felt progress on this front would strengthen his position in the CDU, and the position of the CDU at the polls.[24] Finally, of course, the Germans were

[23] See article by James Reston in *The New York Times*, December 21, 1964.

[24] The German government had recently (in November 1964) put for-

already committed to having a single price at the end of the transition period; what was at issue was not the principle of a common price but the level of the price, the date at which it would become effective, and the subsidy arrangements. Although 1966, as the Commission proposed, or 1967, which the Germans eventually accepted, brought forward the day when German prices would have to be reduced, it was clear that the Germans stood to gain financially from the accelerated schedule, for the French (and Dutch) had made it clear that they would admit no claim for subsidies if the price adjustment were not made until 1970.

The cereals prices and related issues were the subject of intense negotiation at various levels in the Community almost continuously from December when it became clear that the Germans were ready to bargain until December 15. The final "marathon" began at ten o'clock on the morning of December 10; a first package deal, formally presented to the Council by the Commission early the following morning, was not acceptable, mainly because it did not go far enough to meet the Italians. But, after a day's adjournment, the Council resumed its discussions and early in the morning of December 15 the Commission presented a slightly modified package which was accepted.

The decisions reached are available in Community documents and do not need to be set out at any length here. Despite earlier rumors that they would hold out for a rather higher price, the Germans accepted the basic soft wheat price of 425 DM proposed by the Commission. In return for this major concession it was agreed that Germany (and Italy and Luxembourg—whose prices were also above the agreed price) would receive substantial Community subsidies until

---

ward some new proposals for a "political union" of the Six. Dr. Erhard had agreed to formulate a plan during his discussion with General de Gaulle in July. As noted above, Dr. Erhard and Dr. Schroeder were at this time being strongly criticized for being insufficiently "European." The decision to put forward a German plan seems to have been prompted partly by a desire to meet internal German criticism and partly to counter French pressure for a stronger bilateral French-German arrangement.

the end of the transition period. The Germans were also permitted to give additional assistance to their farmers. Despite earlier German opposition to the principle of tapering subsidies, they, in the end, accepted this point. At the insistence of the Germans, supported by the Italians, the date of July 1, 1967, was accepted for the entry into force of the common price, rather than the 1966 date advocated by the Commission. And a review clause was adopted which would make it possible for the prices to be adjusted upward if the value of money changed appreciably between the agreement on price and the time of the review, i.e., July 1966.

In the last stages of the negotiation the Italians proved to have the most reservations, for the Italian situation had developed very differently from the forecasts made when the basic agricultural decisions were reached in January 1962. At that time Italy, like France, confidently expected to be an exporter of agricultural products and to take out of the Agricultural Fund rather more than it put into it. Owing to the rapidly rising standard of living in Italy, the Italians had become net importers; they were thus contributing to the Fund much more than had been anticipated, and taking far less from it. To help correct this situation, it was agreed that surpluses of fruit and vegetables would become eligible for financing from the Agricultural Fund from 1966 and ceilings were set on the Italian contributions to the Fund in 1965 and 1966. It was also agreed that fruit and vegetables, which had heretofore been the one agricultural sector where the Community was following a fairly liberal and unrestricted trade policy toward third countries, should be subject to new rules which would give the Italians a "Community preference" comparable to that given other farm products. The details of how this was to be done were left for further discussion in the new year and proved to be controversial. This backward step toward protection is worth noting, for it illustrated that the Community doctrines of "balanced development" and of equal advantages for all members which have frequently been invoked by the Commission to advance progress toward integration can be used to generalize bad principles as well as good ones.

As has been the case so often in Community affairs, once a general understanding had apparently been reached about what would be done, many of the details were postponed for settlement later, in accordance with an agreed timetable. The package negotiated in December 1964 was a big one and this was, presumably, the reason why the French went along with the Commission's argument that it would be better not to risk overloading it by seeking to settle all the outstanding aspects of the financial regulation.[25] In the past, when the Community spirit was strong and mutual confidence prevailed, the device of agreeing to agree at a later date had proved to be a reasonably effective one. But, as the events in the spring dramatically showed, it is a device that is less likely to work when there is little confidence among the partners that they are, in fact, all trying to work toward the same ends.

The reaction to the successful outcome of the December 1964 marathon was one of great optimism. The statements about the irreversibility of the Community which had been made so often after each crisis had been weathered and each major step forward taken were made again. But this time they were made with new fervor, for a genuine fear of failure had gripped the Community during the autumn. The exuberance was understandable for the Community had done more than simply survive. Despite the very hard line the French had taken during the autumn and the resort to threats and warnings which were totally inconsistent with the Community spirit, the final marathon had gone remarkably smoothly. The Italians rather than the French had tended to be the odd man out, each country had been willing to make some concessions and, as in the past, all had looked to the Commission at the crucial point to bring forward a package which, by skilfully balancing the conflicting desires of the members, embodied

[25] The conclusions reached by the Council that are relevant to the controversy over the financial regulation are discussed in the next chapter.

the maximum amount of agreement attainable. Moreover, it was widely assumed that single prices for the other major agricultural products would be agreed and come into force at about the same time as the cereals prices (i.e., July 1967), that decisions on accelerating the formation of a full customs union for industrial products to keep pace with the agricultural policy would now be taken, and that the imminence of the single-price system for agricultural products would give momentum to the discussions of common or at least coordinated action in the monetary field, since any alterations in exchange rates within the Community would create new and difficult problems once prices in the agricultural sector were not free to vary from country to country. In addition, although no proposals had as yet been put forward, it was quite generally assumed that customs duties would become Community property at the same time as the agricultural levies, for there was a clear lack of logic in differentiating between the two. Once very large sums of money became available and only available for Community programs, the centripetal forces in the Community would of course be enormously strengthened.[26] Finally, of course, there was a very widespread assumption that the French stake in preserving the Community was now large enough and clear enough to give a very hollow ring to any future French threats to break the Community. That the solidity of the Community could still be brought in question was soon to be proved, but even that most perceptive of French observers, Pierre Drouin, felt at the time that the December decisions were a watershed.[27]

[26] Even at this time it seemed unlikely that the French, and other governments as well, would agree to the Commission's gaining full control of the funds. But although it seemed probable that the funds would remain subject to Council control, had very large sums of money become available to the Community for Community purposes only, the power at the center would have been increased.

[27] *D'Une Europe à L'Autre, Le Monde,* December 16, 1964. M. Drouin made a number of interesting and revealing points: first, that Europe had now definitely saved its peasants: *"entre son agriculture et les sirènes du commerce international, elle a choisi"*; second, that although this was cause

It is hardly surprising that the Germans who had made the essential, and most costly, concessions were optimistic that the Kennedy Round would now proceed more rapidly and smoothly, since the ostensible reason for delay on the agricultural side had been removed, and that they also felt the way was open to progress among the Six on political union. Speaking to a press conference on the morning after the settlement, Chancellor Erhard indicated that he felt a sufficiently broad basis of understanding existed so that a meeting of the heads of governments of the Six could soon be held to discuss the various plans for political union that were then before the Six—the German plan, a rather similar Italian plan, and the not very different Fouchet plan.[28]

Although relief that the worst had not happened was understandable, it is rather surprising that the sky appeared quite so blue and cloudless after the December decisions. There was a tendency to exaggerate how much the December agreements owed to the Community spirit and to the tactical skill of the Commission and to overlook the part played by other factors, such as the relationship with the MLF controversy. It is true that the French had made some concessions during the negotiations—principally by agreeing to Community responsibility for subsidies to German, Italian, and Luxembourg farmers, and to new ceilings for the Italian contribution to the Fund. But these were not concessions that cost the French very much to make and the second, at least, was a plain case of simple equity.

Moreover, the French threats during the autumn had left a

---

for satisfaction the inflationary pressures that would result from the choice needed to be recognized; third, that since exchange rate changes were virtually ruled out, the need for common monetary, fiscal, and general economic policy was intensified; and fourth, that the customs union for industrial goods would almost certainly be speeded up to match the agricultural decisions. And finally, he said, the agreement marked the passage from one Europe to another, from that of putting in place community mechanisms to that of "integration pure and simple."

[28] See *The Guardian,* December 16, 1964.

very bad taste. They could not now simply be forgotten. Many Germans had felt that General de Gaulle was hitting below the belt when he threatened them with the denunciation of the Franco-German treaty of reconciliation if they persevered with the MLF. Despite the fact that the treaty had proved to be of little real value—German-French relations deteriorated soon after the treaty was ratified—it was of deep psychological importance to the Germans. In their eyes it seemed to symbolize the German repudiation of the war, and all that had led to it, and to set the seal on the new relationship with France in a way that nothing else had done. Thus even though relations between the two governments were strained and the treaty in some respects a dead letter, the mere existence of the treaty was important. A French denunciation of it would have had a meaning in Germany out of all proportion to the objective value of the treaty.

On the underlying issue of the Community's relationship with the United States, the situation at the end of 1964, although apparently unchanged, had really turned against the French. The MLF was in abeyance, and a confrontation on this issue had been avoided. But the Germans had made no positive concessions to the French in the defense field. Furthermore, it seemed clear that the German government—although prepared to do everything in its power to avoid having to choose between the United States and France would, in the end, choose the United States. For, despite the electoral advantages of choosing to concede to the French on the MLF, the German government had chosen to concede on the domestically unpopular price issue—and to play for time on defense.

The most solid reasons for the optimism at the end of 1964 were, first, that the French stake in the continuation of the Community had been significantly increased and, second, that the decisions taken were bound to increase the pressures for further integration. So they did. But the result was not progress but deadlock.

## CHAPTER TWO

# *The Development of the Crisis January 1965—July 1965*

In his New Year's Eve broadcast to the French people on December 31, 1964, General de Gaulle stressed the theme of French independence: "The year which is just closing has shown, and the year which is beginning will confirm, that while becoming ourselves again in political, economic, monetary, and defense affairs, in other words, while rejecting all systems which, under the cover of 'supranationalism' or of 'integration,' or even of 'atlanticism' would, in fact, keep us under the hegemony which comes to mind, we are fully ready for friendly cooperation with each of our allies, we are helping the union of Western Europe to progress, we remain very active in the giving of aid to developing countries, we are establishing with Latin America . . . ever closer links, we are renewing contacts with China, finally we are extending our relations with the states of Eastern Europe, as their internal evolution leads them toward peace." [1]

General de Gaulle's concern with "independence" was soon to produce the most serious crisis in the Community's history, but the year 1965 began auspiciously. The Community was basking in the afterglow of the unexpectedly quick settlement of the cereals prices in mid-December. The fact

[1] *La Documentation Française,* January 12, 1965. My translation.

that the MLF/ANF proposals appeared to be sidetracked, perhaps indefinitely—an impression which was strengthened by President Johnson's State of the Union message—was regretted by some of the more Atlantic-minded "Europeans." But it seems to have been welcomed by the Commission and by others who, like them, gave an overriding priority to building up the Community, for with the abatement of American pressure for an early agreement on the nuclear plan the prospect of a crisis on the defense issue between the Germans and the French, with the inevitable, if unpredictable, repercussions in the Community, had receded. There was a mood of extreme optimism in the Community and a feeling that a watershed had been crossed. It was confidently expected that 1965 would see agreement on a new acceleration of the Community timetable with mid-1967 accepted as the target date for the completion of the customs union and for the coming into effect of the single-price system for the main agricultural products. A long train of consequential decisions was expected to follow which would carry the Community irresistibly down the road to economic union. A final settlement of the long-drawn-out argument over the fusion of the institutions of the three communities—EEC, ECSC, Euratom—seemed probable. The negotiations on political union also seemed likely to be taken out of the deep freeze where they had been since April 1962. There was also a very widespread conviction that with the agreement on the cereals prices the French stake in the Common Market had been raised so high that further threats from General de Gaulle to break or freeze the Common Market were unlikely and, if made, would not carry conviction.

For the first two or three months of 1965 Community affairs developed normally, if rather more slowly than the optimism at the turn of the year had seemed to promise.

On February 2 the foreign ministers of the Six met as the Council of Ministers of the EEC for the first time since the December "marathon" for a broad exchange of views on the timetable for 1965 and on various proposals about the work of the Community that had been put forward by the Germans, French, Italians, and Commission. No firm decisions were taken at this meeting, but from this discussion, and that at a meeting of the agricultural ministers the week before, some areas of general agreement and some important differences of emphasis emerged. The Council reaffirmed the binding character of those deadlines for decisions on agricultural questions that had been specifically agreed as part of the December package: certain modifications in the fruit and vegetable regulations to be agreed by March 1; Commission proposals on the financial regulation to be made by April 1; the decision on the financial regulation to be taken by July 1; Community financial responsibility to be extended to the fruit and vegetable sector by January 1, 1966. But various other agricultural deadlines which had been proposed by the Commission and supported by the French, such as the dates for the agreement on single prices for fats, sugar, dairy products, etc., were accepted only as working targets, not as binding commitments. Moreover, although there was general agreement that common prices for all the main agricultural products should, in principle, be applied from July 1, 1967 (i.e., at the same time as the common cereals prices came into effect), this was not a firm decision. And the Germans made it very clear that the formation of the customs union and the bringing into effect of various other common policies must proceed in step with the common agricultural policy. Similarly, although the date of July 1967 was felt by most countries to be an acceptable date for the completion of the customs union, no firm decision was taken on this point. The French—perhaps for bargaining purposes, perhaps for more fundamental reasons—felt it was premature to set any date for the final 10 per cent reduction of internal tariffs or for the final step in the unification of national tariffs.[2]

It is clear from the papers circulated by the Commission,

[2] See the leading article in *Le Monde,* February 2, 1965; also *Agence Europe Presse,* January 28, 1965.

by the German government, and by the French delegation that the Commission and the Germans as well as attaching more importance than the French to the completion of the customs union in 1967 also had rather more ambitious ideas about the progress to be made in fields other than agriculture.[3] The Germans in their proposals and in statements made at this and other Council sessions during the first half of 1965 attached great importance to the harmonization of taxation, to the co-ordination of economic policy—particularly short-term business cycle policy, to progress toward monetary union—beginning with agreement on rules to guide the policy of issue banks, to progress toward a common commercial policy, and to the adoption of a common credit policy toward the state-trading countries of Eastern Europe. In addition, the Germans emphasized the need for progress in the negotiations that were under way or in prospect with Austria, Nigeria, Spain, and the Maghreb; they also pushed, as they had done repeatedly, for progress in the Kennedy Round.

The French memorandum was far less comprehensive than the German memorandum; it concentrated particularly on the need to complete the common agricultural policy, above all the financial regulation, and on projects that were designed, essentially, to encourage European industry to organize itself to withstand American competition more effectively. These themes were also the dominant ones in the French comments in the Council discussions on the Community's tasks in 1965. In addition to pressing for the completion of the common agricultural policy, the French emphasized the need for pushing ahead with the work on a European patent, for encourag-

[3] The Commission proposal was a refurbished version of its *Initiative 1964*. The German proposals were contained in a General Memorandum on European Policy circulated to their partners in November 1964; the memorandum was in two parts, economic and political, and the economic section was laid before the EEC Council. The memorandum was printed in the Documents series of the *Agence Europe Presse*, Document No. 288, November 16, 1964. The French memorandum was circulated by the French delegation to the other delegations of the Six in Brussels in January 1965, and excerpts from it were included in the *Agence Europe Presse*.

ing the formation of "European companies," and for Six-country action on scientific and technical research, but they seemed to have little interest in other developments.

Toward the end of February the Council of Ministers held a three-day meeting devoted to various agricultural questions: modifications in the fruit and vegetable regulations were agreed to give the Italians the preference they had been promised,[4] thus meeting the first of the deadlines laid down in December. In addition the ministers fixed the 1965 target prices for milk and the guidance prices for beef and veal which the Six had also promised themselves they would settle by March 1. Shortly thereafter, at the Council meeting on the first and second of March, agreement was finally reached on the main details of the fusion of the institutions of the three communities, an issue which had acquired a symbolic importance out of all proportion to its actual significance.[5]

It is difficult to see why the new-found French enthusiasm for fusion of the executives (a word the French pointedly never used) was so welcome, for it was plain enough that the French were eager to move ahead on the fusion of the institutions partly to cut them down and partly, and more importantly, so that they could move on to the next stage—the revision of the treaties—which the Six had agreed would then be tackled.[6] Nevertheless, the fusion agreement was generally hailed as a Community victory. It was of more real significance that the work on coordinating monetary policy, al-

[4] Although agreement on the fruit and vegetable regulation represented progress in the sense that the first of the deadlines set in December was met, the regulation itself was a backward step in terms of its effect on imports. Under the old regulation countervailing charges could be imposed when imports threatened to disturb the market; under the new regulation, charges would be automatically applied whenever the import price was below the reference price.

[5] The Six governments signed the fusion treaty on April 8, 1965.

[6] See the statements made in French Assembly by M. Couve de Murville and M. Pompidou during the foreign affairs debate in mid-June. It was clear enough that this was the French motivation long before these confirmatory statements were made.

though unspectacular, seemed to be making progress under M. Marjolin's cautious guidance.

Against these successes there were numerous instances of a failure to agree. Progress was slow or nonexistent on transport and on energy policy, but this was not unusual. Discussion on the European patent had run into difficulties because the Dutch wanted a more open system than the others, particularly the French and the Commission, were ready to accept. The French were continuing to resist all moves toward a common commercial policy even though the progress of the customs union made the need for common policies urgent, and the Germans had joined the Commission in pushing for action.

The French continued to interpret the Commission's role as restrictively as the Treaty of Rome would permit; and there were few illusions that General de Gaulle's attitude toward the Community was any more sympathetic than it had ever been. But there was also, during the first weeks of 1965, no very clear sign that the difficulties with the French would become appreciably worse than those the Commission and the Five had been living with for the past few years—with considerable success. Rather less progress had been made than had been hoped, but the pronounced annual cycle which had developed in the Community simply seemed to be running true to form. No big decisions were being taken, but no one felt the time was ripe for big decisions. December has become the high point of the Community year when the major decisions are taken. Sometimes there is a secondary peak of activity at the end of June or early July, just before the summer holidays. In August, nothing whatsoever happens. Normally the Community becomes dormant soon after Bastille Day (July 14) and reawakens about mid-September. From then until Christmas activity and tensions mount, culminating in a year-end "marathon" meeting, when the year's hardest bargaining is done and major decisions are taken. Exhilaration and exhaustion follow. Then come the arguments and disagreements over what was, in fact, agreed in the gray December dawn. Then the cycle begins again. New proposals are discussed, a few decisions may be reached in the early summer, but the most difficult decisions involving the biggest national concessions tend to be deferred to ripen together toward the end of the year.

This cycle was not accidental. It began because the timetable laid down in the Treaty of Rome for bringing the customs union features of the Community into effect set January 1 and occasionally July 1 as the dates when the tariff reductions and tariff alignments and the enlargements in quotas were to be made. But the cyclical pattern might not have become so pronounced had the Commission not found that it was more likely to obtain Council agreement to its proposals if it tied together a number of decisions some of which would favor one country, some another, so that a rough parity of advantage and concession could be maintained. This reliance on the year-end "package deal" with a more or less deliberate build up of pressure has led to a tendency to confuse crises with progress which may, perhaps, have contributed to the miscalculations that culminated in the crisis in the summer of 1965.

The existence of this pronounced cyclical pattern also tended to obscure the fact that a shift in the French attitude toward the Community took place during the spring of 1965. It is difficult to date the shift precisely. It is tempting, but probably wrong, to date it from Dr. Hallstein's premature disclosure to the European Parliament of the Commission's ambitious proposals relating to the financing of the Agricultural Fund. The Commission's rather inept promotion of its far-reaching plan (which is described in some detail below) may well have affected French tactics and precipitated a crisis some months earlier than it would otherwise have taken place. But it seems clear that by 1965 "independence" and freedom of action for France had become more important objectives for General de Gaulle than a "European Europe," doubtless because the experiences of the previous two years had shown that the rest of the Six and the Germans, in particular, were not prepared to accept his view of the role of Europe in the defense field. During the early months of 1965 it was noticeable that although M. Pompidou and M. Couve de Murville still emphasized the Gaullist theme of a "European Europe," General de Gaulle increasingly stressed the need for independence and seemed to have lost interest in even his form of Europe.

It also became clear during the spring that General de Gaulle was taking a much more direct hand in the formulation of French policy than he had previously done. Until then, French ministers such as M. Couve de Murville, M. Giscard d'Estaing, and M. Pisani—all of whom took an active part in the EEC Council—had seemed ready to see the process of economic integration continue. They took care to see that the institutional arrangements were ones that would be acceptable to General de Gaulle and they tried to see that the pace and direction of developments were firmly in the hands of member governments. But they seemed ready to accept a fairly far-reaching form of economic integration even though they must have recognized that this would inevitably limit the freedom of action of the member countries. There was an obvious and inescapable conflict between the progress of the Community and the extreme form of national independence advocated by General de Gaulle. But there seemed to be a kind of tacit conspiracy in the upper reaches of the French government to keep the long-term implications of what was happening in Brussels from coming to General de Gaulle's attention. Or perhaps they were brought to his attention but he did not take them seriously until the Commission's financial proposals crossed the t's and dotted the i's in an inescapable fashion.[7]

Whatever the explanation, the situation changed during the spring and it became clear that General de Gaulle was taking a far closer interest than previously in the positions taken

[7] There are reports that M. Pisani made a point of explaining the full implications of the agricultural policy to General de Gaulle and was given a green light to go ahead at the end of 1963.

by his ministers in the discussions in Brussels. According to an announcement made by M. Peyrefitte after a meeting of the French Council of Ministers on April 21, the Council, "at the request of the President," had adopted procedures governing the participation of ministers in various international bodies, "notably the EEC," and decisions were taken "about the conditions in which instructions need to be given by the whole government." The secretariat of the interministerial committee for European economic cooperation was to keep more closely in touch with ministerial movements and to work out clear instructions which would be put forward "to the Prime Minister and the Council of Ministers." [8] Had General de Gaulle been in favor of real progress in the EEC this action could be interpreted as simply the normal tightening up of interdepartmental machinery that all governments have to do from time to time. But it seems clear that in this case the ruling was not prompted by the desire for efficiency but by the wish to ensure that some of the more "European-minded" of the French ministers did not compromise French freedom of action by agreeing to too much in Brussels.

The nature of the conflict between General de Gaulle's views and the progress of the Community, and also the related question of the connection between economic integration and a political consensus, are considered in the next chapter. The remainder of this chapter deals with the argument over the financial regulation. Although it seems clear that this was a pretext for rather than the cause of the French action, the way the Commission formulated and handled its proposals, the positions taken by the various governments, and the French tactics during the final bargaining are all germane to the subsequent discussion about the significance of the crisis. To make that discussion intelligible, the proposals—which were complex as well as ambitious—will first have to be described in some detail.[9]

[8] See *Le Monde*, April 22, 1965.

[9] The substance of the proposals was contained in a press release P/29 (65) issued by the official spokesman of the Commission; the complete texts were published in a supplement to the *Bulletin* of the EEC, May 1965.

### *The Commission's proposals*

The Commission's submission to the Council was in three parts: the first part contained a proposed regulation on the financing of the common agricultural fund; the second part—known in Community jargon as the "own resources" part of the proposal—contained proposed provisions to be enacted by the Council under Article 201 of the Treaty and concerned the replacing of member states' financial contributions by "Community" resources; and the third part contained a draft treaty modifying Articles 201 and 203 of the Rome Treaty to give the European Parliamentary Assembly some control over the Community budget. The Commission explained in an accompanying statement the logical connection between the three parts and the reasons why it felt all the important subjects it raised in the proposal needed to be considered at the same time. In the light of later developments it is worth noting that the Commission, while arguing that its proposals formed a whole and had to be considered together, did not necessarily assume that final decisions on all its proposals would be taken by June 30, 1965. Some parts were, in any case, linked to decisions which arose in the context of other proposals, notably *Initiative 1964*. The Commission did state that it considered "the provisions about financing the common agricultural policy at the single market stage, and those concerning independent resources for the Community" would have to enter into force simultaneously, on July 1, 1967.[10]

In December 1964 the Council had asked the Commission to do two things: to submit proposals relating to the financing of the common agricultural policy for the period 1965 to 1970, and to submit "proposals on the conditions for implementing Article 2 of Regulation 25 as from the entry into force of common prices for the various agricultural prod-

[10] *Supplement,* cited, p. 5.

ucts."[11] Article 2 of Regulation 25 provided that *in the single market stage* the levies charged on imports from third countries would be the property of the Community and used for Community expenditure. It further provided that the "budget resources of the Community shall comprise such revenue together with all other revenues decided in accordance with the rules of the Treaty as well as contributions of member states in accordance with Article 200 of the Treaty," and that "The Council shall in due course initiate the procedure laid down in Article 201 of the Treaty so as to implement the above provisions."[12]

The first thing the Commission had to decide was when the "single market stage" was to begin: was it to be in January 1970, as some countries had argued in the December debate, or was it to be when common prices came into effect as the French had then argued? The Commission proposed that it should be when the common prices came into effect. The Commission also proposed that common prices and full Community financing for *all* the main agricultural products should come into effect at the same time (i.e., July 1, 1967), arguing that an unbalanced situation would result if the change-over

[11] On July 7, 1965, the Information Service of the Community put out a press statement giving the texts of various relevant Council decisions and regulations. The quotations here are taken from that release.

[12] Article 200 of the Treaty sets forth the scale for national contributions to the budget and to the Social Fund. Article 201, to which considerable reference will be made hereafter, reads as follows:

"The Commission shall study the conditions under which the financial contributions of Member States provided for in Article 200 may be replaced by other resources available to the Community itself, in particular by revenue accruing from the common customs tariff when finally introduced.

"The Commission shall for this purpose submit proposals to the Council.

"The Council may, after consulting the Assembly as to these proposals, unanimously determine the provisions which it shall recommend the Member States to adopt in accordance with their respective constitutional requirements." (There is no authentic English text of the Treaty of Rome. The most carefully prepared version was that done by the British government at the time it was negotiating for accession. All quotations are from that version. HMSO, 1962.)

were made only for those products for which the single-price system had already been agreed (cereals and transformed products—pigs, poultry, eggs). The Commission's concern for a "balanced" development was partly good economic sense: as it pointed out, agricultural production would tend to be distorted if some products benefited from full Community financing and free trade within the Community while others did not. But the Commission was also motivated, as always, by the desire to have its proposals appeal to all the member countries, and for some products the Dutch and Italians were as interested as the French in reaching agreement on common prices. The Commission also argued that Community-wide free trade in industrial goods should be achieved at the same time as intra-Community trade in agricultural products was freed. Again its reasons were partly economic, partly political. The Germans, who had least to gain from the agricultural policy, had always maintained that any acceleration on the agricultural side should be balanced by comparable progress on the industrial side.

The Commission's argument that both the common agricultural policy and the customs union features of the Common Market should come fully into effect on July 1, 1967, was not in the least unexpected: July 1, 1967, although it had not been formally adopted by the Council as the date for anything except the coming into effect of the common cereals prices, had been much talked about as the date when other common prices would enter into effect, and it was the date the Commission was proposing in its refurbished *Initiative 1964* for the completion of the removal of intra-Community tariffs and quotas and for the coming into effect of the common external tariff.

Having decided to recommend that the single market stage begin on July 1, 1967 (with the coming into effect of common prices as the French had argued in December), the Commission then put forward a two-part regulation on the financing of the Fund: the first section provided for the financing for a two-year transitional period lasting from July 1, 1965, to July 1, 1967; the second section contained the rules to govern the financing of the Fund when the "single market stage" was reached, i.e., from July 1, 1967. The first section was quite straightforward, and was, in effect, simply the logical extension of the system applied from July 1, 1962 to July 1, 1965, the contributions of the member states being modified to take account of the decisions reached in December 1964 on the Italian, Belgian, and Luxembourg contributions.[13]

The arrangements for the single market stage were a little more complicated. The proposed regulation dealt first with the measures to be financed by the Fund; this part of the regulation was largely an elaboration of what the Six had already agreed when adopting Regulation 25, but one important, and controversial, new point was added. Regulation 25 had stipulated that the Fund would finance the rebates (subsidies) on exports to third countries. The new regulation introduced an important qualification: exports made in the framework of bilateral or multilateral arrangements were only eligible for rebates from the Fund if these arrangements were of a "Community nature." [14] This provision was logical enough, but it was bound to be opposed by the French who had, for some time, been resisting the taking of any steps toward a common commercial policy arguing that the Treaty required a common policy only at the end of the transition period. Since the Commission was proposing that the customs union should be completed on July 1, 1967, the argument for a common commercial policy on that date was a strong one, but the French

[13] In accordance with Regulation 25 the Fund had been financing "eligible expenditure" under a scale rising by one-sixth a year: the proposals simply continued this scale. Thus four-sixths of eligible expenditure would be covered in 1965–66 and five-sixths in 1966–67. The member states' contributions were fixed amounts adjusted to take account of the new ceilings agreed for the Italians in December and the understanding that the Belgian and Luxembourg assessments would not be increased.

[14] This restriction did not apply to any exports made outside the framework of trade agreements, or similar arrangements.

could, and did, argue that the transition period was laid down in the Treaty and lasted until 1970.

The way the Fund was to be financed in the single market stage could not be dealt with by this regulation since—in the Commission's view—it involved the question of the Community's "own resources." This was a matter on which the Council could not simply approve a regulation proposed by the Commssion, for it had to be dealt with as provided in Article 201 of the Treaty, quoted in the footnote on p. 39 above. In the light of later developments it is worth reiterating that the Commission's reasoning here was not only logical but in line with earlier decisions of the Council. The Commission was, of course, glad to find a way to bring forward the day when the Community had its "own resources," but once it was agreed that the single market stage entered into effect on July 1, 1967, Regulation 25 really did the rest by providing that in the single market stage the levies were to be Community property and, as indicated above, linking this with Article 201 of the Treaty which envisaged customs duties also becoming Community property.

This second part—the "own resources" part—of the Commission's over-all proposal took the form of a series of numbered articles called "provisions" which were to be adopted by the Council. Some of these "provisions" would have required ratification by Parliament in some of the member states. Therefore this part of the Commission's proposal, if adopted by the Council, could only come fully into force after the Council secretariat had been informed that the member states had completed whatever procedures were required by their internal laws.

The first article in the "own resources" part of the proposal stipulated that the agricultural levies and customs duties would accrue to the Community as the Community's own resources from July 1, 1967, in accordance with terms laid down in the next two articles. These introduced a gradual but progressive element into the payment of the customs duties to the

Community, with the result that, although farm levies would become Community property on July 1, 1967, customs duties would not be paid to the Community, in full, until January 1, 1972.[15] These "Community resources" would be incorporated into the Community budget and would "help finance, without distinction, all expenditure included in it."

The Treaty of Rome (Article 199) provides that revenue and expenditure shall be balanced in the budget. The Commission, therefore, proposed that if the receipts from the levies and customs duties exceeded expenditure, payments should be made from the Community budget to the member states; if the expenditure exceeded the receipts, the member countries would make additional contributions. The Commission estimated that the revenue from the agricultural levies and the customs duties would be, in 1972, of the order of $2,300,000,-000: this was substantially above the estimated expenditures.

The third part of the Commission's proposals followed logically from the second.[16] The budgetary procedures laid down in the Treaty were reasonable as long as national governments appropriated funds to the Community, but, the Commission argued, they would not be adequate when large funds accrued directly to the Community and escaped the control of national parliaments. The third part of the Commission's proposal therefore spelled out a new budgetary procedure; this took the form of a draft treaty since it involved modifying Articles 201 and 203 of the Treaty of Rome.

The budgetary process as set out in Article 203 of the Treaty of Rome is as follows. Each of the Community institu-

[15] During the first half of 1967 payments were to be made in accordance with the arrangements agreed for the transition period; in the second half of 1967 the member states were to pay over to the Community all the levies and a proportion of the customs duties, the two together being equal to the amount paid over in the first half of 1967. Thereafter the proportion of the customs duties remaining to the governments would be reduced by one-fifth per year.

[16] It was also consistent with the position that had been taken by the Council of Ministers in December 1963. See below, p. 62, footnote.

tions draws up estimates of its expenditures which the Commission consolidates into a draft budget, attaching an opinion which may contain estimates diverging from those submitted to it. The Council, if it intends to depart from this draft, consults the Commission, and other institutions where appropriate. The Council determines the draft budget, by a qualified majority vote, and sends it to the Assembly, which may propose amendments. If within one month of receiving the draft budget the Assembly has proposed no amendments, the budget is considered to be finally adopted. If, however, the Assembly proposes amendments the budget goes back to the Council which discusses the amendments with the Commission (and other institutions, if appropriate). After these discussions, the Council finally adopts the budget by a qualified majority vote. Thus, although the Commission and the Assembly are both able to propose amendments to the Council, the Council is under no obligation to accept any amendments and it alone has the final say in determining the budget.

Under the new Article 203 proposed by the Commission, the procedure for preparing the budget would be the same, and, if the Assembly agreed with the draft budget, there would, in effect, be no change in the procedure laid down in the Treaty. However, if the Assembly amended the budget, which under the proposed new article it might do by a majority vote, a new procedure would be followed. The budget with the modifications voted by the Assembly would be sent to the Council and the Commission. Within fifteen days the Commission would inform the Council either that it accepted the amendments made by the Assembly or of the changes that it wanted made in them. If the Commission accepted the budget as amended by the Assembly the Council could only set aside the Assembly's amendments by a five-sixths majority. However, if the Commission proposed changes in the Assembly's amendments, the Council could adopt the Commission's version by a simple majority, i.e., by a four-sixths majority. Thus, although the final decision would still rest with the Council, amendments voted by the Assembly and supported by the Commission would stand unless expressly overruled by the Council, and larger majorities would be required to do this than are required to establish the budget under the existing procedure.[17]

The new version of Article 201 proposed by the Commission was also designed to strengthen the role of the Assembly. It will be recalled (see above, p. 39) that Article 201 deals with the procedure for replacing the financial contributions from member states by the Community's own resources; the Commission had been acting under this article in making the proposals in part two of its over-all proposal. An Article 201 was still needed since even were the Council to adopt part two, there might, in the future, be need for an additional source of revenue, or the Six might want to derive some of the revenue from another source; the Dutch were already arguing that a Community tax rather than the customs duties should be used to feed the budget. Under the amended version of Article 201,[18] the Commission's proposals could be adopted by the Council by a qualified majority vote if the Assembly rendered an opinion supporting the Commission's proposals by a two-thirds majority of the votes cast constituting an absolute majority of the members. Otherwise, the Council would have to act by unanimous vote. Provisions adopted by the Council under this Article would, as now, still have to be approved by the member states according to their own constitutional rules, but the Commission proposed adding "until such time as the members of the Assembly are elected in the manner provided for in Article 138 (3) of the Treaty," that is, until the members were directly elected. In its explanatory memorandum the Commission pointed out that when the Parliament was elected by direct universal suffrage the power to create independent

[17] Under the present procedure the Council establishes the budget by a qualified majority vote. See Article 148. In some circumstances, a three-sixths vote is a qualified majority.

[18] The Commission made it clear that the procedure outlined in the amended version of Article 201 was not to apply to its present proposals but only to future proposals.

revenues which at present rests with the member states would have to be completely transferred to the Community.

The Commission's proposals were internally consistent and well constructed and had the member countries been prepared to take a giant step toward economic union and really to shift important power to the Community institutions they pointed the way in a logical and coherent fashion. But General de Gaulle had made it abundantly plain in speech after speech that he was opposed to "integration" and wanted to curtail rather than to enhance the power of the Community institutions. Moreover, although each of the Five was attracted by various parts of the Commission's proposals it was clear before the argument was even begun that they were too divided, too cautious, and too reluctant to push matters with the French to the breaking point, to give the plan as a whole any real chance of success. The Commission was generally felt to be trying for too much too soon. From the time the proposals were first put forward there was thus little expectation that any very far-reaching decisions could be reached by the summer; certainly there were no illusions that the plan as a whole would be accepted by the end of June.

It is difficult to be sure why the Commission decided to act as it did. Until the spring of 1965 the strategy of the Commission and of "Europeans" generally had been to avoid confrontations with the French; to keep strictly to the letter of the Treaty and to count on General de Gaulle's reluctance to violate solemn undertakings; to lay the infrastructure of future action, as in the work being done on monetary questions and on economic planning, so that rapid progress could be made whenever a more sympathetic French government came to power, but not to try to force the pace; and to rely on the slow but seemingly relentless process of integration which had been set in train to enmesh the French irrevocably in the Community. The only questions on which the Commission had previously felt it prudent to be bold were those on which it could count on strong French backing. What led the Commission to depart from this cautious policy of outsitting de Gaulle? A number of factors all seem to have played a part: euphoria, miscalculations, the personalities of some of the Commissioners, sensitivity to accusations that the Commission had tended to play a French game, and fear.

As noted above, there was elation after the decision on the cereals prices in December 1964 and perhaps too little recognition of how much that decision owed to factors other than the "Community" spirit. There was also overconfidence stemming from the prevailing view that the French stake in the Common Market was now so high that the French could no longer afford a break. French interests were, of course, heavily engaged as the subsequent opposition of the farmers, the *Patronat,* and other groups to the French boycott of the Community made plain, but it was a little naïve to assume that in General de Gaulle's calculations economic interest would outweigh political independence. It is now no secret that Dr. Hallstein and Dr. Mansholt were the prime movers within the Commission and that M. Marjolin argued strongly that the proposal was unwise, although, in accordance with the collegiate character of the Commission, he eventually went along with the majority view in the Commission. It is also no secret that the Commission had been criticized in both Germany and the Netherlands for being too "French." It had become a commonplace in "European" circles to talk of the *de facto* alliance between the Commission and the French government, the "Pope" and the "Emperor." Some people were untroubled by this situation and felt that the progress of the Community owed a great deal to this alliance; others were bothered by it and felt the interests of the rest of the Six were too often slighted.

There was also fear that the French were planning to freeze the Community once they had secured the agreement they wanted on the financial regulation. During the spring of 1965 the French seemed to want three things, and only three things—the completion of the common agricultural policy, cooperation on research and scientific development, and arrangements to make the development of European companies legally easier. Their record on everything else tended to be negative and on some things, for example commercial policy, it was very negative indeed.[19] As noted above, the agreement on the fusion of the executives which was sometimes cited as evidence of the French desire to strengthen the Community was really evidence of a desire to weaken it by cutting the staff and bringing forward the day when the treaties would be rewritten. The fact that the details of the financial regulation still had to be agreed gave the Five and the Commission some bargaining power with the French, and it is understandable that, given the trend of French policy, they should have tried to exploit it. Nevertheless, it is difficult to believe that the Commission was wise to try for so much or to hold to its proposals for so long in the absence of very clear and very strong support for the proposal from the German government. A showdown with the French may have been inevitable as General de Gaulle implied in his press conference on September 9, 1965, but the crisis in June came on the wrong issues and in the wrong way.

On March 23 the Commission members were in Strasbourg for a meeting of the European Parliament. While there the Commission held one of its regular weekly meetings and completed its discussion of its proposals on the financial regulation which, in accordance with the decision taken in December 1964, it was required to submit to the Council of Ministers by April 1. The following day, March 24, Dr. Hallstein outlined the Commission's proposals to the European Parliament where they were widely acclaimed by all except the Gaullist deputies. Dr. Hallstein recognized, in his statement to the Assembly, that the normal procedure would be for the pro-

[19] The agreements reached on transport in May were, perhaps, a partial exception. However, in reaching agreement the Commission was deliberately bypassed, and the agreements reached envisage a kind of cooperation that is consistent with General de Gaulle's conception.

posals to be sent to the Council before being described to the Assembly. He justified his action on the ground that since the substance of the proposals had already leaked out it was only courteous for him to explain the broad lines of the proposals to the parliamentarians rather than leaving them to read about them in the press. But his statement also suggests that he was not unhappy to have this excuse.[20] The Assembly was not at this time formally asked for its views; this was done by the Council in May. Nevertheless, the parliamentarians, eager to express their support, adopted a resolution which "insisted" that the first steps should be taken to make both the agricultural levies and the customs duties Community resources on condition that the European Parliament should be given the power to fix receipts and expenditures deriving from these Community funds. In its resolution the Parliament also underlined the need for the Community to adopt a common trade policy so that any calls on the fund for subsidizing exports would be for exports which came within a general framework having the approval of the Community as a whole. The Assembly also asked that the "principle of a fair distribution of charges be respected." [21]

During the summer and autumn the Commission was slashingly attacked by the French for having unveiled its proposals to the Assembly before they had been formally transmitted to the Council, let alone discussed by the Council. The Commission clearly acted imprudently in so doing, but it was worth noting that it had escaped French criticism when it had employed very similar tactics earlier on projects supported by the French. Thus both the Mansholt Plan and the Marjolin proposals for "medium-term planning" had been presented to the Assembly and had acquired considerable public backing before they were formally considered by the Council of Ministers.

[20] See Parlement Européen, *Débats,* Compte Rendu, March 24, 1965.

[21] See Parlement Européen, *Débats,* Compte Rendu, March 24, 1965, p. 191.

The Council of Ministers held a two-day meeting on agricultural questions in mid-April. This session was largely devoted to discussing a number of technical agricultural problems, such as the proposals for organizing the sugar and fats market. The ministers did, however, agree to send the Commission's proposals on the financial regulation and related matters to the Assembly for its opinion, as required by the Treaty. The French had already made it plain that they felt the Commission had dealt with problems that went far beyond those that needed to be settled by July 1, 1965, and it was understood that the forwarding of the proposals to the Assembly implied no endorsement of them.

The first formal exchange of views on the proposals by the Council of Ministers took place in mid-May; as usual this discussion had been preceded by discussions by the Committee of Permanent Representatives. These first discussions confirmed the hostility of the French to many aspects of the plan, and they also revealed that there was no solid consensus in support of them among the Five. The French position was, essentially, that the only question that needed to be settled by June 30 was the way the common agricultural policy should be financed from July 1, 1965. This could be done quite simply: to the extent that the levies were not adequate they should be supplemented by budgetary contributions from the member states.[22] The Commission had, in the French view, gone well beyond its instructions in raising questions such as the assignment of customs duties to the Community and the strengthening of the powers of the Parliament. The three parts of the Commission's proposals should be separated: part one should be discussed, but parts two and three should be shelved.

The others felt, in contrast, that the Commission's proposals formed a whole and that the three parts were closely interrelated and should not be separated. They were also generally sympathetic to the idea that the Community should acquire its own resources, at some time. And they felt there

[22] See *Le Monde* of May 2–3, 1965.

should be some strengthening of the role of the European Parliament. But there the agreement among the Five ended. All of them thought the Commission's proposals raised vast questions which required study and could not be quickly settled, and all of them had reservations about various aspects of the proposals.

The discussion by the Council of Ministers in mid-May was largely procedural. The others were not prepared to agree to the French position that only part one of the Commission's proposals needed to be discussed, and the communiqué after the meeting indicated that the document as a whole would be remitted to the permanent representatives for study. But it was generally accepted that the Six would begin by examining the way the common agricultural policy would be financed. It should be noted that in these early discussions the French supported the Commission's view that the change-over to the single-market stage should take place when the common prices for agricultural products went into effect and that this should be in July 1967 (this was the position the French themselves had taken in the December 1964 discussions), while the Germans and the Benelux representatives felt the change-over to the final single-market system should not be made until the end of the transition period laid down in the Treaty. The Italians, in these first discussions, apparently took no firm position on this point, but right from the start they argued that any new financing arrangement that was agreed upon should be limited to one year and the problem looked at again later. The Italian position on this point arose largely from the fact that the original financing arrangements had worked out very disadvantageously for them, contrary to the general expectation.

Just before this first discussion by the ministers, the European Parliament had a long and rather emotional debate on the proposals on which it had now formally been asked to give an opinion. By a vote of 76 to 0 (10 Gaullists abstaining) the Assembly adopted a resolution stressing the "complementary and indivisible" nature of the proposals and strongly endorsing most of the Commission's suggestions. However, the parliamentarians felt the Commission's proposals for strengthening the powers of the Assembly were inadequate and proposed various amendments which, *inter alia,* gave the Assembly, rather than the Council, the final word in determining the budget.[23]

It was rather unfortunate that this debate was held before the first discussion in the Council, for the debate was somewhat irresponsible and the kind of action called for by the parliamentarians went beyond what even those governments that were most committed to strengthening the powers of the Assembly—the Dutch and the Italian—seem to have wanted. Moreover, both Dr. Hallstein and Dr. Mansholt in defending the Commission's proposals before the Parliament tended to become overcommitted to certain features of their plan. On the parliamentary issue, in particular, they found themselves with little leeway, for in explaining why they could not (or would not) change their own proposals to bring them into line with the more radical suggestions of the parliamentarians they inevitably endowed their own proposals with too much status and became committed to defending them as an irreducible minimum.

Between the Council session in mid-May and the session in mid-June, when the ministers really began their substantive discussions, the Commission's proposals were intensively discussed by the Committee of Permanent Representatives and by various expert groups and also between the member governments outside the Community framework. The most important discussions were those between the French and Germans—at expert level, at foreign minister level, and finally at the top level during General de Gaulle's visit to Bonn on June 11 and 12.

[23] For text see European Economic Community, *Bulletin,* No. 6, June 1965, pp. 55 ff.

Before turning to the EEC Council discussions in June it is worth looking briefly at the Franco-German conversations and at one or two other developments affecting the Community. Although at the end of 1964 the German agreement to the cereals prices and the abatement of U.S. pressure on the MLF had seemed to promise an improvement in French-German relations, differences between the two countries multiplied during the spring of 1965. On a long list of important subjects French and German policies were at odds: the organization of defense; the test-ban treaty; NATO; German reunification; credits to Eastern Europe; political union among the Six; the development of the European Community; Vietnam. But at this time perhaps the main source of tension was General de Gaulle's flirtation with the Russians. In his February 4 press conference General de Gaulle had gone rather far in suggesting that German reunification was a European problem which should be settled primarily by Germany's neighbors, by implication, at least, ruling out any appreciable role for the Germans as well as the United States in such a settlement. The reception given by the French government to Mr. Gromyko at the end of April had seemed to the Germans to be unnecessarily cordial, and they had been particularly annoyed by his parting reference to French-Russian "agreement" on the permanence of Germany's eastern frontiers.[24]

From time to time in the past the Germans had been worried by signs of British "softness" on Berlin, or they had had their suspicions that the United States might do a deal with the USSR over their heads, but hitherto they had felt they could count on rocklike support from General de Gaulle in their relations with the Russians. Now they were far less sure. This new turn in French policy silenced the so-called "German Gaullists" and enabled Dr. Schroeder to re-establish his au-

[24] Although General de Gaulle had said some years earlier that he felt the Oder-Neisse line should be permanent, this was not the same thing as his appearing to agree on the line with Mr. Gromyko.

thority over German foreign policy. This, in turn, may well have had a bearing on the way French policy developed during June and July.

The Germans were also becoming increasingly troubled by General de Gaulle's scornful repudiation of "integration" at any level and in any context—economic, military, political, European or Atlantic—and his elevation of independence into a supreme national goal. In his television broadcast on April 27 General de Gaulle had once again apotheosized "independence": "However big the glass which is proffered from outside, we prefer to drink from our own, while at the same time clinking glasses with those around us." Not only was this attitude a block to constructive international action on almost every front, but it threatened to arouse dangerous nationalist feelings in Germany.

The Germans, like others, were also becoming increasingly unsure about French intentions in the Common Market: there had been numerous disturbing signs during the spring that once the French had obtained the agreement they wanted on the financial regulation they would refuse to agree to common policies in other fields—commercial policy, taxation, energy, etc.—and would generally seek to slow down the further development of the Common Market. At the end of March the French had also annoyed the Germans as well as the Italians (who had thought they had French agreement) by abruptly rejecting a suggestion which the others were ready to accept that the foreign ministers of the Six meet in Venice to reopen discussions on political union.

The Germans were deeply troubled by the deterioration in their relations with the French and were very reluctant to accept at face value the multiplying signs of French unwillingness to see the Community develop toward a true economic union. And, at German suggestion, the usual summer meeting between the German Chancellor and the French President was brought forward. Perhaps the French realized that they were losing valuable support by pushing the Germans too hard, for both the preparatory meeting between M. Couve de Murville and Dr. Schroeder at the end of May and the full-dress meeting between General de Gaulle and Dr. Erhard (with rows of cabinet ministers on both sides) on June 11 and 12 were apparently more amicable than anticipated.

Community affairs occupied a prominent position in both sets of meetings. The Commission's proposals, although not a package that the Germans themselves were prepared to buy outright, could at least be used to smoke out French intentions. From the scant information that was made public about the Franco-German discussions during late May and early June it seems clear that the Germans felt rather reassured. There were no illusions that the French would yield on those aspects of the Commission's proposals to which they were most adamantly opposed, i.e., giving the Community the proceeds of the customs duties from July 1, 1967, and increasing the Parliament's power over the budget, but the Germans had their doubts about the Commission's proposals on these points, too. The French seemed likely to accept July 1, 1967, as the date for the completion of the customs union in industrial goods, and, perhaps, even to agree that customs duties should eventually become Community property and to accept a rather anodyne German formula on strengthening the Parliament.[25] It also seems reasonably clear that the French told the Germans that they were going to urge 1970 rather than 1967 as the date for the single-market stage so that M. Couve de Murville's switch of position in mid-June came as no surprise. (See below pp. 58–59.) There was apparently no hint that the Community would face a crisis if the talks continued beyond midnight on June 30. Quite the contrary; one of the few consistent themes in the press reports was that there would be no crisis in June on the financial regulation. And once again there were the usual French hints that if all went well there

[25] The German formula on the Parliament would merely have allowed the Parliament to recommend changes in the amounts allocated to various purposes, not to alter the total.

might, after all, be a summit meeting on political union before the end of the year.

Before returning to the discussions in Brussels, it is worth noting that the Commission's proposals had gained considerable support during the spring from various Community and European organizations.

Early in May, M. Monnet's Action Committee for a United States of Europe met in Berlin. This meeting had been carefully timed to coincide with the anniversary of V-E day in order to give the Germans a positive "European" way of countering the anti-German speeches that were expected to mark the occasion in Eastern Europe and a way of avoiding embarrassment vis-à-vis their partners in Western Europe. By a happy coincidence the fifteenth anniversary of the declaration on the Schuman Plan (May 9) could be commemorated simultaneously. Dr. Erhard and Herr Brandt were both present for the main meeting at which Dr. Erhard made a strong "European" speech—strikingly different in tone from General de Gaulle's "independence" speech at the end of April. As usual at meetings of the Action Committee, a lengthy declaration and several resolutions were adopted expressing the Committee's views on the outstanding issues confronting the Six. The Commission's proposals for giving the Community its own resources and for strengthening the control by the Parliament were endorsed, although, significantly, the endorsement was a cautious one supporting the "principle" rather than the details of the Commission's proposals. M. Monnet normally spends several months carefully preparing the declaration, discussing it at length with members of his committee. The document is therefore one in which every word has been chosen with care. As in all such documents the significance of the omissions and nuances of tone are very apparent to those who have worked on them, but they are seldom obvious to the casual reader. Thus the caution with which the Commission's proposals had been endorsed was much less widely noted than the fact that they were endorsed by a group which represented practically all the non-Communist, non-Gaullist, political parties and trades unions in the Six countries.

The enthusiastic support given the proposals by the European Parliament, in March and again in May, has already been commented upon. The Council had also sent the Commission's proposals to the advisory Economic and Social Committee for its opinion on the "economic and technical aspects." Rather surprisingly, in view of the position of the French government, the Economic and Social Committee supported the Commission's proposals unanimously, save for the abstention of one member of the French employers' group who said he had not yet had time to give the matter adequate study. It is worth noting that the Committee, although agreeing that customs duties should go to the Community, as the Commission had proposed, suggested that consideration also be given to other sources of revenue, e.g., a Community tax, for it felt that trade policy might be distorted if the Community depended solely on charges levied on imports for its revenue.[26]

The Commission's proposals also received a warm endorsement from some fifty delegates of the Socialist parties of the member countries who met in Brussels at the end of May, although, as was to be expected, they supported the European Parliament in urging that the Parliament be given more power than the Commission had proposed. And, like the Economic and Social Committee, they felt that the Community's revenue should not come indefinitely only from charges on imports.[27]

Thus by the time the Council of Ministers held its first substantive discussion on the financial regulation and related questions the Commission's proposals had already attracted strong support from the European Parliament, from the Economic and Social Committee, from the delegates of the Socialist parties, and, more circumspectly, from the Action Commit-

[26] See *Agence Europe Presse,* May 28, 1965.

[27] The Resolution of the Liaison Bureau of the Socialist Parties of the European Communities was reproduced by the *Agence Europe Presse* as Document 322, May 31, 1965.

tee. They had also been strongly supported by the Dutch Parliament and by the Italian Parliament and by parliamentary groups in Germany, although the Bundestag had yet to take formal action. It was clear that a lot of hard bargaining lay ahead, but a crisis in the summer seemed very improbable. The Agricultural Fund could function for another year before it ran out of funds, and those who wanted to use the agreement on further financing to extract commitments of other kinds out of the French seemed, for once, to be in a relatively strong bargaining position. No one thought that the Commission's proposals as a whole stood any chance of being accepted. The most likely eventual compromise seemed to be the usual Community formula of firm commitments on the points of particular interest to the French and rather weaker, more distant, understandings on the other questions. But the eventual compromise, or crisis, whichever it was to be, and a compromise seemed more likely, was expected to come toward the end of the year, in traditional Community fashion, not in June, if only because it was assumed that General de Gaulle preferred the CDU to the SPD enough to let the affairs of the Six ride until after the German elections in September.

### *Discussions in the Council of Ministers, June 1965*

The ministerial discussions on June 14 and 15 reached no conclusions, but they were marked by an important shift in the French position. As noted above, the French had been supporting the Commission's proposals that the levies should become Community property when the single-price system came into effect for the principal commodities on July 1, 1967. In fact, the bringing forward to July 1967 of the date for the payment of the agricultural levies to the Community had been suggested by M. Pisani in December 1964 and was—for obvious reasons—warmly supported by the French financial authorities.[28] In the Council discussions in mid-June, M. Couve

[28] See *Le Monde,* June 17, 1965.

de Murville reversed the French position and argued that there was no need to rush things; the single market stage need not come into effect until the end of the transition period laid down in the Treaty; until then the Fund could continue to be supported by national contributions. He thus neatly cut through the knot that tied together the three parts of the Commission's proposals. If the levies were not to become Community property until 1970, no problem of parliamentary control arose until then. Meanwhile, an agreement could be reached on the financing of the Fund from July 1, 1965, to January 1, 1970, without any of the "irrelevancies" raised by the Commission. By this maneuver the French not only cut the knots tied by the Commission but they also outflanked the Dutch government which had hitherto stressed that its own hands were tied by the resolution of the Dutch Parliament making an increase in power of the European Parliament a *préalable* for the acquisition by the Community of its "own resources." This argument had had some force because the implementation of Article 201 of the Treaty and the acquisition of "own resources" by the Community would have had to be ratified by the Dutch Parliament.[29]

As M. Couve de Murville made very clear to the National Assembly the following day, the French were not proposing that the date for the adoption of single prices for cereals and the other major agricultural products should be postponed until 1970; on the contrary, the French still intended that the substance of the common agricultural policy should come into effect on July 1, 1967. As M. Couve de Murville also explained to the National Assembly, he had, as yet, taken no

[29] On February 2, 1965, the Second Chamber of the Netherlands States General had declared that there could be no question of an attribution of independent revenues to the Community pursuant to Article 201 of the EEC Treaty unless the European Parliament were given a central position in the budgetary process of the EEC. As one of the arguments for proposing an increase in parliamentary powers the Commission used the fact that it had to take into account the Dutch government's position vis-à-vis its own parliament.

firm position on the final date for the completion of the customs union.

In the press conference that he gave, as chairman of the Council, following the June 14–15 meeting, M. Couve de Murville said that none of the Six was ready to support the Commission's proposals. This was accurate, but tendentious, because it disguised the fact that the Five, although not prepared to accept the plan *in toto,* did support the principle of "globality," that is they accepted the Commission's argument that the proposals followed logically from one another and formed a whole. Moreover, they all felt *some* progress should be made on all aspects of the plan even though some of the Five governments might have been ready to consider as "progress" undertakings that were little more than commitments to consider favorably in the future.

By the end of this mid-June meeting it was clear that the French were determined to get an agreement on the financing of the Fund for the entire period from July 1, 1965, to January 1, 1970, and that they were in no mood to make any meaningful concessions on parts two and three of the Commission's proposals. By advocating the postponement to January 1, 1970, of the payment of levies to the Fund they showed that they were ready to pay hard cash to prevent the Community having its own resources and the parliamentary point from arising.[30] Earlier there had been some feeling that the French might agree simply to a one-year extension of the existing arrangements to permit more time for the discussion of the Commission's proposals. It was now clear that they were not interested in an interim arrangement and further discussion but that they wanted to postpone until 1970, at the earliest, any consideration of the problems of "own resources" and of the consequential strengthening of the powers of the Parliament and of the Commission. Nevertheless, the French tactics at the Council meeting, the statements made by M. Couve de Murville in opening the foreign affairs debate in the National

[30] See *Le Monde,* June 17, 1965.

Assembly the following day, and that by M. Pompidou later in the same debate, all seemed to indicate that the French wanted an agreement, not that they were searching for a pretext for a break.[31]

When the Council resumed its consideration of the Commission's proposals at the end of June, the French still seemed to be bargaining hard to get agreement on the financing of the Fund until 1970 without making any meaningful concession on either the "own resources" point or the strengthening of the powers of the institutions.

The crucial end-of-June session was in three parts: the foreign ministers and agriculture ministers met on June 28; then, on June 29, most of the foreign ministers[32] went to Luxembourg for a meeting of the WEU Council and the discussions were continued—during June 29 and the morning of June 30—by the agriculture ministers; finally, on June 30–July 1, the last phase of the session was held attended by both foreign ministers and agriculture ministers from most countries.[33]

The first day's discussion opened with a long statement by Sig. Fanfani, the Italian Foreign Minister. He restated the Italian view that the Commission's proposals formed an indivisible whole and that the first part could not be decided upon out of context. Since he felt it was clearly impossible to reach an over-all decision by June 30, he suggested two possible

[31] The occasion for the debate was the government's request for ratification of the fusion treaty. As the Foreign Minister explained, he was intentionally broadening the debate to cover foreign policy generally, with particular reference to Europe.

[32] As usual, and presumably to show French contempt for the organization, M. Couve de Murville did not attend the WEU meeting; France was represented by M. Habib Deloncle. Significantly, M. Couve de Murville was in Paris on the 29th.

[33] Although M. Spaak represented Belgium at the first and third parts of the Council meeting, Belgium had a caretaker government at the time and he was only empowered to take decisions consistent with earlier commitments undertaken by the Belgian government. This made it easier for him to support the narrow view of the scope of the negotiation taken by the French, which he tended to do.

courses of action: either the Council could adopt a stopgap regulation extending the present arrangements for financing the Fund (with a few essential changes), thus giving time for a further consideration of the whole set of proposals, or it could agree on a work program, committing itself to take decisions by specified dates on the various parts of the Commission's proposals. Such a timetable, he suggested, might be worked out by the Committee of Permanent Representatives and adopted by the Council in July. Dr. Luns, the Dutch Foreign Secretary, was in general agreement that one of these two approaches should be adopted. Herr Lahr, State Secretary in the German Foreign Office, again emphasized, as the Germans had throughout the consideration of the Commission's proposal, the importance of linking progress on the customs union, on tax harmonization, and on a common commercial policy with progress on agriculture. He felt this could be done by adopting an over-all timetable, as the Italians proposed, and he indicated his readiness to continue negotiating into July. M. Couve de Murville then reiterated the French case: the financial regulation must be completed by June 30 in accordance with previous undertakings; the other points raised by the Commission were irrelevant and out of order; and they unnecessarily complicated a straightforward decision. He apparently warned his colleagues—without being very specific—that if the decision on the financial regulation were not reached as had been agreed by June 30, matters would take a serious turn. The Dutch and the Italians both reacted strongly against the French assumption that only the one undertaking the French were interested in had any validity; and Mr. Luns pointed out the importance the Dutch attached to the declaration made by the Council on December 23,1963, on an increase in the powers of the European Parliament.[34] Dr. Hallstein also answered, not for the first or the last time, the French charges that the Commission had exceeded its instruc-

[34] In the course of the December 1963 marathon meeting, the Council, at Dutch initiative, inserted the following statement in the minutes of its discussions: "In a discussion of the workings of the European Agricultural

tions and introduced irrelevant new "political" conditions.

Despite the fact that the opening positions remained as far apart as ever, some progress seemed to be being made when the ministers turned from general statements to the consideration of particular points. Thus, although no formal decision was taken, there seemed to be fairly general agreement that July 1, 1967, should be accepted as the goal for the introduction of common prices for the main agricultural commodities and for the completion of the customs union for industrial goods. There was also some apparent progress toward an agreement, in principle, that, at a date still to be agreed on, the agricultural levies and customs duties should become Community property. However, the French position on what the Community budget should finance was very restrictive. They appeared to contemplate Community financing of very little except agriculture and the operating expenses of the institutions, in contrast to some of the other delegates who felt the Social Fund, the Development Fund, the Euratom research budget, etc., should eventually be financed by Community funds. Since all the governments supported the provision in the Treaty stipulating that receipts should not exceed expenditures, the restrictive nature of the French view of expenditures that should be eligible for Community financing was rather more significant than their apparent agreement to the principle of the Community having its own resources at some time in the future.

The ministers of agriculture, meeting as the Council on

---

Guidance and Guarantee Fund, the Council emphasized the great importance it attaches to the question of strengthening the budgetary powers of the Parliament. It will deal with this question at its session in February 1964 together with the reports submitted to it on the merger of the Executives and the widening of the Parliament's functions." Commission, Press documentation, August 4, 1965. This problem was not resolved during the discussion on the merger of the executives. In a declaration to the Council on December 1, 1964, which was subsequently released to the press, the Dutch Foreign Minister said: "This I can say, that none of my colleagues here must harbor the illusion that the Dutch Parliament would cooperate, without proper guarantees of genuine parliamentary control, in the procedure of Article 201 of the EEC Treaty which is necessary to enable farm levies to be paid to the Community. This will therefore be for 1970 at the latest." (Source: the same.)

June 29 and during the morning of July 30, also made a certain amount of progress, particularly in establishing an ambitious timetable for deciding on the common prices for the main agricultural products so that the single-price system could come into effect, as provisionally agreed, on July 1, 1967. Again, available accounts of this session suggest that the French ministers were bargaining very hard but in good faith and that they were, at this stage, neither playing for a break nor anticipating a break.

The permanent representatives also met on June 29 to see whether they could make further progress before the foreign ministers reconvened on the 30th, but this meeting apparently yielded little. The Italian proposals for an over-all timetable were discussed, but the French were clearly not interested in this approach to the problem. The Germans made specific proposals on the way progress on commercial policy and progress on the harmonization of taxation should be linked with agriculture and the formation of the customs union, but no understandings were reached.

The final session of the Council began in the afternoon of June 30. Apart from the two big problems—"own resources" and parliamentary powers—the largely technical problems of the scales to be adopted for contributions to the Fund and the rate at which the Fund would take over payments for expenses eligible to be financed from the Fund had still to be settled. These were matters of particular interest to the Italians for, as already noted, the rapid rise in the standard of living had meant that Italy had become a net importer of agricultural products (imports of meat had risen particularly sharply) rather than a net exporter as had been assumed when the original agreement on the Fund was reached.

The Italians throughout the negotiations took a very tough line, arguing that the existing arrangements for feeding the Fund and for paying out from the Fund should simply be renewed for a year or two respecting, of course, the ceilings on Italian payments into the Fund which had been agreed in December 1964.[35] Most of the other delegates were ready to go further and to agree that so far as expenditures were concerned the practice of increasing the Fund's responsibility for eligible expenses by one-sixth a year should be continued: thus the Fund would become fully responsible (six-sixths) for payments in July 1967 when, in accordance with the agreement already tentatively reached, most of the common prices were to come into effect. The argument about the scale to govern country contributions to the Fund was more complicated, for here there was the usual conflict between the Germans who wanted the contributions to be according to a fixed scale and the French who wanted the contributions to be related to the country's imports. In addition, of course, discussion about the scale of contributions could not be separated from the question of the number of years that country contributions would be necessary or, put the other way around, from the question of the date when the Community would receive the levies and the import duties directly. Although the Germans, and probably the others, would have agreed to a financing arrangement for two years without getting much from the French in return, they were not prepared to agree to arrangements for four and a half years (i.e., until January 1, 1970), which was what the French were now insisting on, without some reasonably firm undertakings from the French on other points.

No record of the Council discussions during the critical night of June 30–July 1 has, of course, yet been made public. But from the available information various points seem to be reasonably clear. On the basis of the progress made during the discussions among foreign ministers on June 28 and the ensuing discussions among the agriculture ministers the outlines of a compromise had seemed to be emerging composed of the

[35] It is worth noting that the Italian minister at the Council meetings was Sig. Fanfani. One reason for the tough Italian line throughout the negotiations may have been his desire—for internal political reasons—to show that he could get more for Italy by resisting the French than Sig. Colombo (who frequently represented the Italians) had done in the past by being more conciliatory.

following elements: July 1, 1967, would be accepted as the date for the completion of the customs union for industrial goods and for the establishment of single prices for the main agricultural products, and a timetable for reaching decisions on these latter would be agreed. The single-market stage within the meaning of Regulation 25 would not, however, be reached until the end of the transition period or until a separate decision to this effect was taken by the Council. The principle of the Community having its own resources at the end of the transition period would be affirmed; this date might be brought forward by decision of the Council. In the meantime, the Fund would be fed by national contributions. The financial regulation would be renewed for a period still in dispute. Some undertakings on fiscal harmonization and on progress toward a common commercial policy would be part of the final decisions. Something would be said about an eventual strengthening of the powers of the Parliament, but this point had not really been reached, and no formula on this point was yet in sight.

During the afternoon and evening of June 30 the French position hardened. On a number of occasions M. Couve de Murville, the chairman, apparently sought to narrow down the discussions to the renewal of the financial regulation; he also repeatedly emphasized the sanctity of the June 30 deadline and warned that a failure to agree would have serious consequences for the Community. In his efforts to settle the financial regulation, and only the financial regulation, M. Couve de Murville was supported by M. Spaak, and, to some extent, by the Luxembourg Foreign Minister, M. Werner. But his insistence on the financial regulation, and only the financial regulation, and his veiled threats about the consequences of a failure to meet the deadline aroused strong opposition from the Dutch, the Italians, Dr. Hallstein and, in the end, from Dr. Schroeder as well.

During the first two and a half days of the negotiations the Germans and the French had been in sufficient harmony to give substance to the rumors that they had, in effect, reached agreement during their numerous bilateral discussions, the most recent being a discussion between Herr Lahr and M. Wormser in Paris on June 22. But this coalition conspicuously fell apart during the night of June 30–July 1.[36] The Germans had apparently been given to understand on a number of occasions that the French did not regard the June 30 deadline as sacred and that they would be prepared to keep on negotiating beyond it; they also had, they thought, French agreement to formulas, at least, on the other aspects of the Commission's proposals. During the night of June 30–July 1 the French Foreign Minister seemed to be going back on both understandings. Accordingly, as the French position hardened the Germans switched their support to the Italians and Dutch, and this, in turn, annoyed the French, and led to later French accusations that the Germans had been the ones to go back on the understandings reached before the meeting.

One incident during the evening attracted much comment. This was the fact that at a time when M. Couve de Murville was refusing to discuss anything but financing of the Fund, Dr. Schroeder ostentatiously drew from his pocket a Bundestag resolution adopted a few hours earlier expressing strong support for an increase in the powers of the European Parliament. This gesture was interpreted as a warning to the French that some concession on the parliamentary point would have to be made and this, apparently, infuriated the French.

Views differ on who first provoked whom and on how the blame for going back on earlier agreements should be apportioned; but there is no disagreement that the relations between

[36] Many of the press reports after the de Gaulle-Erhard meeting indicated that the French were no longer attaching importance to the June 30 deadline. See, e.g., *The Observer,* June 13, 1965, and *The Financial Times,* June 14, 1965. But at that time there seems to have been considerable confusion on the German side about whether or not the French were prepared to agree to an interim arrangement only on June 30. See *Le Monde,* June 15, 1965, and *The Financial Times,* June 15, 1965. For Herr Lahr's comments on this discussion with M. Wormser see report from Bonn in *Le Monde,* July 3, 1965, and *The Times,* July 3, 1965.

the French and the Germans deteriorated during the evening.

The issue on which the negotiations ostensibly deadlocked was the length of time for which the arrangements covering the payments to and payments from the Fund should be agreed. The French and Italian positions were the farthest apart, the French insisting on an agreement covering the full four and one-half years to January 1, 1970, the Italians arguing for a one-year renewal, or, at most, a two-year renewal. The position of the others varied with the prospects for commitments on the related questions to which they attached particular importance. The Italian arguments for a short renewal seemed to be less rooted in the desire to extract other commitments out of the French than in concern lest they should once again find themselves liable to pay more and eligible to receive less from the Fund than was equitable.

Rather late in the evening the French produced a new scale of payments to the Fund designed to help the Italians, and, presumably, to buy them off. The French proposal was not only very generous to the Italians but was also more disadvantageous for the French than earlier proposals, for the French would have picked up a disproportionate share of the reduction in the amount to be paid into the Fund by the Italians. The new French formula nevertheless retained the two features the French felt essential for any scale: first, that it should last until the end of 1969, and second, that an increasing part of the national contribution should be related to imports.[37] It is not clear whether the French proposal was seriously intended to advance the negotiations: it was undoubtedly generous but it was apparently presented in a take-it or leave-it manner, very late in the discussion, and seemed to some of those present to be too crude an attempt to buy Italian support to be taken seriously.

As the evening wore on the French seemed more interested in being able to record a failure than they were in finding

[37] The details of the formula were given in *Agence Europe Presse,* July 1, 1965.

a compromise. Suggestions that the Council be adjourned and continue its discussion later were rebuffed by the French. So, too, was an offer from the Commission to put forward amended proposals. Finally, shortly before two o'clock in the morning of July 1, M. Couve de Murville declared that it was obviously impossible to reach agreement and brought the meeting to an end, despite the fact that all delegations, save the French, were ready to continue to negotiate or to resume negotiations later in the month. It was widely assumed that some time during the evening the French delegation had been instructed by the Elysée to break the negotiations once the deadline of June 30 had safely expired.[38]

There is no agreement on when the French decided to break off the negotiations. One of the more plausible suggestions is that M. Couve de Murville was told when he visited Paris on June 29 that he should break rather than make any significant concessions, that after the Germans began backing the Dutch and Italians he decided he would have to give some general undertakings on parts two and three of the Commission's proposal if he were to get what he wanted on part one; and that the Elysée then confirmed by telephone the instructions given the previous day to break rather than to compromise.

As is customary after Council meetings, M. Couve de Murville, as chairman, gave a short press conference. He put forward the French view that solemn undertakings had not been fulfilled and that there was no point in further discussions. "Each government must draw the consequences." He further made it clear that, in the French view, the provisional agreements on the timetables for agriculture and the industrial customs union now had no validity. In reply to a question about whether the existence of the Common Market was threatened he replied: "I did not say that. We shall see." This and other comments during the press conference seemed to confirm the view that the French delegation had been in-

[38] See *Le Monde,* July 2, 1965, and July 3, 1965.

structed by the Elysée to bring the negotiations to an end with the deadline unmet and that the French ministers themselves were in the dark about what would happen next.

The immediate reactions of the other governments and of the Commission was to play down the crisis and to emphasize that progress was being made and that, given a little more time, agreements could have been reached. They also pointed out that it was totally out of keeping with the traditions of the Community to say that the negotiations had failed and undertakings had been violated because agreement had not been reached by midnight on June 30. "Stopping the clock" was an honorable tradition and one which the French had themselves initiated during the first agricultural "marathon" at the end of 1961.

M. Couve de Murville reported to the French Council of Ministers later in the day on his return from Brussels, and at the end of the meeting M. Peyrefitte issued a statement which bore all the marks of having been dictated by General de Gaulle.[39] After giving the French view of the breakdown, this stated ominously that "the government has decided, as far as it

[39] The full text read as follows: "Following the failure of the Brussels negotiations, the Council took note of and deplored the fact that the commitment made three and a half years ago to complete the financial regulation before June 30, 1965, had not been fulfilled.

"It noted that the European Economic Community thereby found itself in a crisis all the more serious in that it was in consideration of the financial regulations that the French government had agreed, in January 1962, to pass to the second stage of the Treaty of Rome, and in that the decisions concerning a common grain price, adopted on December 15, 1964, had been taken on the basis of the formal and renewed assurances that the financial regulation would be completed, as agreed upon, before June 30, 1965.

"The Council also noted the general agreement concerning the timetable proposed by the French delegation that provided for the completion of the agricultural regulations, which are still pending, and the fixing of common prices. This timetable made it possible to envisage for July 1, 1967, the free circulation of agricultural products within the Community, the implementation of single prices, and the establishment at the Common Market frontiers of uniform protection by means of levies.

"The Council took note of the fact that, while France's partners in the Common Market accepted this timetable, on the other hand new political

is concerned, to draw the legal, economic, and political consequences of the situation which has thus just been created." M. Peyrefitte added that no new meeting in Brussels was planned and that everything was now *"au point mort."*

On the afternoon of July 1 Dr. Hallstein also held a press conference: he opened with a short statement and then answered questions. He summarized the points which had seemed to be accepted and stated his personal view that the negotiations were about at the halfway mark when they were stopped. He said quite categorically that "it was not possible on the basis of the stage of the negotiations that had been reached that morning to state that an agreement on the points still under discussion was impossible."[40] In his opinion the chances of success had been good enough so that the right course of action would have been to do as the Council had done before and to stop the clock and to continue with the discussions. He indicated that the Commission was now reviewing the record in the light of the Council's discussions and might modify its proposals before the Council meeting scheduled to take place on July 26. In replying to questions, Dr. Hallstein also answered the charge that the Commission had been derelict in its duties and too dilatory about modifying its proposals.[41] He maintained that the time for new proposals had not come, that the negotiations had been broken off

---

and economic conditions raised on the occasion of these final negotiations had prevented agreement on the Community's financial responsibility.

"The emergence of this crisis is all the less justified in that the French delegation had made proposals with the aim that France assume a share of the financial burdens, which were considered excessive by some of its partners, and had, on the other hand, agreed to completion of the customs union for industrial goods on July 1, 1967.

"In such circumstances the government has decided, as far as it is concerned, to draw the legal, economic, and political consequences of the situation which has thus just been created." From English text released by Press Service, French Embassy, London.

[40] My translation from French text issued by Commission's Spokesman's Group. The phraseology was strikingly similar to that used by Dr. Hallstein at the time of the veto on British membership.

[41] See, e.g., *Le Figaro,* July 2, 1965.

before all the points had been thoroughly discussed,[42] and that, in any case, the Commission was, as always, playing an active part in the discussions right to the end. He also, in answer to another question, in effect confirmed press reports that the Commission had, toward the end of discussions, offered to amend its proposals but had been rebuffed by the French.

French representatives attended meetings in Brussels as usual on July 1 and 2 (Thursday and Friday) but on the following Monday two Council working parties were canceled because the French delegates had been instructed not to take part, and on Tuesday morning, July 6, it was formally announced by the Secretariat of the Council that the Deputy Permanent Representative for France (M. Maurice Ulrich) had informed the Secretary-General that the Permanent Representative, M. Boegner, had been instructed to return to Paris and that, for the present, the French delegation would not be taking part in Council meetings or in meetings of the Committee of Permanent Representatives. Moreover, it would not send observers, as heretofore, to negotiations being conducted by the Commission on the instructions of the Council. The negotiations with Austria, Nigeria, etc., fell into this category; it soon became apparent that the French boycott applied as well to participation in the special Article 111 committee that advised the Commission on the Kennedy Round negotiations. It was also stated that the French delegation would not take part in committees or working parties preparing projects or carrying out investigations with a view to economic union: the Medium-Term Economic Policy Committee and the Fiscal Harmonization Working party were cited as examples. The official announcement concluded with the statement that "the attitude of the French government on the question of technical committees dealing with day-to-day matters, such as the management committees and Fund committees, will be noti-

[42] This was a reference to the fact that the parliamentary question had not been discussed in any detail.

fied at a later stage." [43] In fact French delegates continued to attend meetings of the management committees and also attended a few other routine discussions at a working level. At a somewhat higher level they also attended meetings of the Councils of Association with Greece and Turkey. However, they stuck rigorously to the rule of taking no part in any discussion leading to or involving new decisions.

The French also decided to boycott a meeting of the Six finance ministers which had been scheduled to meet in Stresa on July 19–20. This was somewhat surprising since the meetings of the finance ministers do not come within the Community framework, strictly speaking, although M. Marjolin normally attends them. The July meeting (which was eventually canceled) was expected to discuss the coordination of the views of the Six on various questions having to do with the reform of the international monetary system, and it might have been supposed that French interest in having support from their partners in the Group of Ten discussion early in August and in the IMF discussions in September, together with the fact that the meetings were of the intergovernmental character approved by General de Gaulle, would have led the French to attend.

The French boycott of most of the Community's activities made it impossible for even the most optimistic to deny that the very existence of the Community was in jeopardy. However, even after it became clear that the French government was determined to build up the crisis rather than to overcome it, the Five and the Commission were at pains to keep open all lines of approach to the French, to avoid anything that could be interpreted as provocation or ganging up, and to make it as easy as possible for the French to return to the negotiating

[43] *Agence Europe Presse,* July 6, 1965. See also *Le Monde,* July 7, 1965. The management committees (*Comités de gestion*) advise the Commission on the day-to-day operation of the common agricultural policy. The French had, of course, a strong interest in having these committees and the Fund committee continue functioning.

table.[44] In the days immediately after the breakdown, the danger seemed to be not that the Commission and the Five would be too intransigent, but that they would go too far in the other direction and make humiliating and far-reaching concessions which might save the Community but only at the cost of drastically altering its character and of encouraging the French to use similar tactics again.

For the next few weeks there was a great deal of diplomatic activity, but little came of it, for the French showed no disposition to resume negotiations on any terms. M. Spaak had earned the approval of the French for his support during the evening of June 30, and for a short time it seemed possible that he might emerge as peacemaker.[45] However, although he, like Mr. Luns and Sig. Fanfani, had discussions with the French while they were in Paris on July 12 for a NATO meeting, it was clear enough that the French were not interested in resuming negotiations.

A few days earlier President Saragat of Italy and his Foreign Minister, Sig. Fanfani, had visited Bonn in accordance with plans made before the crisis. The Italians and the Germans were in agreement that the previously scheduled meeting of the Council should be held as planned on July 26, whether or not the French attended, and that the Commission should prepare new proposals as it had offered to do on the night of June 30–July 1. After various other discussions among the Five and with the Commission on how to proceed, it was decided that the Community should continue to function as normally as possible and that every effort should be made to take up the negotiations at the point at which they had been broken off. This would not, of course, preclude bilateral discussions with the French, but the actual negotiations should, it

[44] Dr. Mansholt, unlike the other members of the Commission, was outspokenly critical of the French, as he had been after de Gaulle's veto on British membership.

[45] The French approval of M. Spaak was very apparent from the official French account of the negotiations on June 28–30, 1965, issued by the French Embassy in London on July 9, 1965.

was generally agreed, be carried on in Brussels within the Council. These procedural discussions were important for by this time it was clear that the Community process itself, not simply the status of the Commission, was under French attack.

The French had asked that a meeting of the ECSC Council scheduled for July 13 be canceled, but the Five, with the rather reluctant agreement of Belgium and Luxembourg, decided to go ahead with it and the Council met for the first time with an empty chair. However, the Five were careful to take no decisions, thus avoiding any legal difficulties about the position of decisions taken in the absence of one member. As the EEC Council was to do later in the month, the ECSC Council began the so-called written procedure for a number of matters requiring decision, that is the proposed actions were circulated to the member governments, including France, with autumn deadlines for reply.

On July 22 the Commission adopted its new proposals on the financial regulation.[46] To allow for greater flexibility in dealings with the French, the new proposals were in the form of a memorandum rather than in the usual form of draft Council actions. Wherever possible the Commission incorporated the agreements that seemed in prospect when the negotiations were broken off; on the points that were still at issue its new proposals went as far as they decently could to meet the French. July 1, 1967, was proposed as the date for the realization of the customs union for industrial goods and for the introduction of free trade and common policies for agriculture including common prices for the important commodities. The ambitious timetable for settling the agricultural prices which had been tentatively agreed by the agriculture ministers was retained. January 1, 1970 (rather than July 1, 1967), was proposed as the date when the Community should acquire its "own resources" and, accordingly, the scales pro-

[46] A summary of the memorandum was issued as a press release by the Commission: P-58, July 1965. The *Agence Europe Presse* published the full text as Document 332, July 28, 1965.

posed for feeding the Fund and for the assumption of expenditures by the Fund were for the full four and one-half years from July 1965 to January 1, 1970. This met the main French point. The Commission proposed that the rate at which the Fund would take over responsibility for export rebates and interventions on the market should, in principle, be at the rate of one-sixth a year resulting in full responsibility in July 1967. However, they made this conditional on the Council's reaching decisions on the regulations for key commodities before the end of 1965; if this were not done the Commission felt that the rate should be a slower one, namely one-tenth a year which would result in the Fund becoming fully responsible in mid-1969.

When it turned to the problem of financing the Fund, the Commission pointed out that its original proposals had been based on the assumption that it was proposing scales for two years only, and that the Italian ceilings had in any case been fixed for those years by the Council in December 1964. It now proposed a new scale: in this new scale a declining proportion of the member states' contributions would be keyed to a fixed distribution scale and an increasing proportion to imports, as the French had been insisting, although the proportion of the total keyed to imports was rather smaller than the French had been advocating. Moreover, starting from these principles (and the ceilings agreed by the Council) the Commission produced a table which set out the percentage of the total resources of the Fund to be borne by each country each year. They hoped in this way to meet the Italian objection that they were being asked to buy a pig in a poke and thus to overcome their objection to an agreement for the remainder of the transition period.

The form of the Commission's memorandum was significant at many points; its own views were put forward in a much less rigid way than heretofore, but at the same time it still tried to commit the Council to important principles. Thus when the Commission dealt with the politically explosive question of "own resources" it first reiterated its own view that it would be logical to provide for the allocation to the Community of the income from the agricultural levies and the customs duties as soon as the customs union came into being and customs duties and levies on intra-Community trade were abolished. It recognized, however, that in the light of opinions expressed at the Council it was probably impossible for the Community budget to be financed by Community resources before 1970. The Commission pointed out that if the customs duties and levies were not to go to the Community an equalization scheme should be adopted before July 1, 1967, when the customs union and common price system were to come into effect. This was straightforward enough and sufficiently in line with the Council's discussion so that it was unlikely to be disputed. The Commission then pointed out that: "Community expenditure will be financed as a general rule by resources of the Community itself as from 1970. Accordingly, in addition to levies on agricultural imports from third countries, in conformity with Article 2 of regulation No. 25, further resources will accrue to the Community, notably income from the application of the common customs tariff. After examining the advisability of allocating to the Community resources not arising from external trade as well, the Council, in keeping with Treaty Article 201, will enact the necessary provisions in good time, on a Commission proposal. In so doing, it will take into account the economic and social situation in the member states, and the need for a just division of charges within the Community." [47] The Commission hoped to satisfy those who attached importance to the Community's having its own resources by getting Council approval of this procedure; but it refrained from asking for any immediate specific commitments.

The Commission was even more judicious and conciliatory to the French in its comments on the powers of the European Parliament. Here it simply noted that discussions were

[47] *Agence Europe Presse,* Document 332, July 28, 1965.

broken off before this point had been discussed in full and reserved its right to put forward new proposals at a later stage.

The Commission then noted that in the Council discussion a number of other matters had been raised—approximation of taxes, trade policy, social policy, and regional policy, in particular. Out of deference to the French it was careful not to link progress on these matters directly to the financial regulation. Instead, it dealt with them in a separate part of the memorandum, and simply indicated a few broad general principles. These established the parallelism that the Germans and the others were anxious to achieve, but the way they were presented left it to the Council to decide when, how, and if, to give effect to the general principles. There was nothing in this part of the memorandum that had to be approved or rejected; however, general approval of the memorandum by the Council would obviously give some assurance that specific decisions on these points would be forthcoming.

The Council of Ministers met as scheduled on July 26 to consider the Commission's revised proposals and other questions, and generally to discuss further the way to proceed in the absence of the French. Shortly before the Council meeting it had been announced that General de Gaulle would not make his usual summer broadcast until September 9. It was clear that French intentions, whatever they might be, would not be known until then.

Dr. Hallstein explained the Commission's thinking in devising its memorandum and the substance of the new document was discussed in a preliminary way, the Dutch, Italians, and Germans apparently feeling it went rather too far to meet the French.[48] The memorandum was, however, sent to the permanent representatives for study prior to the next meeting of the Council in October. There was much discussion but little agreement about how to induce the French to return to the negotiating table. The Dutch, Italians, and Germans continued to maintain that any negotiations must take place within

[48] See *The Financial Times,* July 28, 1965.

the framework of the Community and according to the procedures laid down in the Treaty; the Belgians and Luxembourgers were less sure and apparently felt that the only way forward might lie in a summit meeting of the Six.

There was, at this time, no agreement among the various legal experts in the member countries and in the Community on whether the Council, meeting without the French, could take legally valid decisions. Some argued that it could take decisions requiring only a majority vote; others, that all Six members needed to be present even though the decisions might require the votes of only four or five members. There was also no agreement on the possibility of taking the French to the court for violating Article 5 of the Treaty.[49] It was generally felt that it was premature to try to settle these legal points. No decisions were taken at the July meeting; the few routine points requiring decisions in the near future were handled by the written procedure.

M. Pompidou, rather than General de Gaulle, spoke on the French television at the end of July: he restated the French view that the other Common Market countries had broken their undertakings and, even worse, raised a large number of political and economic matters which were both new and untimely. Looking ahead, he was, once again, scathing in his references to the Commission but hardly illuminating, perhaps because he had not yet been privileged to hear General de Gaulle's intentions and, like others, was waiting to learn on September 9 what the French price for a settlement would be: "For the future, we shall see, there are solutions for everything, and the next months will show toward which one we can go. But what is certain is that if one wants there to be a Common Market, there must be a fair financial regulation and a common market for agriculture. What is certain, furthermore, is that we will not agree that the whole French economy should be directed from outside without the government being

[49] Article 5 requires member states to "abstain from any measure which would jeopardize the attainment of the objectives of this Treaty."

able to exercise the responsibilities it assumes toward the French people. Common sense warns us and experience has shown that we cannot leave to a Commission which has no political function the question of deciding the standard of living of the French and at the same time the future of our agriculture and industry. We certainly do now want to prevent the formation of Europe; I even believe that we are the country which is pushing the hardest for its realization, but it will come only from the resolute cooperation of the countries which make it up. This is our position, and we will stand by it." [50]

[50] See *Le Monde,* July 29, 1965. My translation.

CHAPTER THREE

# *The Meaning of the Crisis*

### *The escalation of the crisis*

In his press conference on September 9, 1965, General de Gaulle made explicit what everyone had known to be true but had been reluctant to face. The crisis was only peripherally about the regulation for financing agriculture and much more profoundly about the way the Community functioned: "What happened in Brussels on June 30, in connection with the agricultural financing regulation, highlighted not only the persistent reluctance of the majority of our partners to bring agriculture within the scope of the Common Market, but also certain mistakes or ambiguities in the Treaties setting up the economic union of the Six. That is why the crisis was, sooner or later, inevitable." [1]

In General de Gaulle's view the principal mistakes were, of course, the provisions for the progressive introduction of majority voting and the role given to the Commission—"this embryonic technocracy, for the most part foreign." He had two objections to majority voting: first, that "France would be exposed to the possibility of being overruled in any economic matter whatsoever, and therefore in social and sometimes po-

[1] The quotations here and elsewhere are taken from the English version of General de Gaulle's remarks in the EEC publication, *European Community*, October 1965.

litical matters, and that, in particular, all that has been achieved by French agriculture could be threatened at any moment, without France's let or leave," and, second, that majority voting would strengthen the role of the Commission, because of the provision in the Treaty that Commission proposals can be amended only by unanimous action. General de Gaulle made it quite clear that he fully understood the importance of this innovation in the Treaty and that he was not prepared to accept it. It was also clear that in his view any real delegation of power to an independent, non-French body was unthinkable: "Moreover, after this same date [January 1, 1966], the proposals made by the Commission in Brussels would have to be accepted or rejected in their entirety by the Council of Ministers, without the states being able to change anything, unless by some extraordinary chance, the six states were unanimous in formulating an amendment. We know that the members of the Commission, although appointed by agreement among the governments, are no longer responsible to them, and that, even on the conclusion of their terms of office, they can only be replaced by the unanimous agreement of the Six, which, in effect, renders them immovable. One can see where such a subordinate position could lead us, if we allowed ourselves to deny, at one and the same time, our freedom of action [i.e., give up the right of veto] and our Constitution, which lays down that 'French sovereignty resides in the French people, which exercises it through its representatives and by means of referenda,' without making any sort of exception at all" [i.e., powers cannot be delegated].[2]

It is worth noting in passing that General de Gaulle assumed that "unanimity" among the Six governments, either in amending proposals from the Commission or in agreeing on new commissioners, would be extremely difficult to find: this was a rather revealing recognition of the difficulties of working by unanimity by its foremost exponent. It may also have reflected an assumption on General de Gaulle's part that on

[2] The same. Bracketed explanations added.

many issues French views were likely to be in conflict with those of its partners.

It is also worth noting that General de Gaulle led up to his analysis of the "mistakes" in the Treaty by a number of inaccurate and tendentious comments on the negotiations of the Treaties of Paris and Rome, blaming the inclusion of the provisions to which he took particular exception on the fact that the treaties had been negotiated while France was weak and before "we had decided to take our destiny into our own hands." This assertion was too much for many Frenchmen.[3] It was true that the French had negotiated from weakness, but they had done so brilliantly with the result that the EEC Treaty, in particular, not only contained more hard concessions to France than to any other country, but it also revealed on every page the effectiveness of the French in persuading their partners to accept French ideas and concepts. The Treaty of Rome is a very Gallic document. But it is not, of course, a Gaullist document. And that was the trouble.

Once again, as he has done in practically every major address since 1960, General de Gaulle ridiculed those who had "dreams" of a European federation, a "project devoid of all realism," and put forward his alternative of "organized cooperation between the states, evolving no doubt toward a confederation." In May 1960, when General de Gaulle in outlining his views on Europe during a press conference said that "the path to be followed must be that of organized cooperation between states, while waiting to achieve, perhaps, an imposing confederation," [4] many of the strongest "Europeans," including men such as M. Monnet, who were skeptical of General de Gaulle's European policy, attached a great deal of weight to his use of the word "confederation" and read into it signs of a willingness on General de Gaulle's part to contemplate the eventual evolution of his kind of Europe into their kind of Europe. By the autumn of 1965 there were no such

[3] See, for example, Pierre Uri in *Le Monde,* September 15, 1965.
[4] See Camps, *Britain and the European Community,* cited, pp. 302–303.

illusions. General de Gaulle's speech was read everywhere as a fundamental attack on the Community method, on those innovations in the Treaty of Rome that set it apart most sharply from traditional international organizations, and as a warning that there would be no resumption of French participation in the Community until these key features in the Treaty had been changed.

General de Gaulle also made it clear that he was only prepared to discuss these matters with governments, not with the Community institutions: ". . . France for her part is ready to join in all exchanges of views on this subject which are proposed by the other governments. Should the occasion arise, she envisages the reopening of negotiations at Brussels as soon as agriculture is brought fully within the scope of the Common Market, and as soon as people are ready to have done with the pretensions which ill-founded, Utopian myths raise up against common sense and reality."

The press conference brought out into the open the fundamental differences between General de Gaulle and the rest about the institutional structure of the Community which, although everyone knew they existed, had been skirted with considerable success since General de Gaulle returned to power in 1958. It also raised doubts about whether enough common ground could be found to enable the Community to continue. This time the crisis was clearly going to be a long one, and it might not in the end prove to be soluble. Nevertheless, although General de Gaulle's comments angered and depressed "Europeans" everywhere (including many rather lukewarm "Europeans"), it cleared the air of false hopes by making the confrontation with General de Gaulle open and inescapable, not least in France.

General de Gaulle's attack on the treaties also tended to make the Five more cohesive than they had been and more conscious of the points on which they were in agreement among themselves. During the final stages of the negotiation on the financial regulation at the end of June, everyone had made mistakes and afterward there had been a good deal of self-reproach and mutual criticism. In retrospect, the pre-midnight tactics of the Dutch, Germans, and Italians seemed to many people to have been unnecessarily provocative. And the Commission was felt by many (including some of its own members) to have tried for too much and to have held on to its proposals for too long before offering to put forward modifications. The French refusal to "stop the clock" and the French boycott of most of the work of the Community during the summer tended to make these feelings of guilt on the part of the others pass more quickly than they might otherwise have done. The press conference by lifting the controversy on to a new plane made irrelevant the earlier tactical mistakes and errors in judgment. More importantly, it forced the Five to define their real differences with the French.

It has been one of the strengths in the French position in the continuing dispute that has gone on intermittently since General de Gaulle's return to power that views about the way "Europe" should be built have not been strongly polarized around a "Gaullist" view, on the one hand, and a "European" view on the other. On the contrary, there has been a broad spectrum of views, or, rather, a series of spectrums, for positions have varied with the particular points at issue. One of the curious features of the French tactics during the autumn of 1965 was that by deliberately and rather crudely escalating the crisis they practically forced the Five to come together in opposition to themselves.

It was clear enough from the Commission's July memorandum that the financial regulation could be settled largely on French terms any time the French were prepared to return to the conference table. It was also clear that, despite the anger caused by General de Gaulle's press conference, the Five were prepared to meet any reasonable French demands on the functioning of the Community. The French, however, showed no signs of being willing even to discuss their demands with their partners.[5] Moreover, shortly before the EEC Council of Ministers met (as Five) at the end of October, the French government once again appeared to be deliberately fanning the flames of controversy. This time it was M. Couve de Murville who seemed to be pushing up the price for a settlement in a long speech on foreign affairs to the National Assembly on October 20th.

In opening that part of his speech that concerned Europe, M. Couve de Murville made much more explicit than General de Gaulle had done the connection between the crisis and the lack of progress among the Six on political union: ". . . political Europe is still pending. Only time will tell whether we are merely up against a delay. In the meantime, doubtless because the political evolution of Europe has not progressed in step with its economic evolution, economic Europe is in a state of crisis." [6] Apart from this central point, which is discussed further below (see pp. 91–92), M. Couve de Murville made a number of rather exaggerated charges against the Commission and then dealt in considerably more detail than General de Gaulle had done with the institutional features of the Treaty to which the French objected.

In commenting on the Commission's handling of its proposals he made the point that rather than being discreetly in-

[5] During September M. Spaak sounded out his partners on a plan for proposing to the French that the foreign ministers of the Six meet as a Council of Ministers but without the Commission being present to discuss both the financial regulation and the provisions in the Treaty to which General de Gaulle had taken exception. His proposal met with a rather mixed reception. It was generally agreed that at some point there would have to be a meeting with the French without the Commission being present, but there were differences of view about the subjects that should be discussed in the Commission's absence, the precise nature of the meeting, and the timing of any initiative. The French soon made it plain that any meeting before the French election was out of the question, but the idea of proposing some kind of meeting of the Council without the Commission being present persisted, and a variant of M. Spaak's proposal was eventually agreed upon by the Five and accepted by the French. (See below, p. 92.)

[6] Own translation from French text in *Le Monde,* October 22, 1965.

formed and consulted beforehand, "as would have been normal," the governments learned of the proposals because they were "stated publicly and in detail on March 24, before the Assembly in Strasbourg." The Commission had acted imprudently, but M. Couve de Murville overstated his case: the French government, like other governments, knew a good bit about the proposals before Dr. Hallstein made his speech, although the consultations with governments had not been so full as customary. Similarly the presentation to the Assembly, although unwise, was not out of line with previous practice.

When he turned to comment on the substance of the Commission's proposals for giving the Community its own resources, M. Couve de Murville stated that in his view the Commission's objective had been to transform the nature of the Community "into what the Commission has apparently always wanted, namely . . . a real political authority, decreasingly controlled by the responsible governments. This was the meaning of a permanent appropriation of funds much in excess of its foreseeable expenditure. It was also the meaning of the apparent transfer of powers to the Assembly, which in reality would have tended to turn the Commission into an arbitrator between the Assembly and the Council of Ministers."

Once again the French Foreign Minister had a point, but again he exaggerated. The Commission's proposals would, if adopted, have increased, rather modestly, its own power as well as that of the Assembly.[7] It was also true enough that ever since the revival of discussions among the Six on political union, Dr. Hallstein, in particular, had been emphasizing the political character of the EEC. He had never been modest about the role of the Commission, which he had clearly seen as that of a "real political authority" as M. Couve de Murville said. And, as president of the Commission, he regarded himself as entitled to many of the courtesies normally accorded to heads of governments. However, as the French Foreign Minis-

[7] See Chapter Two, p. 45.

ter himself made plain, whatever the Commission's hopes may have been, none of the other governments was prepared to accept the proposals in full. The most that could have been agreed upon had the negotiations been allowed to proceed in the normal way was a very modest increase in the roles of the Commission and the Assembly, not the wholesale transfer of authority to an "irresponsible technocracy" that spokesmen for the French government always portrayed themselves as resisting.

M. Couve de Murville then turned to the changes in the Treaty of Rome the French seemed to want: "A general revision (*révision d'ensemble*) has become necessary in order to define the correct conditions for cooperation among the Six . . . . clearly what has shown itself to be at issue was the very functioning of the Brussels institutions." M. Couve de Murville then analyzed in some detail the way he felt the Commission should work and set out more explicitly than had been done before the French objections to majority voting. And he made it perfectly plain that until the role of the Commission and the question of majority voting had been settled there could be no discussion of the financial regulation and no resumption of full French participation in the Community. Although in June the French had made much of the fact that the Commission and the Five were introducing "political questions" into a technical discussion, M. Couve de Murville now insisted that these political questions must be settled before the technical discussion could be continued: "A political agreement is necessary before the discussions can be resumed on concrete, technical problems."

Several points made by M. Couve de Murville in his discussion of the role of the Commission and the voting provisions should be noted. In the first place he accepted the fact that the Treaty of Rome and subsequent decisions taken under the Treaty limited French sovereignty. But these, he said, were limitations on sovereignty taken "freely and consciously" and by the authorized representatives of France:

Supranationality, in European jargon, is a very different notion. Essentially it enables decisions concerning a country to be taken by authorities other than its own. This is the case when such a decision can be made by an international organization or by foreign governments. In other words, this is the case if one leaves a question concerning France to the judgment of a Brussels Commission or of a majority of governments when the French government is not part of the majority. . . . I say that, in our view, the conclusion forced upon us by the lamentable experience which we have just undergone is that French interests have no other defender than the French government, and that our agriculture in particular can no longer entertain the illusion that it will find elsewhere a knight errant to whom to entrust its future.

He then shed some light on how the French thought the Commission should function:

The Brussels Commission is charged with submitting to the Six governments proposals for the decisions which they have to make. And commentators have always dwelt on the inherent advantages of a system whereby such an organization, described as independent, is called upon to present the European point of view against the narrow national views of each government. . . . We have never disputed that it could be useful to put forward an objective view of the problems and of their solution. But what is above all necessary, in order to arrive at a solution, is to obtain general agreement, or in other words to find a compromise. This is the chosen field where the Commission can and must use its talents. To put it differently, it is up to the Commission before all else to look for ways of bringing the points of view closer together.

In other words, M. Couve de Murville was saying that the Commission should function as a normal international secretariat. It should not, as it had done with conspicuous success in the past, try to find solutions that represented a "Community solution" but should simply help the governments come to a compromise between conflicting national interests.

M. Couve de Murville then turned to the issue of majority voting.

Until the present time, apart from specific measures of an administrative nature, the Six must make decisions by general agreement, that is to say unanimously. Such is the case, in particular, when the Commission's proposals are accepted or altered. From January 1, 1966, this would change: these proposals could still be amended only unanimously, but they could be accepted by a majority. This, in the present state of relations between the Six, and keeping in mind what has just occurred, seems inconceivable.

In discussing the majority-vote question M. Couve de Murville referred to the fact that he had said (in 1963) that it would be very difficult to imagine that on an essential economic question, such as the price of cereals, the Council would make a decision against the will of one of its partners. And, he continued,

This statement had, at the time, been given a mixed reception. The German government, however, took it up on its own account in December 1964, just after the prices had been agreed, by asking that the result that had been obtained should not be threatened in the future by a majority vote. Nobody either did or could resent this. In the same way, how could we accept that decisions taken so far unanimously, particularly in agricultural matters, should be threatened by a majority vote?

Had M. Couve de Murville rested his case simply on these two points—that decisions reached by unanimous vote should not be changed by majority vote and that none of the Six was really ready to have matters that affected "their vital interests" decided by majority—his remarks would not have created much dismay, for as he pointed out there was a good deal of agreement among all the Six governments on these questions. But the link between majority voting and the role of the Commission, the call for a *"révision d'ensemble,"* and the categorical rejection of the delegation of any authority to an international body clearly indicated that although he had, naturally enough, used the strongest cases to illustrate his point, the French wanted a more far-reaching agreement from their partners than would have been the case had they been concerned only with "safeguarding their vital interests." And again, as he had done at the beginning of his comments on the European crisis, M. Couve de Murville suggested that events might well have taken a different turn if the French proposals on political union had been accepted:

Perhaps the situation would have been different if, as France has been proposing for the last five years, the beginnings of regular political cooperation could have been established between the Six. No doubt the climate of relations would then have been quite different. Frequent meetings, including some at the highest government levels, would have made it possible to discuss all matters in an atmosphere of trust, to seek to bring points of view closer together on a political basis, in short, to avoid clashes, to conclude agreements, and to proceed in such a way that the clause providing for a departure from unanimity would have remained in the realm of theory.

Finally the French Foreign Minister underscored what General de Gaulle had also indicated: it was now up "to the responsible governments, to them all and to them alone, to discuss the matter and seek an agreement."

There were differences of view about just how various passages in M. Couve de Murville's speech should be interpreted: the phrase *"révision d'ensemble,"* in particular, gave rise to much speculation, being read by some to mean a general revision of the Treaty, by others much less drastically. Some thought that the French might ask for formal revision of those provisions in the Treaty that enabled decisions to be taken by majority votes; others, that some kind of "gentleman's agreement" that no country would be voted down on a matter of "vital interest" would be enough. It seemed probable that some limitations on the Commission's right of initiative and on its powers to deal directly with third countries would also be demanded. It also seemed probable that agreement on the French proposals for a "political union" might be a further French condition for the settlement of the crisis.

One of the reasons for the hardening of the French position may have been the fact that the German elections were now over. Dr. Schroeder was to continue as foreign minister and no appreciable concessions had been made by Dr. Erhard to the so-called "German Gaullists." Moreover, at this time it seemed probable—although it proved not to be the case—that some variant of the MLF/ANF might soon become a live issue once again. General de Gaulle had seemed to be hoping for a changed German attitude when he gave his press conference on September 9: "Who knows, in fact, if, when, and how the policies of each one of our partners, after some electoral or parliamentary development, will not finally come round to facing the facts which have once more come to the fore?" M. Couve de Murville, although he made no direct reference to the Germans, began his remarks by recognizing that the "conjunction of policies and efforts" which was the condition of success of "an economic and later political organization" of the Six had not yet been achieved "either because only mediocre attention is paid to our own political aims, or because more importance is attached to other links—which are quite justified, we agree—but which should not be dominant to the extent of becoming exclusive."

A Council of Ministers meeting of the EEC, the second since the French boycott began in July, was held a few days after this new statement of the French case. It was at this session that the Five finally agreed on a version of M. Spaak's earlier proposal for a meeting without the Commission. They also reached substantial agreement among themselves on the Commission's July memorandum on the financial regulation. At the conclusion of their discussions a formal statement was issued which was of far more importance than the usual Council communiqué. The Five governments first solemnly reaffirmed "the necessity of continuing to implement the Treaties of Paris and Rome" and stated that "the solution of the problems confronting the Communities must be found within the framework of the Treaties and of their institutions." The statement then noted that the Five had discussed the Commission's memorandum on the financial regulation and had agreed on the "fundamental principles which, in their opinion, should enable negotiations among the Six to succeed." The president of the Council had been instructed to inform the French government and "to appeal urgently to it to resume its place in the Community's institutions." The statement indicated that the Five were convinced that it would then be possible, "following the Community procedures, to adopt the regulations required in order to complete the common agricultural policy within the framework of the balanced development of the Community."

The Five thus made it plain that discussion of the financial regulation must continue to take place in the usual way on the basis of a proposal from the Commission and in the presence of the Commission. The fact that the statement dealt with this point before the "political points" raised by the French was presumably meant to indicate their readiness to settle the financial regulation whenever the French wanted. The "balanced development of the Community" referred, of course, to the second part of the Commission's memorandum and reflected the fact that the Five intended to maintain the link between completing the Common Market for agriculture and completing the customs union for industrial goods and making progress on other fronts—tax harmonization, Kennedy Round, common commercial policy.

The last part of the Council's statement dealt with the fundamental institutional questions raised by the French. Since the form as well as the substance of the statement was the result of much thought and discussion among the Five it is worth quoting in full:

Taking into account the statements made by the President of the French Republic on September 9 and by the French Minister for Foreign Affairs on October 20, the delegations also instructed the President of the Council to invite the French government, within the framework of the Treaty of Rome, to join them in a special meeting of the Council of Ministers at Brussels. As an exception to the usual practice, this meeting could be held with only the ministers present, as provided for by the Council's rules of procedure. The agenda should be restricted to an examination of the general situation of the communities. It would be highly desirable that this meeting should be held as soon as possible.[8]

The proposal for a special meeting with the French, as it emerged from the discussions at this session of the Council, was thus rather different from the proposal originally put forward by M. Spaak: the special meeting was brought firmly within the framework of the Community; the invitation to the French would come from the president of the Council; the meeting would be a meeting of the Council of Ministers; it would be held in Brussels; and the agenda would be restricted to an examination of the general situation of the Communities. The discussion of the financial regulation would, in contrast, take place according to the normal Community procedures and in the presence of the Commission.

Although the proposal for a special meeting of the Council naturally attracted the most public attention, the reaffirmation of loyalty to the treaties and to the institutions established by the treaties was the most important feature of the statement, for it showed that there was now a solid core to the common position of the Five and certain agreed principles they were now prepared to defend.

It seems probable that M. Couve de Murville's speech in the National Assembly helped the Five to agree among themselves that they would stand on the principle of "no revision of the treaties." At this time the French seemed to be badly overplaying their hand. Rather than capitalizing on the confusion that reigned during the summer, first General de Gaulle and then his Foreign Minister drove the Five together and practically compelled them to define a common position from which to bargain with the French. These were very curious tactics, so curious that it seemed not improbable that General de Gaulle had decided that continued French participation in

[8] Quoted from text in *European Community,* November 1965.

a community built on the Treaty of Rome pattern was inconsistent with the kind of "independence" he sought, and that he was, therefore, ready for a break unless the Five were prepared fully to accept his views.

Mystification and dismay at French tactics and fear that the French government might really be preparing to take France out of the Community were not confined to the Five. Within France there had been growing criticism of French action since the boycott began in July. And there was as little certainty and almost as much alarm about the ultimate aims of French policy there as elsewhere. For example, Maurice Duverger, writing in *Le Monde* at the end of October, said there were three possible interpretations of the French government's European policy: General de Gaulle might simply be raising the stakes to be in a strong position for the ultimate bargaining; or he might be trying to dominate the Community; or he might already have resolved on a break. Nothing, he felt, pointed conclusively to any one of the three, although M. Couve de Murville's statement in the National Assembly seemed to him to point slightly toward a break.[9]

During the summer (1965) the farm groups in France had been unusually critical of French policy, and they had been unwilling to accept the government's assertion that it was acting in the best interests of the farmers first in calling a halt to the negotiations and then in boycotting the Council and other meetings. An exchange of letters between the leaders of the four large farm organizations and M. Pompidou, which was released at the end of the summer, revealed the resentment the farmers felt both at the tactics used by the government and at the substance of the government's position.

At the end of July the farm organizations had written the Prime Minister asking him to state his views on the Commission's revised memorandum. M. Pompidou had replied very curtly that the negotiations were the responsibility of the government. Incensed by this brusque treatment, the farmers'

[9] See *Le Monde,* October 28, 1965.

associations had circularized the members of the National Assembly pointing out that the preamble of the Constitution gave interest groups the right to make known their views on matters of concern to them and stating that they considered the Commission's new proposals were an adequate basis for the resumption of negotiations.[10] During the summer the farm organizations had also informed the French government that in view of the crisis they could take no further part in certain of the work then under way on the Fifth Plan. On October 21 the largest of the farm organizations (FNSEA) made its opposition to the government's policy even plainer by pointing out to its members that it would be foolish to support the government in the forthcoming election since it was not acting in the farmers' interests.[11] Finally, on the eve of the French presidential election, the farm organizations put out a White Book which although largely noncontroversial in tone drove home the point that the continuation of the Common Market was considered to be essential: "Any extension of the Brussels crisis would be a tragedy for agriculture and for the whole French economy." [12]

During the summer and fall of 1965 the farm groups were the most outspokenly critical of the government's handling of the crisis; but, as fears grew that General de Gaulle might really be planning to push his demands to the point of a break, criticism came from the *Patronat,* the trades unions, virtually all political groups except the UNR, from most of the non-Gaullist press, and from many influential Frenchmen who had not heretofore been publicly critical of General de Gaulle.

The objective of a "European Europe" was widely accepted in France. But for some time there had been growing concern among thoughtful Frenchmen at the glaring contradictions in General de Gaulle's European policy. France needed partners, above all Germany, if she was to build a

[10] See *Le Monde,* September 2, 1965.
[11] See *Le Monde,* October 23, 1965.
[12] See *Le Monde,* November 4, 1965 and November 6, 1965.

"European Europe"; yet General de Gaulle seemed bent on alienating the Germans and driving them into even greater dependence on the United States. Few Frenchmen had any illusion that General de Gaulle could persuade his partners to choose French hegemony in place of American hegemony, whereas a European community, effectively, if not formally, led by France had been within his grasp. "Independence" for Europe had been a popular theme; General de Gaulle's new emphasis on "independence" for France was not, for it was rightly seen to put the future of the Community in jeopardy.

By the time the French presidential election campaign officially opened in November, it was clear that the opposition had an important issue in the European crisis and that the efforts of the government to blame the crisis on the overweening ambition of the Commission and the recalcitrance of the Five had not been so successful as had been hoped. The contrast with the reaction after the veto on British accession was very marked. Then the manner of the veto had been criticized, but within France there had been almost no concern at the fact of the exclusion of the British and widespread acceptance of the French government's assertion that she was really acting in the best interests of the Community in keeping out the "unready" British. In contrast, in the summer of 1965 criticism was widespread for a number of reasons. French interests were threatened. The action of the government was not a single dramatic act which was soon a matter of history but a continuing attitude with consequences which were daily becoming more apparent. Moreover, the farmers and other interest groups in France were directly engaged in Community affairs: they knew from their own connections with similar groups in other countries and from their representatives on the Economic and Social Committee of the Community what the facts were and how the French boycott was likely to affect the progress of the Common Market and their own interests. The Common Market and its institutions had become factors in domestic life; the Community was not something "foreign" that the government could simply be left to deal with on its own, whatever M. Pompidou might say.

The government's European policy, and particularly its handling of the crisis, was clearly an issue in the French election, although the argument still continues about how significant a factor it really was. In "European" circles the first reaction to the "putting into ballotage" of General de Gaulle on December 5 tended to exaggerate the importance of the European issue. This interpretation was soon contested by analyses of the voting which gave domestic social policies pride of place in accounting for General de Gaulle's surprisingly low poll in the first ballot. They also cast doubt on how much of M. Lecanuet's unexpectedly good showing he owed to his strong "European" line and to M. Monnet's endorsement of him.[13] Whatever the eventual verdict of the psephologists, it is a fact that all the opposition candidates felt it important to be critical of the French government's handling of the crisis and to show their support for the Community.[14] It is also a fact that the government felt it desirable to become rather more optimistic about the chances of a settlement during the campaign than it had been shortly before. Between the first and second ballot, especially, there was a very marked effort to put the government's European policy in a favorable light, and to hold out the prospect of an early settlement.

The first reasonably encouraging French statement was made by M. Peyrefitte on November 17, after a meeting of the French Council of Ministers. The conditions for a resumption of negotiations had, he said, been improved by diplomatic exchanges with the Italian and German governments. These, together with statements made by M. Spaak, showed that three of the Six now wished to settle the dispute, as did France.

[13] For M. Monnet's endorsement of M. Lecanuet see *Le Monde*, December 3, 1965.

[14] See *Le Monde*, December 2, 1965, for the replies of the principal opposition speakers to a question about their European policies.

And, he added, it now seemed probable that the foreign ministers would soon meet.[15]

The French had made no formal reply to the communication sent to them after the Council of Ministers meeting at the end of October, but it was clear from diplomatic exchanges that some meeting would be held somewhere after the French election. When the EEC Council met again at the end of November (still without the French), the Five reaffirmed their October statement, but they also went a little further to meet the French and empowered the chairman (Sig. Colombo) to "make known the common position of the Five governments to the French government." This came a little closer to the bilateral negotiations the French had wanted and the others had resisted, although Sig. Colombo was clearly given his mandate in his capacity as chairman of the Council and the major purpose of his exploratory talks with M. Couve de Murville (which were held in Rome on December 8) was to try to settle the time and place of a meeting of the Six, not to negotiate on the substantive points at issue. The press reports after the Rome discussions indicated that a little progress had been made and, on December 16, just before the second ballot in the French election, M. Pompidou was confidently predicting that agreement on a meeting would be reached soon after the election.[16]

General de Gaulle dealt with European problems at some length during one of his television broadcasts in the interval between the two ballots. He spoke in a rather different tone than he had in September, if with little change in substance. He seemed ready to settle the financial regulation for agriculture, provided it was not "adorned" with political conditions. For the rest, he reiterated his well-known view that Europe could only be built by cooperation among states, dismissing again as "myths and chimeras" the "supranational" approach. As M. Couve de Murville had done in his speech to the Nation-

[15] See *Le Monde,* November 18, 1965.

[16] See *Le Monde,* December 18, 1965.

al Assembly he referred to earlier French efforts to persuade their partners to coordinate their foreign policies and indicated that if the Common Market surmounted its current trial ("I very much hope we will do so") it would be necessary to take up again the question of political cooperation among the Western European states. One of the most remarkable features of the broadcast was that in this connection and in five other places he rather conspicuously referred to the English, or England, suggesting, more than once, that at some not-too-distant date the British would be part of the Europe of which he spoke.[17] These and other hints to the British at about the same time were looked at askance by many "Europeans" who feared some kind of deal might be in the making, for example, an agreement to lift the veto on British membership in the Community in return for the formal abandonment of majority voting. As discussed in Chapter Five, the British refusal to rise to the flies cast over them by General de Gaulle did much to convince "Europeans" on the Continent that the position of the Labour government was changing and becoming markedly more "European."

General de Gaulle was assumed to be bidding for M. Lecanuet's votes, and indications of a more cooperative French approach were regarded with considerable skepticism until after the voting was completed on December 19. However, after the re-election of General de Gaulle, the French government continued to show signs of being willing at least to talk with its partners, and just before Christmas an official re-

[17] See *Le Monde,* December 16, 1965. "Si nous arrivons à surmounter l'épreuve du Marché commun—j'espère bien que nous le ferons—il faudra reprendre ce que la France a proposé en 1961 et qui n'avait pas réussi du premier coup, c'est-à-dire l'organisation d'une coopération politique naissante entre les Etats de l'Europe occidentale, et à ce moment-là il est fort probable qu'un peu plus tôt, un peu plus tard, l'Angleterre viendra se joindre à nous, et ce sera tout naturel. Bien entendu, cette Europe-là ne sera pas comme on dit supranationale. Elle sera comme elle est. Elle commencera par être une coopération, peut-être qu'après, à force de vivre ensemble, elle deviendra une confédération."

The television interview took place on December 14, 1965.

ply to the October communication from the Five was finally given to the Italian Ambassador in Paris. Shortly thereafter it was announced that the Six would meet on January 17 and 18 at Luxembourg.

The Five had originally insisted that any meeting must be held in Brussels. The French had been strongly opposed to Brussels, and, at one point, were known to be urging Venice, for they wanted to turn the meeting into an intergovernmental discussion outside the usual Council framework. Luxembourg (which was, in the end, apparently suggested by the French) was slightly less distasteful to the French than Brussels, which was tainted, in their eyes, by being the seat of the Commission. Acceptance of Luxembourg was a minor and defensible concession for the Five to make: it is one of the official seats of the Community, the Council customarily meets there from time to time, and on January 1, 1966, the Luxembourg government assumed the chairmanship of the Council of Ministers. There was also something rather appropriate about returning to the spot where the first Community of the Six had its headquarters for a meeting which promised to be one of the historic encounters of the Six.

During the autumn of 1965 the Five had been much firmer than most observers, and the French government, had thought likely. They had handled a difficult and complex situation with restraint and skill: they had neither given anything away nor been provocative. It is perhaps arguable that the Five might have been a little bolder during the autumn and that they went rather too far in refraining from taking any action which would give the French plausible grounds for claiming that the Five were violating the Treaty by taking decisions in the absence of one member.[18] But probably caution was a

[18] There was much argument within the Community about the legal position of decisions taken in the absence of one member. Many, but not all, of the Community lawyers were prepared to defend the thesis that the Community institutions must be able to exercise their full powers and that, accordingly, the Five could legally take decisions requiring a unanimous vote as well as decisions requiring majority votes.

condition of unity among the Five and that, above all, was necessary.

As a consequence of their prudence the Community machine ticked over, but it only ticked over. The French adhered strictly to the position that they would participate in carrying out decisions that had been taken before July 1 but would not take part in any new work. A number of routine decisions were accordingly taken by the written procedure. The strict adherence—by both sides—to the rule of taking only implementing decisions meant that by the end of the year the Kennedy Round negotiations were effectively stalled. The work of the Special Agricultural Committee of the Community had come to a halt in the summer, and, in the absence of decisions on the policies and prices to be applied to sugar, fats and oils, dairy products, etc., the Six could not comply with the agreement reached earlier in the year to table offers on the agricultural side of the Kennedy Round by September 16, 1965. The mandates already given the Commission left a little room for negotiations during the fall on the industrial side and on a cereals agreement, but by the end of the year the Commission had exhausted its authority and needed new instructions if the negotiations were to continue. Similarly, new instructions from the Council were required if negotiations with various third countries were to be continued. The important agreement with Nigeria had been awaiting Council approval since the summer.

The perhaps rather excessive caution followed on all sides also led to some anomalies. For example, the Commission's punctilious observance of the letter of previous decisions, combined with the French government's consistency in refusing to take part in any new decision, however trivial, led to the curious result that a Commission proposal on the regulation to be applied to oranges was allowed to go through although it was opposed by all the governments save Italy.

The Five and the Commission were not only very cautious about taking legally doubtful steps and careful to avoid creating new problems which might make the French return more difficult, they were also scrupulously fair to the French. And in the disbursements made from the various Community funds there was no suggestion of penalizing the French.

The Five and the Commission also tried very hard to find an answer that would be acceptable to the French to the very thorny problem of the adjustments in the external tariff that were required at the end of the year. A problem arose because of the expiration of the agreement—which had been made by the Six governments at the time they made their second alignment in external tariffs—that they would use as the basis of the alignment the common external tariff reduced by 20 per cent. They had made this agreement on the assumption that the Kennedy Round would be completed, or far enough along by the end of 1965, so that this reduction could be confirmed as part of that negotiation. This, of course, had not proved to be the case. All kinds of expedient were examined to try to find a way for the low-tariff countries to avoid having to raise their external tariffs (which they were not prepared to do) without violating the Treaty. In the end the problem was simply stated to be in the process of examination; the French, in effect, accepted this state of affairs, and intimated that they would not make an issue of the technical violation of the Treaty it probably implied, provided the situation was regularized by April 1, 1966.

At the end of the year the French, like the rest of the Six, cut their internal tariffs by 10 per cent as required by the Treaty. There had been doubt until the last minute whether the French would, in fact, make the cut. Although the Treaty required a tariff cut on January 1, 1966, the acceleration in earlier cuts meant that intra-Community tariffs were already down to the level originally envisaged for January 1, 1966. The French might, therefore, have argued that the cut rerequired on January 1, 1966, had already been made. This sign of good will on the part of the French was, however, offset to some extent by their last-minute refusal to agree to the

Community budget by the written procedure, despite the fact that the Five had deliberately scaled down their proposals to make them acceptable to the French.

The French boycott during the summer months had not been particularly serious, for this is always a slack period in Community affairs. But by the end of the year there was no disguising the fact that the situation could not continue for much longer. Either the French would have to return or the Five would have to take their courage in their hands and make decisions on their own. As the year ended, it was far from clear which would happen.

### *The Luxembourg meetings*

When the French and the Five finally met in Luxembourg on January 17 and 18, the French demands were set forth in some detail for the first time. As anticipated, the French asked for far-reaching changes in the way the Commission operated and for the effective elimination of majority voting. Of the two, there seemed to be rather more room for bargaining and compromises on the proposals they put forward concerning the Commission than there was in their position on majority voting. For the latter was, quite simply, that they should always retain the ultimate right of veto.

The French views on the role of the Commission were set forth in a ten-point document circulated by M. Couve de Murville to serve, as he explained, as a basis for discussion.[19] Taken together, the changes proposed were very far-reaching and the tone of the document was gratuitously insulting. However, the French had clearly been careful to couch their proposals in terms which could be accepted without requiring a formal modification of the Treaty of Rome. This was not, as M. Couve de Murville candidly pointed out, because they were opposed to amending the treaty, but because the Five

[19] M. Couve de Murville's "decalogue" was fully reported in the press. See, e.g., *Le Monde,* January 19, 1966. The text was later released by the Information Service of the European Communities.

had made it plain they would not accept changes in the Treaty and it was clear that changes would not be ratified by some of the parliaments.

The main effects of the French proposals would have been first, and most importantly, to circumscribe and to make far less effective, but not to eliminate, the Commission's right of initiative; second, to curb the slow accretion of power by the Commission that had been taking place; and third, to stop the Commission imputing to itself the role of an embryonic European "government."

Heretofore the Commission has, very consciously and frequently successfully, used its right of direct access to the European Parliament, to interest groups, and to the press to mobilize public support for its proposals and thus to create pressures on the member governments which have limited their effective area of choice. As described in Chapter Two, the Commission's attempts to rally support for its financial proposals were bitterly attacked by the French, notwithstanding the fact that similar activities by the Commission in support of proposals having French approval (for example, to bring pressure on the German government to accept the single cereals prices) had escaped French criticism.[20]

In his "decalogue" M. Couve de Murville sought to put an end to these lobbying activities on the part of the Commission. In the first place he proposed that, before definitively adopting proposals of particular importance, the Commission should consult governments at an appropriate level. This, in fact, had been the normal Commission procedure, although it was true that the consultations on the financial regulation had not been as thorough as usual. How limiting acceptance of this French proposal would be would depend largely on how such a provision was drawn; some formulations would simply make the customary practice obligatory, others could introduce a government veto on the Commission's right to propose. The next

[20] For further details about the way the Commission has made its right to propose more effective by mobilizing public support for its proposals see Camps, *What Kind of Europe?* cited.

French proposal was that the Commission should never inform the Assembly or the public of the nature of its proposals before they had been submitted officially to the Council, nor should the Commission on its own initiative ever publish its proposals in the *Official Gazette* of the Community. Taken together, these limitations would reduce the effectiveness of the Commission as the "motor" of the Community. Some governmental restlessness about the Commission's tactics is understandable—and it has not been limited to the French government—but the ability of the Commission to push and prod governments by appealing to public opinion over the heads of the governments has unquestionably been an important factor in the success of the Common Market.

The next two proposals put forward by the French were really designed to stop powers slipping into the Commission's hands as a consequence of the way the Commission drew up its proposals or directives for Council approval. In a sense the French were here criticizing the Council for its laxity as much as the Commission for its unbecoming ambition. Thus the French pointed out that the Commission tended to draw its proposals too broadly; by approving them the Council endowed the Commission with general rather than specific powers. The French argued that the right of Council review should be retained when tasks were delegated to the Commission, and that any executive powers given to the Commission should be clearly circumscribed and no room left for discretionary action by the Commission. The French then pointed out that when the Commission drafted its directives for Council approval, it sinned in the opposite direction and drafted them too restrictively, with the result that the member states had far less leeway than the Treaty appeared to give them in determining the way to carry out the directives.[21]

[21] Article 189 of the Treaty provides that: "Directives shall be binding, in respect of the result to be achieved, upon every Member State, but the form and manner of enforcing them shall be a matter for the national authorities."

The French were, of course, right that these practices tended to transfer powers to the center and to limit national freedom of action. But precisely this kind of gradual growth at the center was foreseen by the drafters of the Treaty of Rome. And, far from having occurred behind the backs of the governments, it had been taking place in large measure as a result of decisions of the Council.

The French also put forward various proposals which although primarily of symbolic importance had some substantive overtones. Thus the French objected to the practice that had grown up for accrediting diplomatic missions to the Community on the grounds that this gave too much prominence to the Commission; they also objected to the way the Community was being represented in international organizations.

The French memorandum also included various proposals designed to keep the Community's information policy under stricter government control and to curb the freedom of speech of the commissioners. Again, although the Commission's "style" was ostensibly under attack, the French proposals were designed to reduce the independence, and effectiveness, of the Commission.

One of the remarkable features of the Communities has been the fact that, until the crisis, the very vigorous information policy carried on by the Commissions and the High Authority has escaped governmental criticism. From the earliest days of the European Coal and Steel Community large sums have been spent on "information," much of which has been excellent propaganda for the European idea. High Authority and Commission officials have cooperated with the Community information services to make it possible for the press, students, and other interested groups to get a detailed understanding of how the Community functions and of the nature of the problems with which the institutions deal. Largely as a result of these activities the Community has been an alive and interesting organization in a way no other international organization has yet become. The hold that the Common Market now has on the popular mind throughout the Community owes a great deal to the energy and sophistication of the information services. Perhaps, at times, the information services have come a little too close to providing "European" propaganda rather than simply information; perhaps at times individual commissioners and some of the Community publications have gone rather too far in criticizing governments. But the fact that information has been provided so efficiently and so liberally and that the commissioners speak freely and can and do criticize the member governments has helped make the Community a living organization and one that arouses intense interest and support. It seems probable that the French proposals were designed not only to save the government embarrassment, but also, more broadly, to damp down the fires of European enthusiasm, and to weaken the popular appeal of the Community.

Finally the French proposals urged a revision of the procedures for Community expenditure, without, however, providing specific suggestions.

The first discussions among the foreign ministers indicated that the "decalogue," although far from satisfactory as it stood, contained points that were worth discussion and might conceivably be reworked into an acceptable document.

The French position on majority voting at the first Luxembourg meeting was, in contrast, very rigid and seemed to offer little room for compromises. The Five were prepared to try to find a formula to make it clear that a country would not normally be voted down when its "vital interests" were at stake, but, by insisting that any country must itself have the sole right to determine when a question involved its vital interests, M. Couve de Murville made it plain that the French were insisting on a veto and that they would accept no formula that allowed a majority vote ever to be taken against their will.

During the discussion at the January 17–18 meeting the French also proposed a timetable for reaching agreement not only on the two points which were at the center of this discussion—majority voting and the role of the Commission

—but also on the fusion of the executives of the three communities, the budget for 1966, the financial regulation, and the unresolved points concerning the external tariffs. The timetable was so clearly designed to meet French needs, and only French needs, and to preserve French bargaining power at every move, that it raised fears that some new French ultimatum might be in prospect. It also escaped no one's notice that acceptance of the French timetable would have meant that the Five would have agreed to the termination of the existing Commission before any agreement had been reached on the members of the fused Commission, thus weakening their bargaining power in an argument which promised to be long and arduous.[22] The absence of any reference to other outstanding problems, and particularly the Kennedy Round, was also noted.

As had been generally expected, no agreements were reached at this first Luxembourg meeting except that a second extraordinary meeting should be held at the end of the month to try again to find a basis for resuming the normal life of the Community. Meanwhile the permanent representatives were to try to bring the opposing positions closer together.

Two features of this first meeting of the Five and the French were significant. First, the fact that the solid front of the Five had held, thanks in part to French obduracy on majority voting; and second, the fact that Dr. Schroeder, the German Foreign Minister, had taken a very firm position in opposition to the French and had been turned to by the rest of the Five as their natural leader. Heretofore the Germans had been reluctant to assume the role as leader of the Five in opposition to the French, and the others had been ambivalent about having the Germans assert their leadership. Now they welcomed Dr. Schroeder's firmness.

Before this first encounter of the Six, the French had again

[22] The term of office of Dr. Hallstein, and most of the other members of the Commission, has expired, but, under the Treaty, the Commission members continue in office until replaced. Agreement to the French proposal would have opened the way to an interregnum.

seemed to be going out of their way deliberately to antagonize the Germans. Three episodes are worth recalling. At the NATO meeting in December (1965) the French had annoyed the Germans both by their refusal to go along with the customary statements on German reunification and also by their attempts to play down and weaken the McNamara Committee. In the second place, it was announced, shortly before the Luxembourg meeting opened, that General deGaulle would visit the Soviet Union later in the year. This had been anticipated, but the timing of the announcement was odd. About the same time the French also announced that they were liberalizing their imports of industrial goods from the Soviet bloc.[23] This, too, was a rather strange prelude to the resumption of participation in the Common Market, for the question of a common commercial policy had been on the Community agenda for a long time and for the past year the Germans had been stressing the need for a common policy toward Eastern Europe. The French action underlined their determination to keep their hands free and was consistent enough with Gaullist concepts, but it was not a move which was calculated to reassure the Germans on the eve of an important negotiation.

It is difficult to know how to assess the German firmness at the first Luxembourg meeting and to measure with any exactitude how far it was dictated by their understandable annoyance with the French and how far by "community mindedness" and a genuine desire to preserve the essential features of the treaty. It seems probable that the developing attitude of the British (discussed in Chapter Five) also had some effect on the Germans, and on the rest of the Five, although again the impact this made can be variously interpreted. Those who have questioned the depth of Dr. Schroeder's and Dr. Erhard's commitment to the Community of the Six suspect that their firmness may have owed something to the fact that the prospect of a break and a subsequent deal with the EFTA countries was not wholly unattractive. Whatever the motives for firmness, and they were undoubtedly mixed, the conse-

[23] See *The Times,* January 13, 1966.

quence of the German position was to commit Dr. Erhard and Dr. Schroeder to the Community and to the Treaty of Rome in a way neither of them has been personally committed heretofore. And it made the French face the fact that, contrary to their expectations, they could not dictate the terms of a settlement: there was a price the Five were not prepared to pay for French participation. The strength of the German commitment to defend the treaty was underlined just before the second Luxembourg meeting when Dr. Schroeder outlined to the Bundestag the German government's position. He was supported in his firmness by all three parties—CDU, SPD, FDP—thus making it abundantly clear to the French that they could expect no change in the German position at the second encounter.

During the interval between the two Luxembourg meetings the permanent representatives, with the French participating, had held a number of meetings in Luxembourg and had made substantial progress toward an agreement on the document concerning the Commission. These surprisingly harmonious discussions foreshadowed a change in the French position. By the time the Six foreign ministers met again on January 28 it was clear that the French instructions were to put an end to the crisis and to resume their place on the best terms possible, but not to risk a break.

The second Luxembourg meeting was a very different encounter from the first, for, from the start, it was clear that the French were now ready to bargain. In the end agreement was reached surprisingly rapidly on the three main subjects: majority voting, the role of the Commission, and the calendar, i.e., the order in which various outstanding Community subjects were to be handled. The texts of the principal decisions have been published, but it is worth commenting on a few of the main features.

The understanding reached on majority voting was the most important—and least satisfactory—aspect of the settlement. The decision had four paragraphs. The first paragraph stated:

When issues very important to one or more member countries are at stake, the members of the Council will try, within a reasonable time, to reach solutions which can be adopted by all the members of the Council, while respecting their mutual interests, and those of the Community, in accordance with Article 2 of the Treaty.[24]

The second paragraph contained a unilateral declaration by the French government:

The French delegation considers that, when very important interests are at stake, the discussion must be continued until unanimous agreement is reached.

Paragraph three then put on record the fact that a difference of view existed on what should be done if it proved impossible to reach agreement:

The six delegations note that there is a divergence of views on what should be done in the event of a failure to reach complete agreement.

Finally, paragraph four stated that the six delegations considered that this difference of view would not prevent the Community from resuming its work in accordance with the "normal procedure." [25]

During the discussion, M. Couve de Murville apparently maintained that the French would not only regard as invalid any decision taken by a majority vote on a matter which they considered to be inappropriate for a majority decision, but that they would not join with others in putting another country in a minority on an issue it declared was in this category, i.e., involving "very important interests." [26]

It is also worth noting that during the discussion the Germans argued that any decision that should have been taken during the period of the boycott and would at that time have

[24] Article 2 sets forth the general aim of the Community.

[25] The quotations are from the text put out by the London office of the European Communities' Information Service (no date).

[26] Given the way votes are weighted in the Community, the curious result of this French position is to make France and Luxembourg the only countries against which a majority decision could, technically, be taken.

been taken unanimously should still be subject to a unanimous vote. Their purpose in so doing was to ensure that the outstanding agricultural regulations, and particularly the prices for dairy products and the arrangements for sugar, should be agreed unanimously. The German statement gave M. Couve de Murville a welcome opportunity to point out that all the Germans need do to protect themselves was to accept his view on majority voting. But, in the end, it was agreed that not only the financial regulation but also a number of the outstanding agricultural decisions would be taken by common agreement. To the surprise of some delegates the French did not press for the inclusion of the Kennedy Round in this special list; it is not very surprising that they failed to do so, for this would have detracted from the force of the general French position that all important decisions must, of course, be decided unanimously.

The French have thus put the others on notice that if they resort to a majority vote in a situation in which the French feel a unanimous decision is appropriate there may be another crisis. The Five have refused to change the treaty and have reaffirmed their own support for the principle of majority voting. As discussed further below, the decision in itself has done no more than make explicit a situation that was known to exist.

The document that was agreed upon concerning the role of the Commission was much milder both in tone and in substance than the original French paper: even the Commission —in its chastened mood—did not feel that acceptance of the new document would weaken its role significantly or impair its effectiveness.[27] It was clear enough that after the events of the summer the Commission was going to move very circumspectly in the future in any case, and, to some extent, the new document guarded against the kind of pretensions and ex-

[27] The ministers agreed that the "practical measures of collaboration" on which they had agreed should be discussed with the Commission and "established by joint agreement on the basis of Article 162 of the Treaty." (This discussion had not taken place when this book went to press.)

cesses which the Commission would now not dream of committing. On the key point of the Commission's right of initiative the new version stated: "It is desirable that the Commission, before adopting a proposal of particular importance, should, through the Permanent Representatives, make appropriate contacts with the governments of the member states, without this procedure affecting the right of initiative which the Commission derives from the Treaty."

The Commission's scope for stimulating public support for its proposals may, perhaps, be somewhat more restricted in the future than it has been in the past, but the formal limitations do not appear to be very serious. The document stipulated that proposals and other official acts addressed to the Council or the member states should only be made public after the addressees had received the texts and "formally taken cognizance of them." There were also some general provisions for tightening up the cooperation between Council and Commission and on the functioning of the press and information departments which may mean some limitations on the rather surprising degree of freedom that has heretofore been allowed these groups. The stipulation that the Council and the Commission should define the means of increasing the effective control of Community spending may also cramp the Commission's style somewhat. However, unlike the paper originally circulated by the French, the total effect of the document that emerged from the Council was not one that ran counter to the spirit of the institutional concepts embodied in the Treaty.[28]

Similarly the discussions by the ministers on M. Couve de Murville's controversial timetable, or calendar, produced a reasonable enough agreement. The budget was to be settled by the written procedure before February 15. Although the Council of Ministers would begin its work by settling the financing regulation, the discussion of other questions would be resumed concurrently, and the Kennedy Round was specifically mentioned in this context. Discussions were also to begin

[28] Quotations are from the text released by the London office of the European Communities' Information Service.

immediately—in the margin of the Council meetings [29]—on the membership of the new Commission. The governments would agree during the first half of 1966 on the date for depositing their ratifications of the fusion treaty, it being expressly recognized that parliamentary ratification must first have taken place and agreement reached not only on the membership of the enlarged Commission but on the president and vice-presidents.

### *The reasons for the crisis*

It is generally agreed that the French could have achieved at least the substance of the Luxembourg agreement—possibly rather more—without having provoked the crisis. Why, then, did they turn the argument over the financial regulation into the worst crisis in the life of the Community? And why, having deliberately intensified the crisis in September and again in October, did the French accept the kind of settlement they did when they did? Who were the gainers and who the losers? And what will be the effect of the crisis and its settlement on the development of the Community?

Until fairly recently the Community has been at a stage in its development when most of the actions that needed to be taken by the member governments were fairly precisely laid down in the Treaty of Rome. The Six were forming a customs union, and the steps for removing barriers among themselves and aligning their separate tariffs with the common external tariff were, for the most part, defined by the treaty. Recently, however, although the customs union is not yet fully completed, the focus has been shifting to the steps required to transform the customs union into an economic union. The removal of trade barriers is, in a sense, a negative act; the adoption of common policies is a positive act, and one which much more directly and clearly impinges on the role of governments

[29] The discussion on the membership of the Commission is, formally speaking, between representatives of the member states acting in that capacity rather than as members of the Council.

and restricts independent national freedom of action. Despite constant pressure from the Commission and increasing pressure from their partners in the Six, particularly the Germans, the French have adamantly refused to take any real steps toward a common commercial policy although here the Treaty is clear that by the end of the transition period the Six are to pursue common policies, and it is clearly desirable—both for technical reasons and to increase bargaining power with third countries—that the Six should begin moving in that direction. French pressure for a common agricultural policy has been a striking exception to the general picture which has been increasing French resistance to moves toward common policies in whatever field—atomic energy, conventional energy, taxation, monetary questions.[30] But, even in agriculture, the French position has been to try to obtain the advantages of a common policy without making any of the concessions in terms of Community control over the agricultural levies that, as the Commission dared to point out, was the logical corollary.

Participation in a free trade area or an arrangement going somewhat further and providing for a common tariff structure and various kinds of regulatory arrangements can be accepted without any very great limitations on freedom of action in those fields that seem to General de Gaulle to be important—foreign policy and defense. But there comes a point in the process of economic integration when this is no longer true. By 1965 the European Economic Community had reached a watershed; if it was allowed to develop much further, participation in the Community would inevitably have restricted national freedom of action on matters affecting foreign policy.

The strategy of the "Europeans" has, of course, been to put their faith in this "spill-over" effect: to argue, for example, that once the Six had moved some distance toward a common

[30] Transport is, perhaps, a partial exception. However, the kind of common action required in this field is largely of a technical order and has little "spill-over" effect into political fields.

tariff the need for a common commercial policy would become inescapable, and that once the Six had adopted common commercial policies pressures would build up to coordinate other aspects of foreign policy. The crisis and the French boycott of the Community were backhanded confirmation of the correctness of the European analysis about the dynamics of economic integration.

For a long time, although the eventual connection between economics, politics, and defense was always recognized, there appeared to be a kind of tacit understanding among the Six that they would keep their commitments to the Common Market in one compartment, their differences on other matters in another. And, until the crisis, the progress of the Common Market seemed to be demonstrating that a surprisingly high degree of political difference among the member states was, in fact, tolerable—if the will to tolerate it existed. We shall not know for sure until the official records become available—or General de Gaulle completes his memoirs—but it seems probable that the crisis occurred because General de Gaulle was no longer prepared to let the economic development get out of phase with political-defense commitments. If the other members of the Community would not accept the French concept of Europe, France must have independence of action.

If France's partners had shared General de Gaulle's vision of Europe and had been prepared to accept the French view of what foreign and defense policies the Europe of the Six should follow there would doubtless have been no crisis. M. Couve de Murville said as much in his speech to the French Assembly on October 20. The connection he then made between progress on the political side and the development of the Community was not, of course, a new French theme.[31]

By 1965 it was completely clear that the Five, and particularly the Germans, would not accept French views on defense. As indicated above the real lesson of the cereals prices "vic-

[31] See above, pp. 86 and 91. It is also worth noting that on March 25, 1965, M. Couve de Murville when responding to criticisms in the European

tory" at the end of 1964 was not that the Germans had yielded to the French on this point or had put loyalty to the Community above the interests of the German farmer, but that they had stuck to the MLF and were conceding on what they considered to be a far less important issue. The steam may have gone out of the MLF by the spring of 1965, but presumably one of the reasons why the United States felt that it could let the steam out was that it had, by then, few doubts as to where German loyalties lay if they were ever forced to choose between the United States and France. Nor had General de Gaulle.

In this situation it was entirely logical that General de Gaulle should have concluded that a "European Europe" was not a possibility; it was also entirely consistent that in those circumstances he should have wanted to limit the extent to which his hands were tied by commitments to his Common Market partners. The Commission by trying, boldly and legally, but rather imprudently, to outmaneuver the French and to force the pace toward integration by wrapping the financial regulation the French wanted in an ambitious Community package may have helped to precipitate the crisis at the end of June. However, on the assumption that the French wanted to slow down developments in order to maintain their freedom of action "the crisis was, sooner or later, inevitable," as General de Gaulle frankly admitted in his press conference on September 9.

The obvious way to put themselves in a position to control the future development of the Community and to ensure that their freedom of action was not limited to any important ex-

---

Parliament that he had said nothing about "political union" when making his report to the Parliament as chairman of the Council said: "This criticism, speaking as the representative of France, I accept with pleasure. The French government has not been the last . . . to state that the evolution of the Common Market, in particular, if not the other Communities, implies some political developments, and that it is not conceivable that the Common Market will continue (*subsiste*) if, to a large extent and progressively, these developments do not take place."

tent was to do exactly what the French did do: to insist upon the maintenance of a right of veto and to try to curb the Commission so that it could not acquire further power and also so that it would not make it difficult or embarrassing for a government to exercise its right of veto. The Commission by engaging public support in defense of its proposals, and by bundling several proposals together into awkward packages, had demonstrated in the past that it could effectively limit the governments' freedom of action.

On the assumption that the principal French motive was to regain control over the direction and pace of European developments it would have been very surprising had M. Couve de Murville been persuaded to accept some kind of understanding on majority voting based on the recognition that the "vital interests" of the member states must be respected. It was never very easy to believe that fear of being outvoted on an issue that could legitimately be interpreted as a "vital national interest" was, in fact, his main concern.

The treaty provisions for majority voting are important, but there are substantial limitations on the use of majority voting and the prospect of the "vital interests" of one member being overridden are negligible. In the first place, most decisions which are highly charged politically (such as the admission of new members) and all decisions which would extend the scope of the Community to new fields, i.e., beyond the subjects the Six have already committed themselves to settle in common by signing the Treaty of Rome, will always require the unanimous decision of the Council. In the second place, the Council can normally take a decision by a majority vote only when it is acting on a proposal from the Commission. Since the Commission is charged with promoting the Community interest there is a reasonable safeguard that, even though a country may not like a decision that is being taken over its objection, the decision will be one that it feels is, nevertheless, fair and objective. It is relevant to note in this connection that when the treaty was being negotiated the small Benelux countries were prepared to accept a voting system that enables them to be outvoted by the three big countries when the Council is acting on the basis of a Commission proposal: but they insisted that, in other cases, at least one of the little countries must vote with the majority. In the third place, as discussions among the Six have made plain time and time again, all countries can be counted on for evident reasons of self-interest and a healthy fear of the tables being turned to refrain from voting down their partners without very good cause. Finally, the three large countries are well protected by the way the votes are weighted; in most cases they can only be outvoted if they are opposed by all the other member countries save tiny Luxembourg. Thus the risks of any of the large countries being outvoted are not very large and, if it has a reasonably good case, they are tiny. But the French needed more than reassurance that their vital interests would be respected if they were to keep from being progressively and inescapably caught in the process of integration.

Majority voting was, of course, doctrinally repugnant to General de Gaulle, and doubly so when, as in the Community voting system, it tended to increase the power of the Commission. The assumption that there is a common interest that can, and should, on occasion, override a national interest—an assumption that underlies the Community method of decision taking—has no place in the Gaullist view of relations among states. This would have been reason enough to oppose the move to majority voting, but the signs of a changed French attitude toward the further development of the Community that were noticeable in the spring before the crisis broke, General de Gaulle's consistent emphasis on the need for independence (and his dropping of the theme of a "European Europe"), the allusions to political union, and the sheer logic, in Gaullist terms at least, of keeping political and economic developments in phase, suggest that the fundamental element in the French position was the recognition that the *engrenage* was working rather too well and that they needed to take some action to free their own hands.

Although again it is impossible to be sure, it seems probable that until very late in the year (1965) General de Gaulle was prepared to carry his policy through to the point of taking France out of the Community, if the Five were not prepared to give in on majority voting and to take some steps effectively to curb the Commission. But it also seems probable that the French were supremely confident that the Five would give in and that this drastic step would never have to be taken. This was not an outrageous assumption. On the contrary, until the crisis the Five had been very dependent on French leadership, and a Community without the French was, quite literally, unthinkable.

However, during the autumn, thanks largely to the fact that the French overplayed their hand, the Five were forced to fend for themselves. The French boycott of the Community boomeranged badly, for it showed the Five, and the French, that they could act without the French if they had to. And General de Gaulle's attack on the "mistakes" in the treaty and M. Couve de Murville's apparent demand for a revision of the treaty gave the Five a clear issue on which to find and hold a common position—defense of the treaty. It would have been very difficult for them to have found firm enough agreement on anything else, for all of them were prepared to "interpret" the majority voting rules in various ways and most of them were not opposed to some disciplining of the Commission.

Until the first Luxembourg meeting and the emergence of the Germans as the leaders of the Five it had not been clear to anyone whether the common front of the Five would hold when they found themselves at the table with the French. When it finally became plain that the Five were not going to give in on the key point—majority voting—it is understandable that the French changed their position just enough to reach a settlement.

The "European response" in the French election, the attitude of the farm organizations, and of the *Patronat* and other organizations, had shown that, whether or not the issues involved in the dispute were fully understood or considered important, the Common Market was very popular in France. It seems clear, too, that, although General de Gaulle himself may have felt the Common Market was expendable, his ministers did not. Even M. Couve de Murville, who is no "European," had had to admit in answer to a direct question in the National Assembly that the Common Market had on the whole been beneficial for France.[32]

The French no longer had the power to paralyze the Community by remaining outside. The period of stalemate was drawing to a close and signs were multiplying that if they continued to boycott the Brussels meetings the Five would shortly begin taking decisions on their own. The date of January 1, 1966, was important in this connection, for whatever the doubts in Community circles about the validity of taking decisions as Five, the case for so doing became much clearer once a substantial number of matters became eligible for majority vote. The French choice was not, therefore, between maintaining the status quo and returning to the Council table but between seeing the Five resume operations with France or seeing them resume operations without France.

Even less desirable, from the French standpoint, was the prospect that, if they continued to hold aloof, the Five would soon turn to the British. Just how this would happen was never very clear to anyone, but the Five had made no secret of the fact that they were thinking of approaching the British if the French continued their boycott. Some people thought in terms of a deal between the Five and the EFTA, others hoped the United Kingdom would slip into the chair left vacant by the French. There was an obvious tactical element in the interest the Five showed in the British at this time. But the interest was not entirely tactical. Although the British scrupu-

[32] See *Le Monde*, September 14, 1965.

lously refused to be drawn into the argument on either side—perhaps they were rather too scrupulous [33]—by the time the final argument among the Six took place they had made it pretty clear that they were "neutral on the side of the Five." There was little doubt anywhere that if the parting with the French came, the British would be ready to come to some arrangement with the Five.

With the emergence of the Germans as the leaders of the Five and the prospects of some kind of an accommodation between the Five and the United Kingdom the French government presumably decided there were fewer risks in returning to the Community than in continuing to hold aloof. The French had failed in their attempt to rewrite the Treaty of Rome, but they were in a strong position to control developments from the inside. There were good domestic reasons for wanting the Common Market crisis settled before the elections for the National Assembly which were to be held some time during the next year. And there would be other opportunities for trying to change the treaty. It seems probable that it has always been part of the Gaullist strategy to try to remove the "offensive" features from the treaties when, in accordance with the agreement already reached among the Six, a single treaty is negotiated to take the place of the two Treaties of Rome (the EEC and Euratom treaties) and the Treaty of Paris (the ECSC treaty).

Who has gained from the crisis and its settlement? The signs are rather mixed, but there has undoubtedly been a shift against the French in the balance of power within the Community. The French spell if not broken has, at least, been badly cracked. The Five are now five in a way they never were before, even after the veto. If the French were again to walk out it would be easier for the Five to come together than it was in the summer of 1965 and they would be far readier to keep the Community going by taking decisions in the absence of the French. On the other hand, there has also been a shift in

[33] This point is discussed further below in Chapter Five.

power away from the Commission and toward the national governments. This stems less from the agreements reached at Luxembourg in January 1966 than it does from the general feeling everywhere that the Commission acted rashly in the spring of 1965 and from the fact that the Commission played no part in the settlement of this crisis. The governments of the Five handled the crisis, and they handled it very well.

The experience of the crisis will breed caution on all sides. It is true that the French, having decided that the dangers of being outside were greater than the dangers of remaining inside, are unlikely to walk out again. But the Commission and the Five are not likely to put the French to the test. Majority voting may remain on the books, but the prospect of its being used against French wishes is rather more remote than it was before the crisis, and it was fairly remote then. In this situation the French will be in a position to see that the Community develops very slowly and that further integration takes a more intergovernmental, more cooperative, less integrative form.

But the French are not in a position to undo what has already happened. Further progress will doubtless be slow, but until the false dawn of the cereals settlement in December 1964 the common assumption among the "Europeans" was that the most they could hope for was a holding operation until General de Gaulle returned to private life. The outlook after a year of exaggerated hopes and an attack that failed was neither very much better nor very much worse than it was before. Everyone had lost a few more illusions; the Common Market had not broken apart; the Six had decided, once again, to try to live with their differences.

CHAPTER FOUR

# *Britain and the European Community (1963 and 1964)*

### *The reaction to the veto*

After General de Gaulle called a halt to the British negotiations for membership in the EEC in January 1963 there was for a time some feeling in Washington and in European circles close to M. Monnet that the British should try to overbid the veto by putting forward a plan for a European defense community which could, eventually, control the British nuclear deterrent. Whatever the merits of this proposal—and they were debatable—any such British initiative in the spring of 1963 was politically unthinkable. Ratification of the Treaty of Rome could almost certainly have been obtained had the negotiations been allowed to continue.[1] But the political implications of joining the Common Market had been deliberately soft-pedaled by Mr. Macmillan and his ministers and the British people were far from ready for any dramatic new initiative. The Opposition argument that the government had made a series of humiliating concessions in the negotiations had had its effect, and the mood in the country in early 1963 was

[1] For further discussion of this point, see Camps, *Britain and the European Community*, cited, pp. 505–6.

uncertain and confused. Moreover, the veto itself was a stunning shock. There were a few forceful pleas for a British initiative, but the instinctive public reaction to the veto was to draw back from Europe and to take a certain satisfaction in once again "standing alone," not to search for ways to overbid the veto.

It had taken great political courage to decide to open negotiations with the Six, for although it was a farsighted move it was also a gamble. It was a gamble on British opinion developing fast enough and far enough during the period of the negotiations to make the terms of accession politically acceptable, and it was a gamble on those forces within the Community that favored British entry proving stronger than those that opposed British entry. When the attempt failed, Mr. Macmillan had no reserves to fall back on. He had shot his bolt.

Moreover, the Common Market and the kind of political construction that had been discussed in the Fouchet Committee were not only the most that the British government thought was then politically feasible for it to put to the electorate, it seems also to have been the limit of what even the most "European" members of the cabinet then felt was immediately desirable. Although many people questioned both the feasibility and the reality of Britain's role as an "independent nuclear power," the country was not ready for a "nuclear deal" of any kind: a "European" nuclear community, a nuclear deal with de Gaulle, the acceptance of complete nuclear dependence on the United States, each had its advocates, but there was nothing approaching a consensus for any of them. From the evidence available, it seems clear that the Nassau conference was not, in Mr. Macmillan's eyes, the great sellout to the United States that it was portrayed as being by General de Gaulle. On the contrary, it seems to have been a desperate attempt in the face of the collapse of Skybolt to retain a semblance of "independence" in nuclear matters. It was primarily a way of buying time and deferring, until after the accession negotiations had been concluded and the treaty safely ratified, the politically explosive question of any fundamental change in Britain's nuclear role.[2]

Partly because of the way Mr. Macmillan rushed into a new agreement with the United States, partly because of the deliberate Gaullist misrepresentation of the Nassau agreement, and partly because of the British failure to take an initiative in the defense field after the veto, many European and American commentators, and some British ones as well, have claimed that the British government did not accept, or, more charitably, did not understand the political and defense implications of membership in the Community. Probably a more accurate judgment would be that most British "Europeans," whether within the government or outside, accepted the fact that eventually the Six, and Britain, too, if it became a member of the Community, would act collectively in the field of defense, but they felt that the process of integration—economic and political—had a long way to go before this was practicable or desirable.

Although the British government took no major initiative vis-à-vis the Six after the veto, it tried in various small ways to keep the road into Europe open. Bilateral economic committees with Italy and Germany—which had been established after the failure of the free trade area negotiations but had been dormant during the accession negotiations—were reactivated; an economic committee was established with the Benelux countries; and the British mission to the Communities was strengthened. For a time the British tried to persuade the Six to agree to hold regular meetings between the British Ambassador to the Communities and the permanent representatives of the Six. This proposal was supported by the Germans and the Dutch, but it was opposed not only by the French but also by the Commission and by some of the other strong "Europeans," e.g., M. Monnet, for it seemed to them to give the

[2] See article by Henry Brandon in the *Sunday Times,* December 8, 1963. André Fontaine supported this interpretation of Nassau in articles in *Le Monde* on November 18, 1964, and December 3, 1964.

British too great an opportunity to influence Community decisions without having to accept any of the obligations of membership. The French successfully resisted all proposals which held the slightest prospect of eventual participation, or partial participation, by the British in the European Community and for a time they even opposed the resuscitation of the WEU (Western European Union) as a link with the British. But eventually, as one of the elements in the "synchronized working program" [3] adopted by the Six in the summer of 1963, it was agreed that relations with the United Kingdom would be re-established by holding quarterly ministerial meetings within the framework of the WEU and that the subject "exchanges of views on the European economic situation" would appear as a regular item on the agenda at each meeting.

Although the British government made it plain on numerous occasions in the weeks after the veto that it still wanted to become a full member of the Community, statements made by the leaders of the Labour party during this period tended to undercut the official position. In the debate on the Brussels negotiations in the House of Commons on February 11, 1963, Harold Wilson (then the leader of the Opposition) spoke scathingly of the "new Conservative myth" that the

> Government were within an ace of achieving a satisfactory agreement only to find the prize snatched from their grasp by an intransigent Frenchman. Let this myth be nailed once and for all. Even ignoring the long list of unsolved problems . . . the fact is that the terms which have been negotiated, the accumulated totality of vital national and Commonwealth interests already surrendered by the Government, already constituted a national humiliation. . . . We therefore utterly reject this account of a satisfactory agreement sabotaged by President de Gaulle.

Later in the debate Patrick Gordon Walker spoke in similar terms. Although government spokesmen had undoubtedly somewhat exaggerated the imminence of a successful conclusion to the negotiations, the statements made by Labour

[3] See Chapter I, pp. 5–6.

spokesmen during the debate, and repeated later,[4] went much too far in the other direction and gave unnecessary support to the Gaullist position on the status of the negotiations—a position which the Five, and the Commission rather more circumspectly, had already clearly rejected. And, as they had done throughout the accession negotiations, Labour spokesmen continued to emphasize that the only Europe they could contemplate joining was one that was radically different from the Europe the Six were in the process of creating. The dominant impression created by Labour spokesmen in the period after the veto was one of relief that the negotiations were over and the United Kingdom saved from having to accept the agreements that Mr. Heath had striven so hard to negotiate, and of satisfaction that the British were still free to pursue an independent policy and had not after all been "corraled into" an "inward-looking Europe" tainted with Gaullism.

This was discouraging enough for Britain's friends in Europe—particularly as it was then generally assumed that Labour would come to power by the spring or summer of 1964. But, in addition, the position taken on defense questions by both the major parties dismayed many "Europeans." At this time the Labour party spokesmen condemned flatly and without qualification all forms of European nuclear deterrent and any other arrangement which would bring Germany into nuclear partnership with its allies.[5] This included the American proposals for a multilateral, sea-borne, mixed-manned nuclear force (the MLF) which the United States administration had begun pushing with new zeal after the veto. The Conservative government was coolly ambiguous toward the MLF but startlingly clear on the importance of preserving an independent British nuclear deterrent. Although the Conservatives sought to make it plain that, unlike General de Gaulle, they

[4] See e.g., the report of the speech by Harold Wilson at Cardiff in *The Times*, February 23, 1963.

[5] The Labour party's position changed a little after it took office in the autumn of 1964. See below, pp. 146 ff.

wanted to strengthen the NATO and were prepared to go quite far in integrating the British deterrent with other NATO forces, many of the arguments they put forward to justify the need for a "last resort" British control over the deterrent were much too close to the arguments being used to justify the development of the French *force de frappe* to make the distinction seem very significant to many "Europeans." Both the Labour party's essentially discriminatory attitude toward Germany and the Conservative party's insistence on the need for an independent nuclear force became prominent themes during the election debate in 1964. Neither position seemed to many people in the Six to be compatible—at least over the long term—with a primarily "European" role for the United Kingdom.

It is also worth noting that during the first few months after the veto the discussions over the ground rules for the Kennedy Round tended to separate the United Kingdom from the Six. In contrast to the British reactions to the MLF—which ranged from cool to hostile—the government, the leadership of the Labour party, and public opinion generally were strongly in favor of the American proposal for ambitious negotiations in the framework of the GATT which, if successful, would mean not only freer trade between Europe and the United States but a substantial reduction in the "discrimination" between the Six and the Seven. However, there was at this time, not only in the United Kingdom but also in the United States and in the Five as well, great fear that General de Gaulle would follow up his veto on British membership in the Community by sabotaging the Kennedy Round. In the atmosphere that prevailed following the veto and in the light of General de Gaulle's conspicuous contempt for the concept of an "Atlantic partnership" this was inevitable. Nor was it surprising that French motives were highly suspect when, during the spring of 1963, they challenged the linear approach to tariff cutting which the United States was advocating and for which authority had been sought and provided in the Trade Expansion Act of 1962.

In other circumstances, it is quite possible that the British would have sided with the French in the "disparities" argument which dominated the preparatory discussions just before and during the GATT ministerial meeting in May 1963 and throughout the better part of the following year.[6] There was considerable intellectual support in the British government for the idea of harmonizing the tariffs of industrialized countries around agreed, relatively low, norms (e.g., nil for raw materials, 5 per cent for semi-manufactured goods, and 10 per cent for manufactured goods). However, given the political climate in the spring of 1963, any French initiative was bound to be suspect. Moreover, the specific proposal then being advocated by the French would have required the United States to make far greater tariff cuts than the Six; this naturally strengthened the suspicions that the French plan was designed not to advance the discussion but to annoy and to delay and, perhaps, to wreck the negotiations. The possibility of forming a common front with the Six in this area was thus ruled out, and British support in the disparities argument went—with some qualification—to the United States.

The weakness of the Macmillan government which was dramatized by the sordid Profumo affair in the summer of 1963 and eventually culminated in the Prime Minister's resignation in October; the confused state of British public opinion toward Europe; preoccupation with domestic issues; the widespread feeling that the veto would be maintained as long as General de Gaulle remained in power; and, for a time, the assumption that the Common Market was itself in such troubled waters that the problem of relationship was no longer acute, all led to a loss of interest in Europe. And the Gaullists lost no opportunity to turn every sign of British apathy, or of loss of interest, or of support for the United States, into an ex post facto vindication of the veto.

The Five were troubled by Gaullist attitudes toward the Community, toward the British, and toward the United States,

[6] For further discussion on this point, see Camps, *What Kind of Europe?*, cited, pp. 16–20.

but, as described in Chapter One, they soon gave a clear priority to the preservation and development of the Common Market and abandoned their attempts to seek to reverse the French veto. Thus, by the end of 1963 both the British and the Six were mainly concerned with their own internal problems. Hopes of some improvement in commercial relations between the two European groups were pinned on the Kennedy Round.[7] British ministers had resumed their quarterly discussions with ministers from the Six in the framework of the WEU, but the French rebuffed all attempts to use these discussions to promote joint action on European problems or to consider ways of bringing the British into the Community in the future. The British election was imminent (although not so imminent as it was then believed to be) and it was clear that the question of British relations with the Six would remain in suspense until after the new government had taken office. Although many people on both sides of the Channel felt that the question of British relations with the Six was unlikely to be definitively settled while General de Gaulle remained in power, the Gaullists, helped by British attitudes and by ambiguities in British policy, had had considerable success in shifting the burden of proof. Rather unfairly and somewhat irrationally the feeling was growing everywhere in the Six that the next move was up to the British.

### *The 1964 election debate*

The British election was not held until October 15, 1964, and the campaigning period is officially limited to a few weeks. But the 1964 campaign effectively began in October 1963 when Sir Alec Douglas-Home replaced Mr. Macmillan as prime minister. During the first nine months of 1964 British political life was stultified by the imminence and uncertainties of the election.

[7] In the year after the veto British trade with the Six increased. This contributed to the decline in interest in membership.

The European question played little part either in the long period of pre-election sparring or in the campaign proper. On a number of occasions Mr. Wilson taunted the Conservatives with having been willing to break their pledges to the Commonwealth and to join the Common Market on "humiliating" terms. And, in addition to reiterating his own party's attachment to the five conditions put forward by Mr. Gaitskell during the negotiations,[8] he challenged the Conservatives to make plain their position on the Common Market. In the course of a debate on Commonwealth affairs early in February (1964) he specifically asked the Prime Minister whether he would "give a pledge that no Government of which he is the head will consider entry into the Common Market on any terms which would reduce Britain's existing freedom to trade with the Commonwealth." He added that "on behalf of my party, I give that pledge." [9] On this and other occasions, Conservative speakers took refuge in the fact that joining Europe was not a live issue and would not become one again until after the election. However, they were careful not to be trapped by Mr. Wilson into tying their own hands in any possible future negotiation; the furthest they would go was to state that any future government would have to obtain the authority of Parliament before entering negotiations. Mr. Heath in the course of the same debate also made it plain that Mr. Wilson was deluding himself and the country, but not the Continentals, by saying in one breath that he wanted to join the Common Market but only on condition that Britain's freedom to trade with the Commonwealth remained unaffected.[10]

For the most part, however, both parties were silent on Europe; presumably each feared dissensions in their own party and saw more dangers than advantages in making either

[8] These were: safeguards for the Commonwealth, adequate arrangements for the other EFTA countries, suitable arrangements for British agriculture, freedom to pursue an independent foreign policy, and freedom to carry out national economic planning.

[9] Hansard, *Commons,* February 6, 1964, cols. 1386–91.

[10] Hansard, *Commons,* February 6, 1964, col. 1390.

past efforts or future intentions into an election issue. There were strong reasons why the Labour party should have soft-pedaled the question: the standing threat that some of the most pro-European supporters of the Labour party would defect to the Liberals; the natural desire of what, for most of the pre-electoral period, was assumed to be the next government to avoid any further tying of its own hands, particularly on a matter which was so conspicuously "not real" at the time; the fact that it was difficult to berate the Conservatives without appearing to side with General de Gaulle.

The very gingerly handling of the European issue by the Conservative party was probably unnecessary. Their insistence that the "veto was the end of a chapter but not of the book" and their unwillingness to give Mr. Wilson any commitments about what they would or would not do in the future were sensible enough, but it seems unlikely that they would have lost votes by boasting a little about their decision to open negotiations and by underlining with some vigor their determination to try again when circumstances permitted. The Conservative opposition to joining the Common Market had come almost exclusively from the right wing; this group would scarcely have voted Labour or Liberal. And a more outspoken defense of the government's European policy might have attracted—or kept—for the Conservatives a few votes that went to the Liberals. Since the Conservatives were trying hard to present themselves as dynamic and forward-looking, it was strange to ignore the most adventurous and farsighted decision of their thirteen years in office. Probably the main reason for their shying away was simply the instinctive feeling of all politicians that any policy that has failed is for that reason alone a liability. In addition, of course, since no one had any positive prescription for overcoming the veto, it was difficult to show how a right decision in the past could be turned into a positive plan for the future.

The election, like most elections, was fought primarily on domestic issues and basically on the question of which party was more likely to undertake the drastic reform of the British economy that everyone agreed was overdue. Foreign policy played a minor role, except for the issue of the "bomb." The Conservative party, and the Prime Minister in particular, tried hard to make a major issue out of the Labour party's declared intention to get rid of the British independent nuclear deterrent. Since, at this time, the main hope for Britain's eventual entry into the European Community seemed to many people to lie through some nuclear arrangement with the Continent, the argument over the bomb had some relevance to the problem of Britain's relations with Europe. However, the debate was conducted, for the most part, not in these terms but rather in terms of whether or not possession of the bomb was a necessary attribute of a big power, a ticket to the top table, or essential to national survival; and, all too frequently, the priorities seemed to be in that order.

It was possible to read into some of the Conservative statements about the need to retain the bomb the desire to keep the best card they felt they had to secure entry into Europe until such time as it could be advantageously played. It was harder to read any "pro-European" motives into Labour's position, but those who were good at grasping at straws drew encouragement from the fact that the Labour party's willingness to give up the bomb could be seen as a step toward equality with Germany and thus a move that might make an eventual accommodation easier. However, this step toward Germany was more than counterbalanced by the strong mistrust of Germany that permeated the Labour party statements on the MLF.

At this point it is perhaps useful to recall briefly the status of the discussions on the MLF, for although it, like the problem of joining the EEC, was not an issue in the election, the positions taken by the leaders of the two parties during the long pre-election period were rather different, and they frequently had overtones that seemed to many people to be relevant to the "European question."

After the de Gaulle veto on British membership in the Community and the signing of the Elysée treaty of cooperation between France and Germany, the U.S. government became worried that Franco-German cooperation might extend to the nuclear field. With this fear uppermost, the administration advocated with new vigor the proposal for a mixed-manned, multilaterally-controlled fleet of twenty-five surface ships each armed with eight Polaris missiles, a plan which in various forms had been discussed in the NATO without much urgency for a couple of years. For a time the proposal met with more skepticism than enthusiasm in Europe, but by the summer of 1963 the German government (and particularly Dr. Schroeder, the Foreign Minister, and Herr von Hassel, the Defense Minister) had thrown its support behind the plan, partly as a counterweight to France and to pro-French pressures in the CDU–CSU, partly as a way of tightening the U.S. military commitment to Western Europe.

On October 1, 1963, Mr. Macmillan announced that the British were ready to join in a technical examination of the feasibility of the plan although he made it plain that this was without any commitment to participate in the scheme. Eight countries took part in the technical discussions which began during the autumn: the United States, the United Kingdom, Germany, Belgium, the Netherlands, Italy, Greece, and Turkey. There were at this time clear and unconcealed differences of view within the British government about the desirability of British participation in the plan. The Services and the Ministry of Defence ridiculed the mixed-manning concept and strongly condemned the plan as "costly, vulnerable, unnecessary, and destabilizing." [11] On the other hand, the Foreign Office, although deferring to the Defence Ministry's view that the force might be of dubious military value, had become convinced of the political importance of British participation and it became

[11] See Alastair Buchan, "The Multilateral Force—A Study in Alliance Politics," in *International Affairs,* October, 1964, pp. 630–631. See also *The Times,* July 7, 1964.

more thoroughly convinced as signs multiplied that German and the United States, together with one or two of the smaller European countries, might proceed with the plan whether or not the British agreed to do so. The Foreign Office felt that the United States by pushing the proposal so hard had to some extent created a German appetite for nuclear power. But once it became plain that, whatever its origins, pressure for some form of participation in nuclear strategy was building up in Germany, the Foreign Office, like the U.S. administration, was anxious to head off any Franco-German nuclear arrangement. The MLF might not be ideal, but since it appeared to have German and United States' support it seemed the safest available way of satisfying the Germans.

Although little was said about it, the Foreign Office was also fully alive to the relationship between the MLF and the extension of Six-country action to questions of foreign policy and defense. With the revival in the winter of 1963–64 of talk among the Six about the possibility of moving toward some kind of political union, the fear that the Six might soon develop into a political-military community from which the United Kingdom would be excluded again became a factor in British thinking as it had been earlier when the Six first began discussing the Fouchet Plan.[12] However, if the United Kingdom, Germany, and the rest of the Five together with the United States established a multilateral nuclear force of the size under consideration, the scope for a defense arrangement based solely on the Europe of the Six without Britain would be severely limited. There would then be two centers of political power in Europe: an economic group (the Common Market) with strong political overtones, and a defense group (the MLF group) with strong political overtones. At some point the logic of a merger would become irresistible.

The fact that the MLF was an "Atlantic" force and had a built-in U.S. veto was felt by the British to be a source of strength in the plan, not of weakness. As discussed further be-

[12] See Camps, *Britain and the European Community*, cited.

low, throughout the MLF debate the British government—of whichever party—far from agreeing with those Europeans who felt the MLF was only tolerable if it contained a "European" clause, welcomed the retention of the veto as a guarantee against the development of a European nuclear force which might drift, or steer, on to a "third force" tack.

Throughout the pre-election period the Conservative government made no formal commitments to the MLF, but various statements by the Prime Minister and the Foreign Secretary made it clear enough that if the Conservatives were reelected the admirals and the military skeptics would be overruled and a decision taken to participate actively in the formation of the MLF.[13] The Labour party position remained firmly opposed. It was noticeable, however, that as the election grew closer and particularly after their discussions in Washington, in the spring of 1964, both Patrick Gordon Walker's and Harold Wilson's statements opposing the MLF became more carefully worded. The MLF was still described as military nonsense, an inadequate answer to the problems of the alliance, and an unnecessary and dangerous indulgence of the Germans, but there were loopholes and saving phrases which seemed to indicate that some version of the MLF might, in the end, be found palatable if it proved impossible to gain American agreement to Labour's preferred solution of a more effective voice for the British (and the other European allies) in the control of the deterrent.

The election manifestoes of both major parties dealt with the European issue in a very perfunctory fashion. The Conservative manifesto stated that "we remain convinced that the political and economic problems of the West can best be solved by an Atlantic partnership between America and a united Europe. Only in this way can Europe develop the wealth

[13] In a statement made in the course of a foreign affairs debate later in the year after the Conservatives were in Opposition, Sir Alec Douglas-Home said he would have both kept the independent deterrent and made a contribution to the MLF. Hansard, *Commons,* December 17, 1964, col. 593.

and power, and play the part in aiding others, to which her resources and history point the way." However, it then removed any suggestion that some bold new initiative might follow from this assertion by pointing out that "entry into the European Economic Community is not open to us in existing circumstances, and no question of fresh negotiations can arise at present. We shall work with our EFTA partners, through the Council of Europe, and through Western European Union, for the closest possible relations with the Six consistent with our Commonwealth ties." [14]

This circumspect pronouncement was rapturous in comparison with the rather backhanded treatment of the European question in the Labour manifesto. After noting that the Conservative prime ministers (Macmillan and Douglas-Home) had both "declared there was no future for Britain outside the Common Market and expressed themselves ready to accept terms of entry to the Common Market that would have excluded our Commonwealth partners, broken our special trade links with them, and forced us to treat them as third-class nations," the manifesto continued: "Though we shall seek to achieve closer links with our European neighbours, the Labour party is convinced that the first responsibility of a British government is still to the Commonwealth." [15]

The election pronouncements were taken rather more seriously across the Channel than at home. As the election grew closer and Labour statements continued to reveal a lack of sympathy for the Community and downright hostility to the idea of Britain's ever becoming a member, there was a growing feeling on the Continent that if Labour won the election the "British question" would be settled, and settled in the negative for many years to come. In contrast, in the United Kingdom there was a tendency to discount the election statements and Labour's own past record on the European question and to feel that Labour's position on the closely related problems

[14] *The Times*, September, 18, 1964.
[15] *The Times*, September, 12, 1964.

of defense arrangements and on relations with Europe was bound to change, in time, once it had the responsibilities of government.

*The Labour government's first few months in office*

During the long months before the British election was finally held, it was commonly assumed on the Continent, and to some extent in the United Kingdom as well, that very soon after the election the new British government would be asked by its friends in Europe to clarify its views on its European role. If this British statement was negative, or inconclusive, the "British *préalable*" would then be removed and the Six would begin discussions on "political union" in earnest. This view was a little *simpliste* for the differences between the French and the rest about the form the "political union" should take and about its role on defense questions were more of a block to progress on political union than was the uncertainty about the British.[16] Moreover, although there were uncertainties surrounding the British position, much of the French emphasis on the need for a clarification of British views clearly stemmed less from any real interest in the British position than it did from a desire to divert attention from the hard fact of the veto. Nevertheless, disingenuous though much of it may have been, the feeling existed on the Continent that after the election the British government would—and should—be asked by its friends in the Six to make some new statement of its intentions. And it was widely assumed that if Labour won the election any statement of intention would, at best, be too vague and imprecise to carry conviction.

The Queen's speech to the new Parliament [17] confirmed

[16] For further discussion of the "political union" question, see Chapter Six, pp. 222 ff.

[17] The "European problem" was mentioned in a most routine and perfunctory way. "My Government will continue to play a full part in the European organizations of which this country is a member and will seek to promote closer European cooperation." Hansard, *Commons,* November 3, 1964, col. 38.

that Labour's priorities would be, first, domestic problems; second, efforts to reduce East-West tension; and third, an attempt to put new content into the Commonwealth relationship. And the performance of the Wilson government during its first few weeks in office showed alarmingly little concern for European sensibilities. The abrupt imposition of the 15 per cent surcharge on imports, the rumored cancellation of the Concord airplane, the quick trips to Washington by the Prime Minister and other senior ministers, many of the arguments used in support of the ANF (Atlantic Nuclear Force) proposals—particularly the strong emphasis on the importance of a continuing U.S. veto in the nuclear field and the flat rejection of any form of eventual European deterrent—the Prime Minister's emphasis in the defense debate in December (1964) on the differences between Britain and its continental neighbors—its world role and mission east of Suez—all strengthened the impression that Labour had no positive European policy and little sympathy for, or understanding of, the European interest in unity. The Labour government's attitude in those first weeks in office also gave ammunition to the "Gaullists" on the Continent who lost no opportunity to point out that General de Gaulle's veto on British membership had been the act of a "realist": the British were, as he had said, irrevocably tied to the United States; they were uninterested in and unfit for a role in Europe.

The inept way the surcharge was imposed undoubtedly reflected an attitude toward "foreigners" and toward the restraints of international commitments which made it difficult for even the most charitable to envisage a Labour government's coming to accept the far more stringent restraints on independence of action which membership of the European Community involves. And Mr. Wilson's use of phrases such as not being willing to be "dictated to by foreigners" or "corraled into Europe" made matters worse.

But to some extent the bungling of the surcharge was simply a consequence of the Labour party's long years in the wilderness. In this and other contexts Labour ministers in their first months in office showed themselves to be surprisingly unaware of the extent to which, during the last dozen years, an unwritten code of behavior had developed among the European countries—both the Six and Seven. When Labour was last in office, physical controls on trade were commonplace; in 1964 they were not, and the trend toward freer trade by industrialized countries was firmly established. For a major country to reverse that trend so sharply in contravention of a half-a-dozen international agreements and without adequate prior consultation was much more of an affront to the conventions of the day than the Labour government seems to have realized. Certainly Labour ministers were taken aback by the strength of the outcry, particularly, and with most justice, in the other EFTA countries.

The failure to foresee the impact on the EFTA illustrated just how far out of touch the new ministers were with contemporary European feelings. The surcharge effectively wiped out the tariff advantage the other EFTA members enjoyed in the British market as a consequence of the tariff reductions that had been made since EFTA was formed. And the fact that the EFTA countries received no better treatment than the other European countries (and, in terms of prior notice, rather worse treatment than the United States) made a mockery of the frequent assertions by Labour leaders that, unlike the Conservatives, they took the EFTA seriously and intended to make it into a more important instrument. Moreover, the other EFTA countries found the shabby treatment they were given particularly infuriating since it had been a favorite argument of the British government that the EFTA could be built on mutual trust: unlike the EEC, the EFTA had no need of elaborate institutional arrangements and a book-length treaty to ensure that the members lived up to the spirit of the organization and took full account of each others' interests.

Nevertheless, despite a lot of initial fumbling, it soon became plain that events were not moving in quite the way some on the Continent had been forecasting: the Labour government might not yet have a positive European policy, but it seemed, at least, to be trying to keep the European option open. The first indication that a clear Labour "no" to Europe was not going to materialize came very soon after the election. On October 20, Dr. Luns—during a brief visit to London for other purposes—had a short talk with the new Foreign Secretary. Although it was much too soon to expect any very positive indication of Labour's views he was clearly relieved by the emphasis Mr. Gordon Walker put on the virtue of "continuity" in foreign policy.[18] The following month Mr. Gordon Walker's discussions in Bonn did much to convince the Germans that, whatever Labour's pre-election hopes may have been, Labour in office recognized that it could not escape thinking seriously about its relations with Western Europe. Mr. Gordon Walker's statement to the WEU Council on November 16 (1964) reiterating the British desire to participate in any discussions that the Six might undertake on political union was virtually indistinguishable from remarks made by Mr. Butler at WEU Council meetings during the previous year. True, many "Europeans" felt the British position—as stated by both the Conservative and Labour foreign secretaries—was unrealistic and, in certain respects, unhelpful. Thus, the desire to participate in political discussions before entry into the Economic Community—irrespective of the reasons that made entry impossible—seemed to most "Europeans" to indicate an inadequate understanding on the part of the British of the nature of the movement toward unification on the Continent and of the way the "Europeans" still hoped to suck de Gaulle into their version of the process. Moreover, the kind of political union most British spokesmen appeared to envisage was too close to Gaullist organizational ideas to suit the "Europeans," although it was also too Atlantic-minded in orientation to please the Gaullists.[19] Nevertheless,

[18] See *The Times,* October 21, 1964.

[19] See *The Times,* November 17, 1964.

although the Labour government seemed to have no very clear idea about what it meant by "political union," viewed against the earlier position of the Labour party, it was progress in the right direction that attempts were being made to keep a foot in the door.

### *The MLF controversy*

During the autumn of 1964 the gathering storm over the MLF faced the Labour government with a much more urgent need to clarify its European policy than did the possibility of some new move toward political union among the Six. Well before the election was held it had become clear that the new British government would have to take positions in the nuclear argument very quickly and that the rather leisurely renegotiation of Nassau and re-examination of the structure of NATO that Labour had seemed to have in mind were unlikely to meet the needs of the situation that had developed during the spring and summer of 1964. Since, by the second half of 1964, the argument over the MLF had become an important issue among the Six, British action on the MLF could not be kept separate from the question of Britain's role in Europe.

Early in the autumn of 1964, when it looked for a time as though the Conservative party might win the election, there were rumors that General de Gaulle might try to do some kind of nuclear deal bilaterally with the British after the election. Certainly a markedly warmer French attitude toward the British coincided with the Conservative party's pre-election insistence on nuclear independence—which at times had a rather Gaullist ring. Whatever lay behind these rumors, the Labour victory ended this speculation. And soon any hopes General de Gaulle may have entertained—based on the Labour party's past denunciations of the MLF—that British opposition might kill the MLF seemed likely to be disappointed as well. Within a few weeks it became very clear that, rather belatedly, the Labour party was actively searching for a way out of its nuclear dilemma that would be acceptable to Bonn and Washington; it also became clear that in this search the "neutralists" and unilateral nuclear disarmers in the party were receiving scant consideration.

Once it became plain, as it seemed to be during the summer and autumn of 1964, that the United States and the Germans were determined to go ahead with the MLF, despite French objections and, if necessary, without the British, the Labour government really had no choice but to search for an acceptable variant of the MLF. Mr. Wilson was committed to giving up the "independent nuclear deterrent" and reducing defense expenditures. For domestic reasons, he had, therefore, to take some action either to destroy, or sell, Britain's existing nuclear capacity or to put it under some form of international control. Only the latter was really feasible, partly because the building of the Polaris submarines was too far along to be canceled, save at enormous cost, but more importantly because military strength is much more easily given up by politicians who are out of office than by any government in office. The explosion of a nuclear device by the Chinese put a rather different complexion on the situation in the Far East and perhaps accelerated the inevitable shift in position.

The Labour party leaders were strongly opposed to the MLF, particularly in the form then favored by the Germans. They felt that it met no military need, and would thus involve unnecessary new expenditure; that it would be divisive of the Alliance particularly if it contained a "European clause"; that it would give the Germans too great a say in nuclear matters and be provocative to the Russians. Moreover, they felt a "European clause" might lead to proliferation. However, the British recognized that if they held aloof from the MLF discussions it was probable that either France or the United States would eventually form a nuclear partnership with the Germans. Either arrangement would be bad from a British standpoint. A Franco-German nuclear arrangement would open the way to a "third-force" Europe, would give the Russians legitimate grounds for apprehension, and would probably end by destroying the NATO and isolating the British, or perhaps driving them into even greater dependence on the United States. An American-German nuclear arrangement, although in some ways less dangerous, was still objectionable from a British standpoint. It would rule out the development of any strong European "third force," but it would alarm the Russians, and it would strengthen German-American links at the expense of British-American links. There was already enough disturbing evidence that Germany was the preferred partner of influential groups in Washington. In these circumstances, the Labour government had no alternative but to try to put forward a modification of the MLF plan which would be acceptable to the United States and Germany and which would be reconcilable with its own election pledges, and, if possible, with its strongly held views on alliance strategy.

The outline of a plan which it was hoped would satisfy these rather diverse requirements was given the U.S. government by Mr. Gordon Walker during his visit to Washington at the end of October (after the British but before the American election), discussed by him with the Germans during his trip to Bonn for the WEU Council meeting in mid-November, developed further during a weekend of defense discussions among British ministers at Chequers (November 20, 21, 22), and then discussed in more detail by Mr. Wilson with President Johnson and others during Mr. Wilson's visit to Washington in early December. The main features of the plan—which envisaged an Atlantic nuclear force—were foreshadowed by *The Times* on October 24, 1964,[20] and various aspects of the plan became generally known as they were further developed and discussed in Bonn and Washington during the autumn. For obvious reasons, Mr. Wilson was not very forthcoming when

[20] This article was written by *The Times*' defense correspondent, Alun Gwynne Jones, who a few days later became a Minister of State responsible for disarmament questions in the Foreign Office. As Lord Chalfont, he was also one of the Foreign Office spokesmen in the House of Lords.

pressed by the Opposition to discuss the plan in the House of Commons after the Chequers weekend but just before his trip to Washington; he outlined it in considerable detail, however, on December 16 after he had returned from his discussions with President Johnson.[21]

As described by Mr. Wilson at that time, the British proposed that the Atlantic nuclear force be made up of the following components: the British V-bomber force, except for aircraft needed for existing commitments outside the NATO area; those British Polaris submarines which the Labour government had decided were too near completion to be canceled; at least an equal number of American Polaris submarines; "some kind of mixed-manned and jointly-owned element in which the existing non-nuclear Powers could take part"; and "any forces which France may decide to subscribe." This Atlantic force would be under a single authority in which all countries taking part would be entitled to be represented; this authority would be closely linked to the NATO, but would probably not itself be the NATO Council. This new authority, "acting entirely on instructions from Governments," would have the following duties: "to provide the force commander with political guidance; to approve the force commander's targeting and operational plans . . ." (the targeting by the ANF would be coordinated with the targeting of other U.S. forces in the Atlantic area); "to take the decision to release nuclear weapons to the force commander; to develop agreed policy on the role of all types of strategic and tactical nuclear weapons; and . . . to consult and discuss possible contingencies anywhere in the world which could give rise to the possibility of nuclear weapons being used."

The British national element in the force—the V-bombers and the Polaris submarines—would be "committed to that force for as long as the Alliance lasts." The United States, the United Kingdom, and France, if she took part, would have a

[21] Hansard, *Commons,* November 23, 1964, cols. 935–945.
Hansard, *Commons,* December 16, 1964, cols. 429–439.

veto over the use of all elements in the force and over any changes which might at any time be proposed in the control system. "Any other country participating would also have a veto if it wanted, though collectively they could, if they so desired, exercise their veto as a single group." Mr. Wilson made it very plain that he was still strongly opposed to the suggestion of a "European clause," and that he, like the Conservatives, would oppose any scheme in which "either at the outset or at a later date there was any question of the American veto on the use of the strategic weapon being withdrawn, or made subject to any system of majority voting." He rubbed home his objections by indicating that in his view any eventual renegotiation of the veto arrangement with a politically united Europe would amount to the proliferation of nuclear weapons.[22] As further insurance against this possibility, and to make it clear that the constitution of the ANF was a step toward a wider nonproliferation agreement, the British had proposed that the nuclear countries organizing the force should undertake—as part of the basic agreement—not to disseminate nuclear weapons and that the non-nuclear countries should undertake not to acquire nuclear weapons or to acquire control over them; in addition—again underlining their objections to any form of "European clause"—they had proposed that there be a specific prohibition against nuclear weapons passing into the control of any group of non-nuclear countries that might be formed.

Since the Nassau meeting and General de Gaulle's veto, the Continentals have tended to see in all British statements and actions on the nuclear issue signs and portents about British attitudes toward "joining Europe" and indications of their acceptability—or lack of acceptability—as full partners in the search for European unity. Many "Europeans," not simply the "Gaullists", had had their doubts about the consistency of the MLF with progress toward a European political union, and only the inclusion of a "European clause" allowed them to resolve their doubts. The British insistence on the need for an

[22] Hansard, *Commons,* December 16, 1964, cols. 431–433.

absolute American veto for all time and their objection to any form of "European clause," however remote and hedged around with safeguards, seemed to many to go beyond the desire to convince the Russians that the MLF was and would remain consistent with a pledge of non-dissemination and to reflect both a basic lack of interest in being a part of a real European union and a continuing opposition to the development of a European union of which Britain was not a member. Similarly, the suggestion that the mixed-manned element in the force was primarily, at least, for the non-nuclear powers but not for themselves, seemed to belie other statements by Labour ministers, particularly Mr. Gordon Walker, that the government recognized and accepted the fact that Germany should be treated as an equal. This impression that the British nuclear role would still be different in kind from that of other European participants was strengthened by the proposed veto arrangements which put the United Kingdom and France on a par with the United States rather than the other European countries and by the fact that the Prime Minister seemed to envisage a British nuclear role in other parts of the world independent of any kind of collective restraint. In short, the ANF, as outlined by Mr. Wilson, did not do much to narrow the existing differences between the Germans and the British in the nuclear field, nor did it go appreciably further than the Conservatives had already gone in giving up British "independence" in the nuclear field.[23]

The ANF plan proposed rather more participation by the British and other Europeans in the targeting and control of the U.S. deterrent than had the MLF, since some of the existing American Polarises were to be part of the force and the force as a whole was to be jointly targeted with other U.S.

[23] The Conservative government had, in effect, assigned the nuclear deterrent to the NATO subject only to the right to withdraw it in case of grave national emergency; the Labour party's formula was different—the assignment was for as long as the Alliance lasted, but the real difference was insignificant since obviously the Alliance would break up if there were a difference of opinion over the defense of the vital interest of any member country.

forces; the plan also seemed to call for rather more consultation on nuclear strategy generally among the members of the force than has been the pattern in the NATO. And the ANF, like the MLF, would have strengthened the American commitment to Europe by putting very powerful nuclear weapons under joint ownership and control. These aspects of the proposal, and the fact that the British were, at last, putting forward an alternative rather than simply shooting holes in the MLF, were welcomed by the German government. But the minor role for the mixed-manned element, the continuation of a preferential position for the British in the force, the distrust of Germany which still permeated Labour attitudes, the complete opposition to any form of "European clause," and the insistence on the United States' veto—an insistence which seemed particularly gratuitous in view of the remoteness of the possibility that a U.S. government would ever, in fact, agree to give it up—all made the ANF less attractive than the MLF to the German government.

The ANF made the choice between a "European" option and an "Atlantic" option inescapable; it was specifically designed to do so. The MLF was deliberately less clear cut; it gave those who wanted to blur or postpone the choice or to maintain that these were false alternatives the possibility of arguing in these terms.[24] And, essentially, it was this latter argument that the Germans were putting to the French during the summer and autumn of 1964 in a futile attempt to persuade General de Gaulle to return to his previous position of scorning the MLF but acquiescing, or seeming to acquiesce, in German participation.[25]

During the autumn of 1964 there was, as described in

[24] The fact that the MLF—in the words of its most ardent defenders—"kept the options open" may well have been a weakness rather than a strength, for it opened the door to charges that the United States was talking out of both sides of its mouth.

[25] The Germans on numerous occasions referred to the fact that de Gaulle had said that he "understood" the reasons for the German interest in the MLF and that they were taken aback when he later took an intransigent line against German participation. This seems curiously naïve. Doubtless de

Chapter Two, great French pressure on the Germans to opt for a "Europe that was European"—in all respects. French "Europeans" and Gaullists alike agreed on the necessity for a "Europe" which would eventually be "itself" in defense as in other matters and there was bewilderment in France at British assertions that the MLF gave *too much* encouragement to a European group to become "independent" in the defense field. With a few exceptions, even those Frenchmen who opposed General de Gaulle's extreme anti-Americanism and his contempt for an "integrated Europe" tended to have their own doubts about the consistency between German participation in the MLF and progress toward a European political union. In these circumstances, the German government was having an arduous time trying to convince the French, and the strong Francophiles in the CDU–CSU, that the MLF would not destroy the Franco-German relationship and all hopes of a move toward political union in Europe. Pressure from the British for modifications which made the plan less acceptable to important groups in the CDU and more difficult to reconcile with "European" objectives was, therefore, particularly unwelcome. Given the extremely difficult position in which Dr. Erhard found himself, it is scarcely surprising that the German government resented statements such as Harold Wilson's outright rejection of a European nuclear force in his Guildhall speech on November 17 [26] and found the constant British insistence on the importance of maintaining the United States' veto gratuitous and irksome.

The Germans may have been trying to walk a tightrope

---

Gaulle did "understand," but this would not mean that he accepted. Moreover, as in the case of British membership in the Community, General de Gaulle does not waste time opposing things he does not think are "real." He did not think the British were serious until the summer of 1962; thereafter his position hardened. He did not think the MLF was "real" until the summer of 1964; once it became real, his position hardened.

[26] The Germans were upset by Mr. Wilson's categoric condemnation of any separate European nuclear deterrent and "alliances within alliances" in his Guildhall speech, and they also felt Mr. Wilson's position was rather different from what they had expected from their talks earlier in the month with Mr. Gordon Walker.

between the American and the French positions that was bound to break; but it was no help to have the British twisting and shaking the rope. Much of Mr. Wilson's preoccupation with vetoes resulted, of course, from the fact that he, too, was walking a tightrope. His only hope of making the ANF palatable to his own left wing was to present it not only as the end of the British independent deterrent but also as a plan which, far from hindering a wider non-dissemination agreement, was a positive step in that direction. Inescapably but unfortunately, the domestic political pressures in Britain and Germany led the two leaders to emphasize those points on which they differed rather than those points on which they agreed.

By the end of November (1964) it seemed probable that, despite the differences between the British and the Germans about certain crucial aspects of the force, and despite the mounting opposition from Paris, an agreement between the United States, Britain, Germany, Italy, and perhaps one or two of the smaller European countries would be found if, but only if, the United States maintained not only its strong interest in the MLF (or an acceptable variant) but maintained as well a certain pressure on the German and British governments to come to an early agreement. However, about the time of Mr. Wilson's visit to Washington on December 7–9, President Johnson decided that the United States should cease pressing the MLF upon its allies. Various factors seemed to have convinced the President that this was the right course to follow. There was little congressional support for the plan and considerable congressional criticism of the plan. United States' participation in the MLF would have required congressional approval and it would have been difficult for the President to persuade a reluctant Congress that this was required unless he could demonstrate that the force was clearly necessary in terms of national security. The MLF had from its inception attracted considerable adverse criticism from military strategists in the United States and, although the Defense Department was prepared to back it, the military value of the fleet was generally conceded to be useful but not essential. Had there been strong European support for the plan and had it seemed to offer the prospect of strengthening the Atlantic Alliance the President would doubtless have felt able to go to the Congress on these grounds. But this was demonstrably not the case: the French were actively hostile to the plan; the Germans were badly divided on the plan; the British wanted to rewrite it.

There were very few voices urging the President to maintain American pressure; there were a great many urging delay, further exploration of alternatives, attempts to find compromises with the French, and so forth. However, once the President decided to leave to the British and Germans the attempt to find a compromise it was clear that little was likely to happen, at least before the German elections in the autumn of 1965. Given the differences within the CDU, the Erhard government could only just have gone ahead with the plan if it had seemed clear that the alternative was a really serious disagreement with the United States. Similarly the kind of compromises on a mixed-manned force and probably on a "European clause" that Mr. Wilson would have had to make to obtain German agreement to a modified plan were not compromises that could be self-generated, given the state of opinion within the Labour party.

Both Mr. Wilson and Dr. Erhard were anxious to buy time; in December 1964 neither felt an immediate decision on the ANF–MLF was essential; [27] both faced very difficult internal political situations. The reaction to the sudden relaxation of United States' pressure was therefore one of relief, but of relief mixed with some apprehension. For, although both the British and the German governments had resisted and resented United States' pressure, it was clear that the postpone-

[27] Some of the German interest in a quick agreement on the MLF evaporated with the replacement of Khrushchev, for one of the reasons for haste had been to have the agreement signed before he visited Bonn as planned in the spring of 1965. Wilson had fulfilled his election pledge—more or less—by putting forward his plan. It was not *his* fault if other countries would not accept it.

ment of the question would be widely interpreted as a victory for General de Gaulle, not least by General de Gaulle himself. The relief that time had been borrowed and a fresh clash with the French had been avoided was, therefore, mixed with some dismay, particularly in the Foreign Offices of both countries.

The merits and demerits of the MLF have been argued at length elsewhere and are not in any case a primary concern of this study. What is relevant here is the part the MLF–ANF argument played in the argument over the kind of European unity that is being formed and the way the part played by the British government in the controversy revealed its attitude and in turn affected continental attitudes about the British role in Europe.

It is difficult to draw conclusions on these aspects of the question, for both the MLF and the ANF proposals were too full of contradictions to make the attitudes adopted as revealing as they were sometimes made to seem in the heat of the argument. Thus support of the MLF could never really be equated either with being in favor of "European unity" or with being in favor of the "Atlantic Alliance." Some of those whose interest in European unification is above question, e.g., M. Spaak, some members of the Dutch government, some members of the EEC Commission felt the MLF went too far in organizing defense questions on a basis that was inherently inconsistent with the development of a federal united democratic Europe. Others, whose attachment to the Atlantic Alliance is above question, e.g., the Canadian government, Mr. Denis Healey, genuinely felt it held dangers for the Alliance and would prove divisive. Once General de Gaulle had trained his guns on the MLF, there was some tendency to turn the MLF into a kind of symbol of anti-Gaullism and to see in the decision to opt for the MLF a vote for alliance and interdependence and against anarchy and extreme nationalism.[28] But the choice never seemed to most people to be so starkly drawn between good and evil.

[28] See, for example, *The Economist,* December 5, 1964.

British attitudes toward various features of the arrangement under discussion were doubtless revealing; so, too, was the widespread continental attachment to a "European clause"; and the American ambivalence about a "European clause." Had the MLF—with a European clause—been accepted by the United Kingdom and the Five, a form of cooperation between them would have been started which would seem, almost inevitably, to have ensured eventual British participation in the Community. Perhaps this would have come about quite quickly had General de Gaulle decided that the formation of the MLF was the signal to take France out of the Community; more probably it would have come at a rather later date as the result of a merger between the EEC and the European element in the MLF. The fact that neither the Conservative government nor the Labour government really exploited this opening undoubtedly reflected the fact that at this time neither gave an overriding priority to the European relationship. Had the MLF been adopted it would also have been much harder for the two sides of the Atlantic to drift apart, or to be pushed apart by General de Gaulle or some like-minded successors. But it would not have been impossible, for whether or not the agreement had had a "European clause," no agreement is proof against a renegotiation or repudiation if conditions change. It is perhaps worth noting one of the many contradictions in the British argument: although they stressed the divisive consequences of the MLF they were also the strongest critics of mixed manning which was probably the strongest guarantee against a later division.

There are many parallels between the MLF and the EDC. In each case it was easier to form coalitions of diverse interests against the plan than coalitions for the plan; both essentially used defense arrangements for political rather than military ends, and both were open to criticism in terms of military efficiency; in both cases the proponents of the plans were trying to achieve too many objectives and were defending their actions on too many and sometimes inconsistent grounds. The wide range of interests the MLF was said to satisfy—the desire to tie the United States to Europe, the desire to tie Europe to the United States (which is not the same), the desire to integrate Europe in the defense field, the desire to take the United Kingdom into Europe, the desire to "dry up" the British independent nuclear deterrent, the desire to satisfy German nuclear ambitions in a harmless way, the desire to keep the Germans from having any fingers near the triggers of any nuclear weapons, the desire to give IRBM's to SACEUR, the desire to frustrate General de Gaulle's "third-force" aspirations—could, just, be reconciled. But they could only be reconciled at so sophisticated a level that the plan could not arouse widespread understanding and support in Europe, in Britain, or in the United States.

CHAPTER FIVE

# *The Revival of British Interest in the Community*

Early in 1965 British interest in the Common Market revived. There may have been some slight causal connection between this renewal of interest and the disappearance of the MLF/ANF discussions from the center of the diplomatic stage; but there was not very much, for very little of the latent "European" interest in the United Kingdom had been absorbed in that issue. For the most part, the resurgence of interest in the relationship with the European Community was prompted by other developments. To some extent it was simply a product of time. The veto had, understandably, provoked a temporary drawing back from Europe, but the tide in the United Kingdom, once it had turned toward Europe—as it did in 1960–61—could not easily be reversed. Although during the first two years after the veto the European question was scarcely discussed, there was a continuing shift of opinion toward Europe; sooner or later this was bound to become apparent. Perhaps the issue would have come to the fore again in any case by the spring of 1965, but a number of developments accelerated the trend toward Europe and stimulated a revival of interest at about this time.

The shock of the enormous balance-of-payments deficit in 1964, the humiliation of having to borrow $3 billion in

November, and the dramatic difficulties of the aircraft industry each contributed to the new mood. So, too, did the way trade was developing. In the first eighteen months after the veto, trade with the Six had expanded rapidly despite the growing tariff discrimination, but in the second half of 1964 exports to the Community began to level off. Furthermore, although exports to the Commonwealth were marginally higher in 1964 than in 1963, there had been no reversal of the declining trend of exports to the Commonwealth in relation to total exports. Despite the Labour party's campaign talk of plans for expanding Commonwealth trade, very little was heard of these plans once the 1964 election was over. Many of the Commonwealth countries were, in any case, actively seeking to develop new trade outlets: Australia and New Zealand with other countries in the Far East, particularly Japan, and Nigeria and the East African countries with the Six. Expectations about the size of the tariff reductions that were likely to be achieved in the Kennedy Round had also been scaled down during the eighteen months of plodding discussion in Geneva. A useful reduction in tariffs was still hoped for, but by 1965 no one looked to the Kennedy Round to solve the problem of trade relations between the Six and the Seven. Again, although some modest expansion in trade with Eastern Europe had occurred, British imports had increased more rapidly than exports, and the prospect for any substantial expansion of exports was not very bright: the Six and the United States were also seeking to increase their exports to Eastern Europe and the markets were thin in any case.

Although the enormous size of the balance-of-payments problem, the shifts in the pattern of trade, and the pessimistic outlook for the Kennedy Round all gave new emphasis to the commercial importance of coming to terms with the Six, the economic reasons for joining the Community were seen in broader terms in the spring of 1965 than they had been in the late fifties and early sixties when the need to avoid discrimination and to compete on an equal basis in the rapidly growing markets of the Six had been the dominant consideration. The difficulties of the aircraft and computer industries and the need for heavy expenditure on research and development underlined the need for a large and sophisticated industrial base if technologically advanced industries were to flourish. It was noticeable, too, that the same arguments that were prevalent on the Continent, particularly in France, about the difficulties of competing with the American giants, and about the dangers of cooperating with them, were increasingly heard in the United Kingdom. Cooperation with European companies could be cooperation between equals; cooperation with the much larger American companies was frequently simply the first step to take over.

The revival of British interest in the Common Market in the spring of 1965 also owed something to the resurgence of confidence in the Community that was so marked on the Continent after the agreement on cereals prices early in December 1964. Understandably enough, an accommodation had seemed much less urgent while the Community itself was in the doldrums in the months after the veto.

Political factors also contributed importantly to the revival of interest in "joining Europe." The British decision in 1961 to seek to join the Community was taken essentially on political grounds. But the political reasons for joining and the political implications of joining were deliberately played down during the accession negotiations, largely because it was felt that public opinion would respond positively to the economic arguments for joining but much more circumspectly to the political arguments. This may have been a miscalculation. But it was an understandable miscalculation, for at that time comparatively few people accepted, emotionally as well as intellectually, the changed power situation of the United Kingdom. The questioning—in any very profound way—of the ability of the United Kingdom to play a satisfactory role on its own had only just begun. However, once started, the domestic debate over Britain's role in the world did not stop with the veto. The

Conservative party's failure to induce the intelligent voter to believe that the bomb alone was a ticket to the top table, and the Labour party's failure to rouse much but skepticism for an important British role "East of Suez" were both symptomatic of the new uncertainty. There was a growing feeling that the United Kingdom was overextended politically as well as economically. And given this mood of uncertainty, Mr. Goldwater, President Johnson, and General de Gaulle, in their various ways, all tended to bring home the advantages of a primarily European role for the United Kingdom.

The British, like most Europeans, found Mr. Kennedy a very sympathetic president and, particularly after the second Cuban crisis, there was considerable confidence in, and little resentment at, the fact that the American President was ultimately responsible for the safety of the West. It was very easy for the British to feel a sense of rapport with the Kennedy administration, for its style and approach were cosmopolitan. Moreover, while Mr. Kennedy was president, international problems tended to take priority over domestic problems. President Johnson's style and approach are much more characteristically American and his own interest and particular talents lie in the handling of domestic problems. Unlike President Kennedy, he makes the British aware of the differences between his reactions and their reactions. And since it is harder for the British to feel "Atlantic" it becomes easier for them to feel "European." Little things as well as big things have contributed to this feeling of difference, or separateness, between the two sides of the Atlantic, a feeling which has clearly grown since the change in administration. It would have been unthinkable for President Kennedy not to have attended Churchill's funeral: the contrast between President Johnson's apparent insensitivity to the symbolic importance of the event and General de Gaulle's acute awareness of it could not help but strengthen the European tug and weaken the Atlantic tug. More importantly, the growing uneasiness at American policy in Southeast Asia, coupled with the impatience shown by the Johnson administration toward overseas advice, has made "dependence" on the United States less acceptable than it seemed to be when it was less obvious. And the shock of the nomination of Mr. Goldwater was not completely dissipated by the fact that he was roundly defeated. The fact that he could be nominated was enough to make many people take much more seriously than they had before the Gaullists' arguments that Europe must be responsible for its own defense.

Both the weakening of the sense of identification with the United States and uneasiness at the course of American policy—particularly in Vietnam, but also in the Dominican Republic affair—made it easier for pro-European feelings to flourish. In a rather different way, General de Gaulle's constant emphasis on, and object lessons in, independence also had an impact in the United Kingdom. There was comparatively little sympathy for the extreme nationalism and rabid anti-Americanism of the French president, but much for his insistence on the superiority of European civilization and his conviction that Europe should play a larger role in the world—even though he tended to confuse Europe with France.

In December 1962, when Dean Acheson said in a speech at West Point that "Britain had lost an empire but not yet found a role," the British generally felt the accusation was unjust as well as unkind. By 1965 such a statement would have been regarded as so obvious that it would probably have passed unnoticed. The re-examination of Britain's role in the world—which began in earnest after the Suez debacle—had by 1965 reached an almost morbid intensity. The re-examination is not yet completed, but the tide is flowing strongly toward a greater British role in Europe, despite the fact that it is still difficult to see when and how the choice of a European role is to be made effective.

### *Positions taken by the political parties in the spring of 1965*

During the spring of 1965 all three political parties reflected this new interest in coming to terms with the Six, although they advocated rather different lines of approach.

The Liberal party, unlike the Conservative party, had never dropped the European issue and it was not surprising that the Liberals were once again in the forefront of the campaign to take Britain into Europe. In January Lord Gladwyn joined the Liberal party, citing the Liberal party's consistent advocacy of British membership in the European Community as a major reason for his decision. Shortly thereafter he reactivated the Britain in Europe Group and began campaigning for a "declaration of intent" to make it clear to the Six that the United Kingdom wanted to join the Community as soon as the French would permit. The idea of a declaration of intent was formally taken up by the Liberal party in a statement issued in April reaffirming its belief that "for political, economic, and defence reasons this country must become a member of the European Economic Community." In this statement the Liberals indicated that the United Kingdom would be morally bound to consult (at least) with the other EFTA countries and the Commonwealth countries and would also have to work out voting arrangements and a few other questions with the Six before joining. But, they argued, the United Kingdom should state its intention of signing the Treaty of Rome "without any conditions save those inherent in the treaty itself on a given day in the future, say January 1, 1968." On the controversial question of defense, the Liberals assumed that any European union would extend to the defense field, but they opted for an Atlantic nuclear force rather than a European nuclear force.[1]

The Conservative return to advocacy of British membership of the Community was not much more surprising, but it was, of course, very much more significant than the renewal of Liberal interest. Some of the Conservative enthusiasm was "party political" and designed primarily to embarrass the gov-

[1] The statement was slightly equivocal: it spoke of accepting the establishment of an "autonomous political and defence Community" but appeared to envisage the retention of the United States' veto in the nuclear field and stated that "to create two centers of nuclear control within the Western Alliance would be inherently dangerous."

ernment. But most of the Conservative statements about the importance of "becoming European" carried conviction, and support for joining Europe appeared to be more strongly based and more widely spread throughout the party than it had been at the time of the accession negotiations. There was more than a hint of "Gaullism" in the attitude of some of the Conservatives.[2] A few influential Conservatives (e.g. Julian Amery, Peter Thorneycroft) were believed to favor offering General de Gaulle a nuclear partnership in return for his removal of the veto, but none of the public statements made by members of the shadow cabinet during the spring of 1965 took this position. The Conservatives did, however, appear to envisage some nuclear role for the European Community—once the United Kingdom had joined—although their statements, like that of the Liberals, were not very precise on this point.

During the early part of the year (1965) a number of prominent Conservatives—Duncan Sandys, Edward Heath, and Sir Alec Douglas-Home, then the leader of the party, all made important statements on Europe.[3] In addition, early in April the One Nation Group of Conservative M.P.'s issued a pamphlet, *One Europe,* which although not signed by the five members of the group who were on the Opposition front bench was known to have their general support.[4]

[2] The kind of quasi-"Gaullist" thinking that was current in some Conservative circles was reflected in various articles written for *The Guardian* by John Grigg, for *The Financial Times* by Nigel Lawson, and for *The Statist* by J. Bruce-Gardyne. See, for example, *The Financial Times,* March 17, 1965, *The Guardian,* February 18, 1965, and the Bruce-Gardyne letter to *The Times,* January 29, 1965.

[3] In his speech to the Young Conservatives on February 13, 1965, Sir Alec said: "If . . . the Europe of the future will be one of the great constellations of power—economic, military, and political—then Britain must not shirk her role of helping to shape its destiny." *The Daily Telegraph,* February 15, 1965. Sir Alec Douglas-Home, like Mr. Heath who outlined his views a few days later in a speech at Oxford, clearly felt there was no scope for an immediate British initiative and both appeared to accept the then fashionable view that 1968 was a good target date toward which to work.

[4] The five were: Heath, Macleod, Maudling, Joseph, and Powell.

From the tone of these and other statements it seems clear enough that as of the spring of 1965 the Conservative leadership, although convinced that the nuclear issue could not be excluded from any future settlement with the Six, had no very clear agreed line about how it should be handled. The Conservatives were more open minded than the Labour party about the possibility of converting the British nuclear deterrent (or at least part of it) into a European deterrent. But the most outspoken of those Conservatives who took this line, Duncan Sandys, also emphasized the importance of assigning any European nuclear force to the Atlantic Alliance and of integrating its strategic planning with that of the United States; his concept was, perhaps, not very different from that of the MLF with a "European clause." Obviously the Conservatives were as aware as everyone else of the basic dilemma: no nuclear arrangement was likely to prove attractive to General de Gaulle that did not go further than the leadership in all three parties would have felt it was wise to go in straining the Atlantic Alliance and thereby weakening the American commitment to the defense of Europe.

By the summer of 1965 the Conservative leadership had moved into a position of outspoken support for joining the Common Market whenever that became possible, and for working for some kind of political and defense union as well. The fact that Mr. Heath was chosen leader of the Conservative party in preference to Mr. Maudling showed that his known sympathies for "joining Europe" were no liability, and probably an asset. The assumption that under Mr. Heath's leadership the Conservative party would put Europe high on its list of priorities was confirmed by the statement of Conservative policy—*Putting Britain Right Ahead*—issued early in October.[5] Although there were many ambiguities in the Conservative position on the defense aspect of a united Eu-

[5] "We aim to be realists both in our relations with other countries and in our assessment of Britain's place in the world. In maintaining peace, in seeking disarmament, in promoting economic development, in safeguarding and expanding our commerce, in building up our strength to exert political influence in the world, we can best achieve our objectives in a wider grouping.

rope, and particularly on the nuclear issue, Conservative spokesmen were far more explicit than they had been in 1961–62 about the political implications of entry into Europe. And it was clear that their central argument for British membership in a European union—a union that would be economic and political, and would, eventually, embrace defense questions—was to gain strength and influence in the world.

The leadership of the Labour party also said a surprising amount about the British relationship to Europe during the spring of 1965. But, in contrast to the statements made by the Conservatives and the Liberals which carried the argument forward from where it had been when it went to ground after the veto, the Labour government's statements harked back to the past. There was some rather uneasy repeating of the five conditions that Labour had formulated at the time of the accession negotiations. And there was a great deal of talk about pragmatic arrangements and about "bridge building" between the Six and Seven that was strongly reminiscent of the statements made by the Conservative government during the period between the collapse of the free trade area negotiations at the end of 1958 and the change in Conservative policy in 1961.

It is, of course, always easier to advocate bold policies out of office than in office. And it was not surprising to find the

---

"It was on these grounds that Britain sought suitable conditions for membership of the European Economic Community—a prospect unwelcome to the Labour party. It is on these grounds that, when the present difficulties and uncertainities in Europe are resolved, we believe it would be right to take the first favourable opportunity to join the Community and to assist others who wish, in the Commonwealth and in EFTA, to seek closer association with it. Until this becomes possible a future Conservative Government will cooperate with other European countries in joint policies in the common interest."

From *The Times*, October 7, 1965. It should also be noted that in the section of the statement that dealt with agricultural policy, the Conservatives indicated that once back in power they would reshape domestic support systems to bring them more into line with the Community import levy system.

Prime Minister, Mr. Wilson, quoting his predecessor who the year before had dismissed the question of entry into the Common Market as a "dead duck," [6] particularly as in the spring of 1965 not even the most enthusiastic proponents of "joining Europe" could see how it was to be done. But the Labour government during the spring of 1965 did not simply repeat that there was no immediate prospect for a successful negotiation; it seemed to be basically unsure of what policy toward Europe it wanted to pursue.

The first substantial public statement of Labour's view on the European problem was given by Michael Stewart before the British Chamber of Commerce in Brussels shortly after he had replaced Patrick Gordon Walker as foreign secretary. This speech for all its deliberate good will toward the Six—"I am very pleased that my first visit abroad as Foreign Secretary should be to the centre of the European Economic Community. This signalizes the close relations which we want to maintain with our fellow Europeans of the Six"—was disconcertingly reminiscent of speeches made five years earlier, before the Conservative government had reversed British policy. There was the same unwillingness to accept the EEC as a form of international action that was different in kind, not simply in degree, from the type of cooperation that the British had accepted in the EFTA, in the OECD, and in other organizations. There was the same emphasis on "cooperation" and the same shying away from the more committing concepts of "integration" and "union." And there was, too, the same warning against creating divisions: "If these economic divisions persist, they will in time inevitably lead to political divisions." There was also the familiar repetition of the British desire to take part, from the outset, in any talks on forming a political union. Rather curiously, given the general tone of this speech and of other government statements made at this time, Mr. Stewart added: "There is no reason at all to think that we can go less far than the members of the Community together in

[6] Hansard, *Commons,* April 29, 1965, cols. 623–625.

promoting European unity and common policies." [7] This reflected the common British assumption—which was undoubtedly true—that in terms of institutional arrangements they were as ready (or as reluctant) as was the government of General de Gaulle to delegate power to "supranational" institutions. But to "European" ears, the assertion, taken in the context of the speech as a whole, seemed to reflect a gross unawareness of the extent to which the Six, including the French, had already accepted common policies. Moreover, the sharp distinction that the British—as well as General de Gaulle—appeared to draw between economic and political integration was felt by the "Europeans" to be not only unreal but symptomatic of a lack of understanding of (or of a quite deliberate refusal to understand) the process of integration on which the Community was embarked. In short, Mr. Stewart's statement, although it tended to be read in Britain as a rather encouraging sign that the Labour government was beginning to move toward Europe, was received on the Continent with a rather weary feeling that the lessons that had apparently been learned in 1961–62 had been forgotten.[8]

About a week later, in speeches to British audiences, both Mr. Stewart and Mr. Wilson again summarized the government's policy toward Europe. The emphasis was on "bridging the gap," on seeking to establish closer relations through the WEU and Council of Europe, on pragmatic steps and functional cooperation, such as the joint production of new types of aircraft with France, and perhaps other European countries, that had recently been announced by the Minister of Aviation (then Roy Jenkins), and on mutual tariff reductions in the Kennedy Round. Both ministers also sought to put a damper on talk of joining the Community by pointing out again that it was not a live issue at the present time.[9] And Mr.

[7] From the text released by the Foreign Office, February 11, 1965.

[8] See report from Brussels in *The Times,* February 12, 1965, and special article "How Neighbours See Us," in *The Times,* March 4, 1965.

[9] Although there had been a spate of statements about Europe, the effect of the renewal of interest was magnified by the way the British press feeds

Wilson on this occasion, as he was to do again, reaffirmed that he stood by the conditions of entry that the Labour party had earlier agreed upon.[10]

Early in March (March 8–9) Mr. Wilson went to Bonn, for the first time since becoming prime minister. By this time the Germans had already reacted, rather negatively, to the British proposal for an ANF and it was plain that there would be no immediate help from Washington in pressing the Germans to make concessions to the British view. The Defense White Paper had been published at the end of February: this had emphasized the importance of Britain being able to play a role, perhaps even a nuclear role, east of Suez. It had also made it clear that a reduction of British forces in Germany was felt to be necessary for financial reasons and to be sensible on strategic grounds as well.

Despite this unpromising background, the Anglo-German discussions appear to have been friendly and mildly useful, the principal result being the agreement to postpone any cuts in the BAOR (British Army of the Rhine) while the possibility of more German help with support costs was examined. According to his comments to the press at the end of the discussions, the Prime Minister had, once again, confirmed that joining the Common Market was not, today, a "practical proposition" and had reiterated that the emphasis for the present should be on practical links—joint production projects and

---

on itself; the weekend of February 20–21 most of the Sundays and weeklies had "European" leaders. This outburst gave the impression that rather more was afoot than in fact was the case.

[10] Michael Stewart at a press lunch on February 17, and Harold Wilson at Church House, see *The Times,* February 22, 1965. Also see Hansard, *Commons,* February 16, 1965, col. 1003–1004. It may be significant that the Prime Minister, although indicating that the conditions remained, did not restate them. Moreover, on March 18 in a written answer he seemed to be intentionally cautious: "The five conditions we stated in October, 1962, reflect essential aspects of British policy, but we cannot usefully turn these into precise bargaining conditions for a new European negotiation until one is in prospect." Hansard, *Commons,* March 18, 1965, written answers col. 319.

perhaps some action in the tariff field beyond the Kennedy Round.[11]

Mr. Stewart, the Foreign Secretary, went from Bonn to Rome to a WEU Council meeting. Although in his speech in Brussels a few weeks earlier he had expressed confidence that the WEU could be a useful link between the United Kingdom and the Six, some of the limitations of that forum must have become apparent to him during the Rome meeting, particularly the fact that the French have never taken it seriously. Other countries usually send their foreign ministers to Council meetings; M. Couve de Murville does not normally attend, and he was not at Rome. Furthermore, although the WEU meeting took place at a time when it was widely expected that the Six would shortly meet to discuss the German and Italian proposals for political unity, and although Mr. Stewart reiterated the British desire to participate in these discussions from the start, it was made clear to him that the British would not be invited to take part and that the most they could hope for was to be kept informed of the progress the Six were making among themselves.

By the time Mr. Wilson paid his first visit to Paris on April 1 and 2, 1965, it had become clear that, despite the new ferment of British interest in Europe, Mr. Wilson had no intention of seeking to reopen negotiations; partly because he felt the veto still applied, partly because he was not yet convinced that membership was the right answer for the United Kingdom. The Labour government was, however, very ready to pursue with the French and other countries specific joint projects in the aircraft and other industries where the advantages of cooperation were clear to both sides. Since Mr.

[11] About this time there were press reports that Mr. Wilson had revived an old idea and would suggest to the Germans that the Six collectively might join the EFTA as an eighth member. As a comment in *Le Monde* (March 10) made plain any such suggestion would have been interpreted in the Six as nostalgia for the old free trade area—a plan that even the Germans and the Dutch felt was some years out of date.

Wilson was as ready as General de Gaulle to confine British relations with the Six to "tunneling" and "bridging," it is hardly surprising that the talks were reported to be "extremely successful."

Those who specialize in taking political temperatures reported a somewhat warmer climate for Anglo-French relations after this meeting, but there was nothing to suggest that General de Gaulle had altered his view that the British were too Atlantic-minded to make good European partners. In any case, by this time General de Gaulle seemed to be less concerned with strengthening the Europe of the Six than he was in creating some wider, looser concert of power in Europe, stretching from the Atlantic to the Urals but not, apparently, across the Channel.[12]

### *EFTA developments during the spring of 1965*

In addition to trying to put Britain's relations with the Six on a more cordial basis and to find pragmatic ways of bridging the economic gap, the Labour government also sought to repair the damage done to the EFTA by the hasty imposition of the 15 per cent surcharge in October 1964. At the EFTA ministerial meeting in February the British announced that they would cut the surcharge to 10 per cent with effect from April 27, 1965. This decision was obviously taken on purely political grounds in response to strong pressure from the other EFTA governments, for there had not been time for the effect of the surcharge to be gauged.

The British action undoubtedly improved the atmosphere, and after the February meeting the customary statements were heard that the EFTA had emerged from its crisis stronger than ever. This seems unlikely to have been true, for the whole affair of the surcharge had dramatized a fundamental weakness in the EFTA, that is, the fact that it is not a viable eco-

[12] See General de Gaulle's press conference on February 4, 1965, and television broadcast April 27, 1965.

nomic unit. With the best will in the world on all sides, the British balance-of-payments crisis could not have been handled on an EFTA basis. The Italian crisis in the spring of 1964 was not, in fact, handled by the Six, but technically it could have been, for enough resources existed within the area.

The Six, although they cannot isolate themselves effectively from other large industrial countries, are strong enough, as a group, to defy them. It would be possible for the Six to maintain free trade internally while imposing new restrictions against third countries, despite third-country opposition. The EFTA countries could not. Because the British were largely dependent on financial assistance from the Six and the United States, their power to "discriminate" on an EFTA basis was, in effect, subject to outside agreement in a way that similar action by the Six would not be. Thus even in its own internal affairs, the EFTA is very vulnerable not simply to the attitudes of its member countries but also to the attitudes of important third countries.

When the EFTA was formed it was commonly assumed that it would be a temporary organization with a life expectancy of something less than five years. By the spring of 1965 EFTA was well on the way to becoming a full free trade area and most of its members felt that the prospect of negotiations with the Six was still some years off. Nevertheless, the EFTA continued to be regarded as a way station to the "larger Europe" and not as an end in itself: this gave the organization an air of impermanence that those most concerned with EFTA affairs found unsettling and frustrating.

There was, however, no agreement among the EFTA governments about what should be done to improve matters. Some, like the Swiss, felt that the right course was to forget about the Six for a time and to concentrate on building up the EFTA; others, like the Danes, still gave an overriding importance to a settlement with the Six and were anxious to avoid taking any steps that might make that settlement more difficult. Some members felt a strong EFTA would be better able eventually to negotiate collectively with the Six; others felt this unlikely and that the only road to the "larger Europe" lay through eventual separate negotiations with the Six. A discussion of the future of EFTA and of the prior question of the timing and nature of any approaches to the Six took place at the February Council meeting, but the real argument came at the ministerial conference in Vienna at the end of May.

Rather unexpectedly, a curtain raiser for the May meeting took place at the end of April, when Socialist leaders from twelve European countries who were attending a meeting of the Socialist International in London dined together at Chequers with Mr. Wilson. Six-Seven relations were discussed—apparently in fairly general terms by the whole group—and then in considerably more detail by a smaller group.[13] Shortly after these talks Mr. Wilson suggested that the EFTA hold its May Council meeting at head of government level and expressed his own willingness to go to Vienna.

It is clear that the underlying assumption at the Chequers discussion and also at the Vienna EFTA meeting a month later was that there was no prospect of British membership in the Community for some years. Given this assumption, two themes dominated the discussion: how to improve and strengthen the EFTA and how to "build bridges" with the Six. There was clearly an element of domestic politics in Mr. Wilson's sudden upgrading of the Vienna meeting and in the somewhat extravagant statements that appeared after the Chequers discussions. Against the background of the renewed Liberal and Conservative support for joining the Common Market, Mr. Wilson doubtless felt that he had to show that he,

[13] According to *The Times*, April 26, 1965, those participating in the more detailed talks later in the evening were:

Wilson (United Kingdom)
Erlander (Sweden)
Krag (Denmark)
Pitterman (Austria)
Bratteli (Norway)
Brandt (Federal Republic of Germany)

too, was "for Europe." But his EFTA initiative revealed that he had not yet made up his mind what kind of an eventual European solution he sought. He was treading water, not yet swimming purposefully in any direction.[14]

The EFTA Council meeting in May revealed, once again, the differences of view between those countries that felt that bridge building was unproductive, or even counterproductive, and wanted to give priority to the building up of the EFTA and those countries that were anxious above all to find a way of coming to terms with the Six. The Swedes and the Swiss have always tended to be the most active in arguing that the strengthening of EFTA should receive priority, the Danes and the Austrians have been most anxious for a settlement with the Six. But there was little agreement even among those countries who felt that bridge building was a waste of time about how, in fact, EFTA should be strengthened, the Swedes being ready to go much further than the Swiss in turning the EFTA into a kind of replica of the Common Market. Similarly there was very little real agreement about how, if at all, to approach the Six. Most of the Seven felt that Mr. Wilson was badly overestimating the willingness of the Six to cooperate on any basis. Various ideas were discussed, some of them fairly hoary, such as the possibility of tariff reductions on goods primarily traded on a European basis after the Kennedy Round had been completed, the freeing of trade in certain sectors following the United States–Canada precedent in automobiles, and even the formation of a free trade area between the Six and the Seven, despite the unpromising history behind this idea. More limited approaches were also discussed, such as an agreement between the Six and Seven on patents and company law.

At Mr. Wilson's initiative, it was agreed, although with a marked lack of enthusiasm on the part of most other dele-

[14] The fact that much British opinion was a good deal more "European" than Mr. Wilson was reflected in the skepticism with which the British press greeted the EFTA initiative. See, e.g., leader entitled "Old Wine in Old Bottles," *The Sunday Times,* May 2, 1965, and leader in *The Times,* May 25, 1965, and Nora Beloff's article in *The Observer,* May 30, 1965.

gates, that it would be desirable "to seek to arrange meetings at ministerial level between the two groups at the earliest opportunity which offered prospects of a fruitful result." [15] However, the details of how and when this should be done as well as the substantive matters the two groups should discuss were remitted to the Council for further study. So, too, were the various ideas put forward, mainly by the Scandinavian countries, for strengthening the EFTA. It was agreed that both sets of questions would be considered further at the next EFTA Council meeting in Copenhagen at the end of October. It was clear that the Seven were going to move very cautiously and that, whatever Mr. Wilson's ideas at the time of the Chequers meeting, there was not likely to be any dramatic new turn in EFTA affairs either internally or in their relations with the Six.

### *The Commonwealth prime ministers' meeting*

A few weeks after the EFTA meeting, the Commonwealth prime ministers met in London for the first time since the change in the British government. The leaders of the Labour party had been very critical of the handling of the Commonwealth Conference in September 1962 at which Mr. Macmillan had made it plain that he was ready to take Britain into the Common Market even though the Commonwealth countries felt their interests had not been adequately protected by the arrangements that had been negotiated. And during the election it had been a prominent Labour theme that, in contrast to the Conservative willingness to sell the Commonwealth down the river they, a Labour government, would put new content into the Commonwealth and take steps to expand trade with the Commonwealth.

The Labour government's decision to tighten up immigration from the Commonwealth was a bad prelude to the Commonwealth conference. And neither the economic nor

[15] From the communiqué issued after the Vienna meeting. See EFTA *Bulletin*, June 1965.

the political discussions at the conference itself produced any real feeling of Commonwealth solidarity. Where possible, controversial subjects were avoided rather than met head on, and where they could not be sidestepped, e.g., the problem of Rhodesia, the discussion far from strengthening the bonds of the Commonwealth showed up the difficulty of holding it together. In the debate on the Commonwealth in the House of Commons on June 1 Mr. Wilson had said he hoped decisions taken at the conference would reverse the declining trend of Commonwealth trade: nothing that happened at the conference seemed likely to have that effect. It was agreed that a Commonwealth secretariat would be set up which would, among other things, explore ways of expanding trade, but no specific arrangements providing for an increase in trade were made, despite the Labour government's earlier hopes and promises.

Thus by the summer of 1965 the Labour government was far less attracted by both the EFTA alternative and the Commonwealth alternative than it had been while in opposition. It was noticeable that when Mr. Wilson spoke of the difficulties of joining the Common Market, acceptance of the common agricultural policy, and particularly the effect of so doing on the British balance of payments, was being given pride of place.[16] The famous five conditions had clearly become something of an embarrassment to Labour ministers and there were signs of an effort to disentangle from old positions, if not yet of a positive new policy. Despite obvious disenchantment with earlier prescriptions and some rather revealing reinterpretation of their five conditions,[17] the Labour leadership had not

[16] See, e.g., Mr. Wilson in House of Commons on June 1, 1965, Hansard, *Commons,* cols. 1644–1652.

[17] See Michael Stewart's statement at a meeting of the Labour Committee for Europe held during the Labour party conference and printed in *Europe Left,* winter 1965–66. See also Mr. Padley's comments in the House of Commons:

"The five conditions are not the Ten Commandments. They related to the vital interests of Britain and the Commonwealth. They will be interpreted in practical terms in the light of practical affairs as they exist between Britain and Europe." Hansard, *Commons,* August 2, 1965, col. 1043.

yet made up its mind what policy it wanted to follow in Europe. But at this time other questions seemed more urgent. No informed observer—inside or outside the government—felt that the time to negotiate had come. And most people assumed that the next opportunity was unlikely to arise before General de Gaulle had left the stage and the Community had completed its transition period.

### *The British reaction to the crisis in the Community*

Spokesmen for the British government were scrupulously careful to treat the crisis among the Six as a family quarrel and to avoid saying anything that could be interpreted as fishing in troubled waters. There were few ministerial comments on the crisis: when they did comment, the Prime Minister and others expressed their hope and confidence that a settlement would soon be found.[18]

This policy of neutrality, although clearly right during the summer while the argument among the Six was ostensibly about the financial regulation, may well have been rather shortsighted once General de Gaulle had made it plain—as he did in his September press conference—that the argument was over the kind of European Community that should be built. The British could obviously take no direct part in the negotiations among the Six, but had the government been willing to bring its policy into line with that of the other two political parties and declared its acceptance of the principles of the Treaty of Rome and its readiness to join the EEC at an appropriate time, the position of the Five would have been strength-

[18] See, e.g., Mr. Wilson in the House of Commons on July 19, 1965:

"It is not for us to take sides or to express opinions, still less to exploit this serious difficulty which has arisen for advancing a particular conception of a particular doctrine about European unity or about British participation. . . . I think we can be most helpful by not attempting to take sides but by using such influence as we have to make sure that our European friends settle this problem amongst themselves on terms acceptable to them, because by so doing they will not only be helping themselves but peace in Europe." Hansard, *Commons,* July 19, 1965, col. 1141.

ened and the suspicion dispelled that the British government was far from unhappy at the prospect of some curbing of the powers of the Commission and some "interpretation" of the majority voting provisions. This could only have been done convincingly, however, by a government that had clearly made up its mind on Europe. Although there were signs during the autumn that the government's position was changing, it was apparent that Mr. Wilson had not yet made up his own mind about what kind of Europe he wanted to see develop, or about Britain's role in Europe, and that he was primarily interested in keeping his hands free.

A number of influential individuals went out of their way to make it plain that in their view the British interest would best be served by a continuation of the Community on the Treaty of Rome pattern.[19] And on several occasions Duncan Sandys and Christopher Soames (then the shadow Foreign Secretary) both made statements that were plainly designed to reassure the Five that if the break with the French came they could look to a Conservative government to join with them in continuing the development of the European Community.[20]

It was abundantly clear that the Treaty of Rome was not considered by the Conservative leadership to be an unduly ambitious document, and that once in office a government led by Mr. Heath would seize the first opportunity to join the Common Market, but the Conservative position was not wholly without ambiguity so far as the argument between the Five and the French was concerned. During the autumn there were from time to time a number of rather "Gaullist" articles by journalists with strong Conservative party connections arguing that the French were "realists" and that if the Community were reshaped along the lines advocated by the French it would become more acceptable to the British.[21] And Mr.

[19] See, e.g., Kenneth Younger in *The Listener,* November 25, 1965, and numerous speeches and letters to *The Times* by Lord Gladwyn.

[20] See, in particular, the speech by Mr. Sandys at Strasbourg on September 25, 1965, and that by Mr. Soames at Strasbourg on September 28, 1965.

[21] See, for example, various articles by John Grigg in *The Guardian* and by Nigel Lawson in *The Financial Times.*

Heath's interview with General de Gaulle in November was felt by some "Europeans" to be unfortunately timed, to say the least. However, the main reason for the Conservatives' reluctance to take sides in the argument seemed to be simply tactical: since the French veto was the barrier to British membership, siding with the Five seemed likely to worsen the prospects of eventual British membership. There were, too, domestic political considerations in the Conservative position that there was nothing to be done at the present. Mr. Heath was clearly becoming worried that Mr. Wilson would succeed where he had failed and be the one to take Britain into Europe.[22]

Although the British government formally kept to its position of neutrality throughout the crisis, it was plainly becoming increasingly interested in Europe and was watching European developments with close attention. The comments and speeches of the Foreign Secretary, Michael Stewart, were obviously being made with their effect on the crisis much in mind. During the autumn the Foreign Office made little attempt to conceal its view that a settlement on "European" terms was more in Britain's long-term interest than a settlement on "Gaullist" terms, and that a capitulation of the Five to General de Gaulle would not only do nothing to help Britain's own prospects but would tend to increase the difficulties of working with the Six in the Kennedy Round and might well have repercussions in the defense field. Had the decision been theirs alone to take, it seems probable that a "declaration of intent" would have been made, making it clear that the British government was ready to join the Community on the basis of

[22] Mr. Heath in a speech to the Federal Trust conference in January 1966 indicated that he thought there would be no chance to negotiate before 1968. Although some people interpreted this as an indication of a cooling off in Conservative ardor it was almost certainly nothing of the sort, but it probably did reflect Mr. Heath's concern lest Mr. Wilson would steal his clothing and be the one to take the United Kingdom in. The whole tone of Mr. Heath's speech was that of a very strong European, with a political vision of a united Europe as an effective world power.

the Treaty of Rome at the appropriate time. Such a declaration would not, of course, have ensured British membership, unless the break with the French came, but it seemed likely to increase the chances that the settlement would be made near the "European" rather than the "Gaullist" end of the spectrum. It would, moreover, have made it plain that the British regarded themselves as "Europeans" and were rightly concerned with the kind of community that was being built.

The disadvantages for Britain of a settlement on "Gaullist" terms seem not, however, to have been seen so clearly or regarded so seriously in other parts of Whitehall. In some quarters, at least, it was considered to be rather quixotic to suggest a course of action which did not seem likely to improve the prospects for joining the Community, in the short term at any rate, but simply to increase the chances that the French would find it expedient to compromise with the Five.

However, despite differences of view about the right tactics to pursue, the actual performance of the British government during the crisis was clearly reassuring to the Five without being offensive to the French. The government was less forthcoming than it might have been, but it showed an awareness of the nuances of the European situation which was in complete contrast to its actions on taking office the year before.

The way "bridge building" was quietly abandoned was indicative of this new attitude. Despite the publicity given to "bridge building" by Mr. Wilson a few months earlier, the British position at the EFTA Council meeting late in October 1965 was a model of circumspection and the EFTA decisions were deliberately keyed very low. That section of the communiqué that dealt with the discussions on relations with the Six was sensibly anodyne in both form and content. The EFTA countries reaffirmed their conviction that "the possibilities of their final goal, a wide European market solution, would be considerably improved if a dialogue were established between the EEC and EFTA at all possible levels, and EFTA stands ready for this."[23] They reaffirmed their belief that the primary aim so far as European tariffs were concerned was the successful conclusion of the Kennedy Round. And they also indicated that they would like to examine the possibilities of closer cooperation with the Six on certain practical matters: industrial standards and patent laws were specifically mentioned. The readiness of the EFTA to negotiate with the EEC on all matters, large or small, was stressed, but there was nothing in the communication to which the Six had to respond by a particular time, or, indeed, ever.

A few weeks later the Foreign Secretary said, at a meeting of a Socialist group in London, that in his view the wider European unity that everyone desired should be "something resembling more the EEC principle than EFTA."[24] Questioned about this statement in the House of Commons a few days later, Mr. Stewart not only confirmed the gist of his earlier statement but made a notable comment on "bridge building," heretofore one of Labour's favorite expressions: "I never use the phrase 'bridge-building' myself because I think that these metaphors are misleading. . . . There is nothing inconsistent between readiness to join EEC, provided that essential British interests are safeguarded, and the pursuit of practical projects on which we and other countries in Europe can work together. It is that which is commonly described as 'bridge-building,' though I think it is a misleading name. Some of the contacts which we have been able to make with Europe are both useful in themselves and will make the atmosphere more favourable in time for a wider European unity."[25]

Just before the first Luxembourg meeting of the Six, Sir

[23] See *The EFTA Bulletin,* November 1965.

[24] See *The Observer,* November 28, 1965. Nora Beloff commented: "His speech confirmed hints last week from Downing Street that Mr. Wilson is seriously thinking of stealing Mr. Heath's European clothes and bringing Britain into the Common Market as soon as circumstances permit. There have been signs of a shift of opinion inside the Cabinet toward tying Britain more closely into Europe and the Prime Minister himself believes that a substantial majority of his colleagues are now more for than against."

[25] Hansard, *Commons,* December 6, 1965, col. 27.

Con O'Neill, the Foreign Office official responsible for relations with the Community, made an important speech in The Hague in which he was at some pains to show that the government's position had evolved appreciably during the year.[26] And between the two Luxembourg meetings, when it looked as though the Five might be in for a long, hard struggle with the French, the Foreign Secretary, speaking to a meeting of the Federal Trust in London, seemed to be trying to give comfort to the Five without actually taking sides. He made an obeisance to Labour's five conditions, but he managed to soften them and to reinterpret them almost, if not quite, out of existence.[27] The only substantial difficulties either of these speakers now saw in joining the Community arose from the nature of the common agricultural policy, the main problems being the impact on the cost of living and on the balance of payments of adopting the levy system and the Community's price levels. Both speakers were, however, careful to present even the agricultural problem as a matter for negotiation, not as an insuperable obstacle to joining.

Before the Luxembourg meeting of the Six there had been no official approach to the British from the Five, but there had

[26] Sir Con O'Neill was formerly British Ambassador to the communities. The principal part of his speech was reprinted in *The World Today,* January 1966. As well as containing a revealing summary of the way ministerial statements had become progressively warmer during the year, his speech contained an excellent analysis of the difficulties the common agricultural policy posed for the United Kingdom.

[27] "Our policy is, that we are, as we have always been, ready and willing to negotiate for entry into the European Economic Community provided we can obtain the right conditions: we must safeguard what are, for Britain, essential interests, just as the Six members of the Community safeguarded their own essential interests when they were engaged on the mammoth task of drafting the Treaty of Rome. Our minds are certainly not closed to new ideas; and we should interpret the basic conditions we have laid down for ourselves in the light of all the existing facts and circumstances, some of which have changed since the conditions were formulated. There are no inhibitions on our side, provided adequate means can be found to protect Britain's essential interests, and those of our EFTA partners and the Commonwealth, and provided the Community is willing." (From advance text released by the Foreign Office.)

been enough informal contact so that the Five were confident that if the break with the French came they could, after a period of continuing alone, turn to the British in the expectation that some arrangement—perhaps some quite far-reaching arrangement—could be negotiated. There were still many ambiguities in the British position, but the fact that the Prime Minister had never repudiated the increasingly warm comments made by his Foreign Secretary had been duly noted.

The British government had, moreover, won the gratitude of the Five for not having done anything mischievous during the long period of tension among the Six, for having played the October EFTA meeting prudently and quietly, for not having confronted the Five with any awkward choices, and for not having risen to hints from Paris that a victory for General de Gaulle in his quarrel with the Six would make British accession easier. These were, perhaps, negative virtues, but given the long history of mistrust of British intentions among the "Europeans" and the kind of statements about the Community Mr. Wilson and other leading Labour politicians had been making a year before, the government's performance during the crisis was felt by most "Europeans" to be the best proof they had yet seen that the British position had "evolved."

The fact that much of British industry, most of the press,[28] and the declared positions of the other two political parties, were considerably more "European" than the government made the cautious edging of the government toward Europe much more significant and credible than it would otherwise have been.

In 1965, in sharp contrast with the situation in 1961–62, a substantial, informed, and influential body of public opinion was very clearly well in advance of the government. Earlier, at the time of the accession negotiations, the Macmillan govern-

[28] One of the most significant developments so far as the press was concerned was the fact that the *Daily Mirror,* a mass circulation daily with sales of something over five million, had become an enthusiastic advocate of British membership in the Community.

ment was ahead of the country as a whole in its understanding of the development of the European Community and in its decision that for political as well as economic reasons the British should seek to join the Six. There was a tiny group of British "Europeans" prepared to go even further—in the sense of more unconditionally—into Europe than were Mr. Macmillan and the leading "Europeans" in the government. But generally speaking, the Prime Minister, Mr. Heath, Mr. Sandys, Mr. Soames, and the other members of the cabinet who were most instrumental in changing British policy were not appreciably behind the "committed Europeans" in their view of what could and should be British policy.

If one defines the "European" group rather broadly to include all those who were convinced that the Macmillan decision had been right, if belated, it would not in 1961–62 have been very large, although it would have included many of the most influential voices in the country. The group that was utterly opposed to joining was also small, probably considerably smaller than the group that clearly favored joining, and, for the most part, it was less influential. But the vast majority of the British people in 1961–62 was to be found between these two extremes. The Macmillan government's rather equivocal position—that it was not negotiating to join but negotiating to see whether acceptable conditions could be obtained so that the United Kingdom could join—had corresponded to the dominant mood in the country. Those who opposed entry would doubtless have been able to gain some recruits from this large undecided group had the negotiations been allowed to continue and agreements been reached along the lines that seemed in prospect when General de Gaulle brought the negotiations to a halt. But the bulk of the large undecided group would almost certainly have followed a strong lead by the Prime Minister and would have supported a decision to join, not out of strong conviction, and not, exactly, out of apathy, but from the feeling that the choice was a difficult one, the arguments for and against rather evenly balanced, and the decision one that could safely be left to the government. The prospect of "joining Europe" had ceased to be alarming to the British people. It was already something that a majority could contemplate with equanimity, if not with much enthusiasm. But in 1961–62 only a minority was pro-European in a positive sense.

By 1965 the situation was rather different. A substantial part of the undecided group had clearly shifted toward the European end of the scale. The number of those who were convinced that Britain must sooner or later join the European Community was very appreciably larger than it had been in 1961–62; the group that was irrevocably opposed had probably not shrunk very much, but it had gained no important new recruits. Furthermore, not only had many of those who were undecided in 1961–62 come to the conclusion that joining was the right course of action, but the long-term political implications of such a move were far more widely appreciated and accepted than they had been three or four years earlier. In this situation, people on both sides of the Channel were looking for signs of a shift in the government's position and this made them read into Mr. Stewart's cautious statements a much firmer commitment to Europe than the words taken by themselves would have conveyed.

Since the pronounced revival of British interest in the Common Market in the spring of 1965, another British move to join the Community has seemed probable. The edging toward the Community that took place during the crisis appreciably increased the probability. Heretofore British interest in the Community has waxed and waned with the fortunes of the Community: it has been strongest when the Community was flourishing and weakest when the Community was in trouble or marking time. This was not true during the autumn of 1965. The cynics will say that this was because the British saw that there was a possibility of a break among the Six and perhaps an opportunity to fashion a new European group more to their liking. There were clearly some thoughts of this kind:

given the history of the last fifteen years it would have been very strange if there had not been. But there was another reaction as well. Many people had come to feel that the Community was, after all, the kind of arrangement they wanted to join and they felt a vested interest in the Common Market's continued existence.

The fact that the British government did not hold out the bait of some broader, looser arrangement may have been the result of differences of view and indecision within the government rather than of high-mindedness or of a conversion to "Europe." Nevertheless, it reflected, at the least, the fact that there was an important group within the cabinet that wanted to preserve the option of joining the Community. Perhaps the Foreign Secretary created the impression that the British government was rather readier than it was to slip into any chair left vacant by the French. But, whatever the response had it come to the test, the result of the crisis, and of British actions during the crisis, was to give the question of British membership an immediacy that it had not had before. The British had been felt to be a factor in the crisis by the Five, by the French, and, not least, by themselves. As a result, by the beginning of 1966 the British were again involved in Europe in a way they had not been since the veto in 1963. On both sides of the Channel the question no longer seemed to be whether the United Kingdom would become a member of the Community, but how soon it would do so.

### *The election campaign of 1966*

The way the European issue was handled in the British election campaign early in 1966 strengthened the impression that the question was no longer whether there would be a new effort at a settlement but when it would happen and what form it would take. Unlike the 1964 campaign, when both major parties deliberately ignored the issue, the Common Market question provided one of the few patches of interest in the

1966 campaign. As was to be expected, the Conservative manifesto was unequivocal: a Conservative government would "seize the first favourable opportunity of becoming a member of the Community." That section of the Labour party manifesto that dealt with Europe was mildly encouraging,[29] but the effect of this section was counteracted by the flat rejection of an import levy system in the statement on domestic agriculture in another section of the manifesto.[30] Moreover, in his press conference launching the manifesto Mr. Wilson drove home his view that there was no question of adopting the common agricultural system as it stood. This statement was quickly picked up by Mr. Heath and interpreted as evidence that whatever hints Mr. Stewart and others might drop the Labour government had, in fact, no intention of seeking to join the Community.

This was too simple a reading of Mr. Wilson's pronouncement. Until early in 1966 it had seemed clear that a British gov-

[29] "Britain is a member of the European Free Trade Association, which is a thriving organization beneficial to us and to our partners. The Labour government has taken the lead in promoting an approach by EFTA to the countries of the European Economic Community so that Western Europe shall not be sharply divided into two conflicting groups. Labour believes that Britain, in consultation with her EFTA partners, should be ready to enter the European Economic Community, provided essential British and Commonwealth interests are safeguarded.

"The Conservative record on relations between Britain and the 'Six' is one of notorious and abject failure. Yet Conservatives now talk as if they could take Britain into the Common Market without any conditions or safeguards.

"Labour believes that close contact with Europe—joint industrial ventures, scientific cooperation, political and cultural links—can produce among the 'Six' that understanding of Britain's position which is necessary to a wider European unity." *The Times,* March 8, 1966.

[30] "The selective expansion of agricultural production is a key part of the national plan. In particular, it will make a significant contribution to the balance of payments by import saving.

"The record of our farmers and farm workers in increasing productivity is outstanding. We shall not shake their confidence by substituting for the well tried deficiency payments the levies on imported foodstuffs advocated by the Conservatives. This would reduce the farmers' security and push up food prices to new high levels." *The Times,* March 8, 1966.

ernment that sought any radical change in the agricultural system of the Community stood no chance of being taken as a serious candidate for membership. But Mr. Wilson's remarks came after various hints from Paris that the French were becoming disenchanted with the common agricultural policy and were particularly disturbed by the high price levels that were being built into the system.[31] It is probable that Mr. Wilson in making his statement had two purposes in mind: first and mainly, of course, to gain votes by portraying the Conservatives as ready to plunge recklessly into the Common Market without any thought for the consumer, the farmer, or for the balance of payments; second, to build up a position from which, later, to bargain on agriculture. If the French position was, in fact, changing on agriculture, there was no point in becoming overcommitted, as Mr. Heath seemed in some danger of becoming, to a system that had very great drawbacks from a British point of view and which might be negotiable in some respects after all.

The Conservative line throughout the campaign was to play up their own commitment to Europe and to interpret the reservations and qualifications in the Labour position as foreclosing the possibility of British membership in the Common Market. The Labour line was to portray the Conservatives, and particularly Mr. Heath, as hotheaded and impetuous, ready to leap into the Community on any terms. Nevertheless, although European policy was frequently mentioned, it only once showed signs of becoming a major issue. And then it proved to be a three-day wonder. Mr. Heath deliberately chose a day when the WEU Council was meeting in London to reaffirm the Conservative party's commitment to join the Common Market and to work for the political unity of Europe. He challenged Mr. Stewart to ask the ministers from the Six whether they were prepared to abandon the common agricultural policy to please Mr. Wilson. He also, in commenting

[31] See, e.g., *The Financial Times,* February 3, 1966 and, later, March 14, 1966.

on the NATO question which General de Gaulle had just thrust into the limelight, came out strongly for redressing the balance in the alliance: "I believe in Britain, I believe in Europe, and I believe in a partnership and not in people being satellites." [32]

The next day, however, the Foreign Secretary recaptured all the headlines. At the conclusion of the WEU Council meeting, Mr. Stewart, in his capacity as chairman, held a press conference in the course of which he reported that the French veto on British membership had now been lifted. The reasons why Mr. Stewart decided to play up the rather cautious remarks made by the French representative, M. de Broglie, during the Council session are not altogether clear.[33] Perhaps it was simply a political move to outmaneuver Mr. Heath, perhaps it was an attempt to force the French either to confirm or to repudiate the frequent but rather oblique suggestions that had been coming from Paris since November that there was a new French attitude toward Britain. Or perhaps Mr. Stewart really felt M. de Broglie's remarks indicated a new French attitude, although this feeling was not, appar-

[32] This was a rather odd time to choose to seem to be agreeing with General de Gaulle about the dangers of becoming too dependent on the United States, and Mr. Heath's remarks were widely interpreted as being more of an endorsement for General de Gaulle's decision to withdraw from the integrated arrangements under NATO than was presumably intended. From other statements made by Mr. Heath, it seems clear that his own ideas of the way the balance within NATO should be righted are very similar to the "two-pillar" concept supported by many "Europeans."

[33] Reports of what transpired at the meeting indicate that M. de Broglie, in effect, reiterated what M. Couve de Murville had written in a special supplement of *Le Monde* a few days before:

"In Europe, France has launched, with five partners who also wish to set up an economic community of advantage to all, into a great undertaking which has already made considerable progress. Nothing could give clearer evidence of the success of this vital achievement than its extension to Great Britain. The day that country decided to join the Six without reservation, she would be fulfilling the wish of the Europeans, for they believe that the British must in any case share the destiny of the peoples of the continent."

From translation in the *Bulletin of Information,* March 1966, issued by the French Embassy in London.

ently, shared by most of those present. Whatever the explanation, Mr. Heath returned to the charge the next day, accepting the report of a French change of heart at face value and reproving Mr. Stewart and the Labour party for not immediately taking advantage of this new situation.

The following day Mr. Wilson effectively deflated any hopes that his Foreign Secretary's optimism may have aroused. In a speech at Bristol, which was described in advance as an important statement of his views on the European question, Mr. Wilson seemed to be going out of his way to undo Mr. Stewart's painstaking good work. He restated that as a condition of entry "we must be free to go on buying food and raw materials, as we have for one hundred years, in the cheapest markets—in Canada, Australia, New Zealand, and other Commonwealth countries—and not have this trade wrecked by the levies the Tories are so keen to impose." This was rather flat, but so many statements along this line had been made that it came as no surprise. But the following passage did seem to introduce a new and more negative note and to reflect an attitude toward the Community that was markedly different from that of the Foreign Secretary: "The Conservative leaders have been totally evasive on the one central question which they refused to answer during the last set of negotiations. Do they regard any move toward Europe as principally economic, or—as many good Europeans and some Tory front benchers insist—as a step toward political, and, ultimately, military integration? We believe that, given the right conditions, it would be possible to join the EEC as an economic community. But we reject any idea of supranational control over Britain's foreign and defence policies. We are in Europe, but our power and influence are not, and must never be, confined to Europe."[34]

[34] From the press release issued by the Labour party. The tone of these remarks was utterly different from that of Mr. Stewart's talk to the Federal Trust in January, cited above. Perhaps the most striking contrast between Mr. Wilson's strictures and his Foreign Minister's views is revealed by Mr. Stewart's concluding remark: ". . . small wicket gates are opening in the

Speeches made in the heat of a political campaign are one thing; the policies pursued by a government in office another. And the day when any European country was likely to accept "supranational" control over defense and foreign policies was obviously far off. Nevertheless, the statement had a profoundly anti-European ring about it and seemed to reflect an attitude on Mr. Wilson's part that was out of tune with the more European sentiments of some of his colleagues.

Rather curiously, the total effect of the 1966 election campaign was to strengthen the impression that, once the election was over, the progress toward Europe that had been noticeable in the autumn would be resumed. The Labour tactics during the campaign had been to arouse distrust of Mr. Heath's European enthusiasm, but no suggestion was made that a vote for Labour was a way to stay clear of European commitments. On the contrary, the message seemed to be that a Labour government would take the country into the Common Market in a dignified way and on satisfactory terms.

The impression that the Common Market was again on the agenda was confirmed when, early in April, Mr. Wilson reorganized his cabinet shortly after being returned to office with a large majority. Not one minister but two were given special responsibilities for Europe—George Brown, the Minister for Economic Affairs, was put in charge of economic relations with Europe, and George Thomson, formerly Minister of State in the Foreign Office, was promoted to be Chancellor of the Duchy of Lancaster (a largely titular office) and, subject to the over-all responsibility of the Foreign Secretary, charged with the foreign policy aspects of relations with Europe. It was made clear that George Brown would head most British delegations to meetings of European organizations—EFTA, WEU, OECD, Council of Europe, etc.—and that

iron curtain. In the long run, the peace of Europe depends on the encouragement and development of this process. I have no doubt that a prime condition for this will be the military, economic, and political cohesion of Western Europe. . . ." Contrast, also, Mr. Brown's speech on May 6, 1966, quoted below.

George Thomson would accompany him. Both of them would use these and other opportunities to explore the possibilities of, finally, coming to terms with the Six.

A few weeks later George Brown, speaking at length about the European question at the Socialist International Congress in Stockholm, seemed to be going out of his way to soften and put a rather different twist on some of the points in the Prime Minister's Bristol speech. Mr. Brown's gloss on the much-quoted statement that British power and influence were not and must not be confined to Europe was strikingly different in tone from Mr. Wilson's original formulation:

> My conclusion is that it is not only possible and desirable to look beyond the frontiers of Europe if one is to be a good European: it is essential to do so. We believe that the problems which face all of us today exist on a world scale; and they must be tackled on a world scale, where possible by the countries of Europe acting together. If we thought in Britain that it was necessary to forsake these wider interests and obligations in order to become members of the EEC, this would be a formidable obstacle. But this is surely not the case. The really important problems concern all of us in Europe. I am confident that closer integration in the economic sphere need not prove an impediment to any country's influence or efforts but will help all countries to work more closely together.[35]

### *What kind of Europe does Britain want?*

There are clear differences between the kind of Europe that is in Mr. Heath's mind and the kind of Europe toward which the Labour leadership seems to be edging. Mr. Heath's Europe corresponds very closely to the kind of Europe that most of the strongest continental "Europeans" also have in mind: a European group that would be a new center of power closely linked with the United States but having policies of its own. An economic union would be the first objective, but the

[35] From the press release issued by the Labour Party Press and Publicity Department, London, May 6, 1966.

European union would, over time, develop a common defense structure and a common foreign policy in all fields.[36] A reorganization of the NATO and a "two-pillar" Atlantic alliance are plainly part of Mr. Heath's concept, although the nature of the arrangements in the nuclear field remain rather unclear. Institutionally the system would initially be that of the Community, but it would evolve gradually along federal lines.

It is impossible to be sure today what kind of European arrangement Mr. Wilson wants, for his views are obviously undergoing some change and since becoming prime minister he has been deliberately ambiguous. The ambiguity is partly prudence; he obviously does not want to arouse his left wing prematurely or to disclose his cards before the bargaining begins. But it seems doubtful whether he has yet formulated any very clear European objectives beyond the rather grudging conclusion, perhaps best expressed in double negatives, that in the long term the United Kingdom cannot afford not to become a member of a European economic community.

It is clear that most of the Labour leadership (with a few rather conspicuous exceptions) is much less convinced than is most of the Conservative leadership that the best role for the United Kingdom is as a member of a European group which would be a new center of power and which would progressively pursue common policies externally and have a common defense structure. To some extent this dislike of Europe as a new center of power reflects a streak of parochialism in the Labour party and a distrust of all foreigners. But to some extent it is a reflection of another more important strand in Labour attitudes, an idealistic rejection of power and a belief in a kind of "Scandinavian," neutralist internationalism.

To some extent the doubts about Europe as a new center of power also arise because "Europe" still has, in Labour's eyes, the conservative, Catholic, "cold-war" image of the

[36] Mr. Heath made his views clear in numerous speeches during the election campaign. He was also quite explicit in his long speech to the Federal Trust in January 1966.

Adenauer–Schuman–De Gasperi period. There is a feeling that "Europe" should now mean not Western Europe but all Europe. This feeling was reflected in the formation of the "One Europe" group of Labour Members of Parliament in the summer of 1965. This group is worried by any hardening of the division between East and West and is clearly attracted by some aspects of General de Gaulle's conception of a "Europe from the Atlantic to the Urals." It is not a coherent group, and it has no agreed policy. Nevertheless, it undoubtedly represents an uneasiness about the implications of belonging to a Western European power group that is fairly widespread in the Labour party. The concern over relations with Eastern Europe does not seem likely to keep the British from joining the Community, but, as discussed further in Chapter Six, the ability of the members of the expanded Community to reach an agreement on the problem of Central Europe will be one of the factors that will determine how far the Community develops.

Today Mr. Wilson's view of the European arrangement he would really like is probably not very dissimilar from the free trade area of the Maudling era, that is an arrangement that eliminates trade discrimination with the minimum interference with national action in other fields. Nevertheless, the available evidence suggests that he would in fact go a good deal further to "join Europe" and that the Treaty of Rome is no longer considered to be unacceptable, although some of the regulations that have been adopted, particularly for agriculture, raise substantial problems and would, in the British view, have to be renegotiated.[37]

[37] Acceptance of the common agricultural policy as it stands would both raise the cost of food to the consumer and put a substantial extra charge on the import bill. Estimates of the impact on the cost of living and on the balance of payments are difficult to make and vary enormously. Estimates of the "crude" cost to consumers of a switch from the British deficiency payments system to the import levy system of the Community (at the prices agreed or in prospect) run around £400 million per year. A little less than half of this would come from increases in the prices of home-produced food;

The fact that General de Gaulle has put a brake on the federalizing pressures in the Community has clearly contributed to Mr. Wilson's willingness to adopt a more forthcoming attitude toward joining the Community. Mr. Wilson is not a "good European" and there is no point pretending he is. He has "good Europeans" in his cabinet, however, and it seems probable that Mr. Wilson himself will be a better "European" a year or two from now than he is today. Thus far the Labour government has been following the pattern set by the Conservatives with uncanny faithfulness: first, the flirtation with the alternatives to "joining Europe"—the Commonwealth and EFTA—then the disenchantment, then "bridge building," then the cautious acceptance of the idea of membership in the Common Market, on conditions, and with the political overtones played down, ignored or rejected. Perhaps it is too much to expect that the Labour government will overtake Mr. Heath's full-blooded Europeanism very quickly, but a glance backward shows that the evolution of Labour policy on the European issue has been remarkably rapid.

All British governments are subject to similar domestic pressures. All British governments face the same problem of how to match their resources to their responsibilities and aspirations. There is very little real room for maneuver and far less scope for choice than there appears to be. In the end all British governments seem likely to reach much the same conclusions about the main thrust of British policy.

The economic and political reasons that are today compelling the Labour government to look toward Europe seem bound to make them want the kind of Europe that offers not simply a wider area of free trade, but all the advantages that come from being part of a very large economic unit, including, of course, the added strength in bargaining with third

a little more than half from increases in the price of imports as a consequence of the levies. Apart from the saving to the Treasury on deficiency payments (of the order of £175 million) it is very difficult to calculate other offsets, such as possible drawings from the Agricultural Fund. See *The Financial Times,* March 19, 1966 and *The Guardian,* March 18, 1966.

countries. That kind of Europe is not the large, loose Europe some Labour spokesmen still seem to hanker after. Moreover, as the crisis in the Community has shown in a backhanded way, that kind of Europe is, sooner or later, irreconcilable with complete freedom of action in foreign policy.

Today the Conservative and Liberal parties clearly and openly advocate British participation in a European union as the way both to improve the quality of life in the United Kingdom and to make the British contribution to the orderly solution of the world's problems most effective, in short, as the way to maximize British power. The present government does not. But it has no alternative policy. Given this fact and the way informed opinion has been moving in the last few years it seems probable that if the Labour government brings itself to take the first step and finds a way to join the Economic Community, the pressures of public opinion and the advantages to be gained from going further down the road toward collective action will, in a few years' time, turn Mr. Wilson and his government into far better "Europeans" than they look today.

CHAPTER SIX

# *What Kind of Europe?*

What are the prospects for British membership? How will the Community now develop? What kind of "Europe" seems likely in, say, the next decade? These are not questions that can be answered today with any confidence. And a glance back at the number of unforeseen developments affecting the Community that have happened since the beginning of 1963 underlines the folly of making predictions. Nevertheless, the events of the last few years, the interests of the countries involved, and the way attitudes are evolving, both on the Continent and in the United Kingdom, seem to point to a few rather tentative conclusions.

By the spring of 1966 it seemed much clearer than it had at any time since General de Gaulle's veto in January, 1963, that the United Kingdom would eventually join the Community, although when and on what terms remained uncertain. Had the Labour government had a strong, well-defined "European" policy it might well have been able to exploit the NATO crisis precipitated by General de Gaulle early in March, 1966. A British initiative at that time for a European defense community (perhaps comprising a European command structure for European—including British—troops assigned to NATO and a common procurement and supply system) would have been a desirable response to General de Gaulle's challenge. It would have pointed the way to a better balance in the NATO and thus have met that aspect of General de Gaulle's criticism that commanded the most widespread support. It would have confronted the Six with a proposal five countries would have wanted to accept and one that it would have been extremely difficult for the French to turn down without isolating themselves and running the risk of a realignment around the British. But that opportunity came too soon for the Labour government.

The prevailing British view that they must be in a stronger economic position before again seeking to join the Six and the priority now being given to domestic economic problems suggest that the British are unlikely to try to force the issue for a year or two, at least. And little pressure on them to try again seems likely, for a time, from the Six. The Five governments having finally reached a settlement with the French will be reluctant to risk further crises: the Commission, which has always given an overriding priority to preserving the Community, will be particularly reluctant to see a potentially divisive negotiation begin while the repairs made in the Community fabric are still so fragile. The "Europeans" among the Six will be reluctant to have a negotiation with the British begin while General de Gaulle is in power and the policy of the Wilson government is as ambiguous as it is today, for they naturally fear the result of such a negotiation would be to turn the Community into a purely commercial arrangement shorn of its integrative pressures and its "communitarian" features. Moreover, despite persistent rumors from Paris during the winter and spring that the French veto had been lifted, there is a very strong presumption that the veto still applies.

There is a surface plausibility to the view that General de Gaulle may feel that British interests are sufficiently parallel to his own to dictate a change in the French attitude: the Gaullists and the Labour government seem to share a dislike of "supra-nationalism," an ambivalence toward the Germans, a desire for openings to the East, and a recognition of the mutual advantages to be gained from closer cooperation in certain industrial fields, particularly those where government contracting is of crucial importance. But all French official statements continue to insist that the British will only be welcome in Europe if they are ready to join without reservation or conditions. It seems probable that this means not simply accepting the agricultural policy as finally agreed by the Six, but also making a much bigger break with the United States in the defense field than the present British government, and probably any British government, would be prepared to make. Any possibilities there might once have been for an Anglo-French understanding on defense would seem to have been eliminated, for the present at least, by the French government's precipitation of the NATO crisis and by the strong pro-Atlantic character of the British government's reaction to that crisis.

Dramatic overtures from either side in the near future therefore seem unlikely, although they can not be entirely ruled out. The outlook seems to be for probings and informal explorations, but for no definitive move for a year or two, perhaps longer.

Provided General de Gaulle relinquishes power in the next few years it seems reasonably safe to predict that the Community will survive the backwash of the NATO crisis, that the British interest in Europe will continue to grow, and that the United Kingdom will become a member of the Community—accepting the Treaty of Rome and its long-term political implications—soon after a change of government in France. If, however, General de Gaulle were to remain in power for the full seven years of his present term of office (or even longer) there might be great temptations to form new patterns. It is possible that the British would become "European" enough in a few years time so that some British initiative and a realignment around the United Kingdom might be a natural development. It is also possible that the veto would endure, that the Community would remain a customs union of the Six, and that the British would become progressively linked to the European market by industrial ties but would not join the EEC. (The analogy of the Canadian relationship with the

United States suggests itself, although it can not be pressed very far.) It seems rather more likely, however, that the French veto would, in time, be lifted in the sense that negotiations with the British would be given a green light. However, assuming continuing disagreements on defense, a government headed by General de Gaulle would probably seek to use the expansion of the Community to transform it into a loose economic arrangement shorn of its integrative pressures and its political overtones. As described in the last chapter, the views of the present British government about the kind of Europe it needs and wants are changing fairly rapidly. How far Mr. Wilson would go in joining hands with General de Gaulle in turning the clock back might well depend on how soon the temptation to do so arose.

The timing of General de Gaulle's departure from the political scene thus seems likely to be of considerable importance to the way things now develop between the British and the Six. It will also be important to the way things develop internally in the Community. The next section looks at the way the Community of the Six seems likely to develop while General de Gaulle remains in power. It is followed by some speculation about the way things might develop if he were to yield power, even to another Gaullist, some time between, say, 1967 and 1970, and the British were to join the Community soon thereafter.[1]

### *The short-term outlook for the Community*

As long as General de Gaulle remains at the head of the French government it is difficult to see the Six making any sig-

[1] It seems reasonably clear that although many aspects of French policy will not change with a change in government in France, any successor government will be rather more "European" in its policies. All the important opposition leaders have made their position plain on this point. Another Gaullist would doubtless pursue the general line laid down by de Gaulle, but no successor is likely to have quite the same exalted view of France as an independent power as General de Gaulle has had or to have quite his imperviousness to domestic pressures and the wishes of his Common Market partners.

nificant progress toward common policies in fields not covered by the existing treaties or any very rapid progress toward the kind of economic union—with common, community policies supplanting separate national policies—that seemed in prospect a few years ago.

Although for a time in the early sixties the French seem to have hoped that the Five would accept French views as the basis of a collective European foreign policy, it was never very probable that the Germans would have felt the *force de frappe* offered them enough protection so that they could take the risk of loosening their ties with the United States. Whatever the dangers in the past, and they were probably quite small, General de Gaulle had gone so far in alienating the Germans —by his flirtation with Moscow and, more deeply, by his reversal of the earlier French policy of treating the Germans as equals—that this possibility had become very remote before General de Gaulle opened his attack on the NATO arrangements early in 1966. General de Gaulle's press conference on February 21, 1966, and the subsequent French moves to withdraw from the NATO structure would seem to have eliminated any possibility of finding common ground among the Six on defense questions while General de Gaulle remains in power. The alternative road to a common view in foreign policy and defense—that General de Gaulle would modify his own views to bring them into line with those of his partners—has also never seemed very likely; it is almost inconceivable today.

As discussed in earlier chapters, if the Community were allowed to develop into an economic union along the lines envisaged by the Treaty of Rome and spelled out in more detail by the Commission in the Action Program and in its subsequent proposals (both those that have been published and those known to be in prospect [2]) national freedom of action on matters affecting foreign policy would become increasingly

[2] In particular, the Commission's proposals of March 30, 1965, which were the pretext for the crisis, and the plans for a monetary union that the Commission has been working on for some time.

restricted. Perhaps if France's partners had been willing to accept General de Gaulle's view of the policies the Europe of the Six should follow on foreign policy and defense the French would not have objected to the development of an economic union along these lines, for then the restraints on national freedom of action would have been far less important. Since the rest of the Six are clearly not prepared to accept French foreign policies as Community policies it seems probable that the French will continue to oppose—as they had started to do even before the crisis—any new commitments which restrict national freedom of action in any important way. All common policies come, of course, in this category. The French may also seek to loosen some of the more restricting commitments they have already undertaken.

The French can also be expected to continue to oppose the transfer of any real power from national authorities to central institutions, since any such transfer restricts the scope of the national authorities and is inconsistent with General de Gaulle's concepts of how relations among states should be organized. The objection to central institutions and the objection to common policies are closely related, but they are logically distinct. It would be possible, although not very easy, to have common policies elaborated by intergovernmental discussion and implemented entirely by national authorities.

If they were wholly consistent, the French should, of course, also seek to change the character of the common agricultural policy. Although it is economically advantageous for France, it is doctrinally at odds with Gaullist concepts and it gives an impetus to integration in other fields that may be difficult to control. Some of the apparent French interest in British membership during the winter of 1965–66 may well have stemmed from French reflections on the advantages of using British entry as a way of modifying the policy, compensating French farmers for any loss of income by increased sales in the British market. The French can be counted on to continue to insist, as they did in June, 1965, that the contributions to the Agricultural Fund remain under governmental control rather than having the Fund fed directly and automatically by the levies. And it would not be surprising if, under French pressure, the administration of the common agricultural policy were reshaped somewhat to give the representatives of the national governments a greater voice in the management committees. But it is probably too late to make any radical changes in the nature of the policy, for in all the Six countries, and not least in France, agricultural interests are well entrenched in support of a system which at the price levels that are in prospect is exceedingly attractive to the farmers.

Once agricultural prices are the same throughout the Community it will be extremely difficult for the exchange rates of any of the Six to be altered independently of the others. If rates between the member countries are unalterable, or almost unalterable, and trade virtually free, the Six will be driven to cooperate closely on monetary policy and on economic policy generally, whether they want to cooperate or not. The common agricultural policy will also of course limit somewhat national freedom of action on commercial policy. This is particularly true of relations with Eastern Europe, since a number of the eastern countries traditionally export agricultural products to the Six. The fact that decisions were finally taken by the Six on May 11, 1966, to complete the common agricultural policy suggests that the French have concluded that the stimulation the agricultural policy will give to the adoption of common policies can be kept within bounds and that the necessary coordination in other fields can be achieved by cooperative arrangements among governments rather than by the adoption of common policies elaborated and administered by central institutions.

In the optimistic days of 1961–62 the Community was widely expected to have moved by now toward common policies not only in agriculture but in other areas as well, particularly toward a common commercial policy and a common monetary policy. In both areas the Commission has had plans drawn for several years and has been ready to take action whenever the governments would agree to do so. These plans now seem likely to stay in their pigeonholes until the policy of the French government changes.

Given the Community's present level of development and the existence of other commitments governing the conduct of international trade, continued French blocking of any move toward a common commercial policy will probably have rather different consequences than might, at first, be assumed. Thus far the French have seemed reconciled to having the Six act as a unit in their negotiations in the Kennedy Round, although there was a French suggestion at one time that the Community exceptions' list might be supplemented by national exceptions' list and, conceivably, this idea might be put forward again. Commercial relations with many countries—particularly with countries whose main instrument of trade control is today the tariff—will be largely regulated by the outcome of those negotiations. By far the largest part of the Community's trade with third countries comes in this category.

The Community, of course, already has a common commercial policy toward those countries with which it has association arrangements, that is the countries in Africa that are signatories to the Yaoundé convention, Greece and Turkey, and the former Dutch possessions in the West Indies. And it has a partial common policy with a number of other countries with which it has concluded trade agreements, e.g., Israel. The commercial policies of the Six differ mainly with regard to trade with Eastern Europe, those parts of the underdeveloped world that are not associated with the Community and whose exports to the Community are substantially limited by the quotas imposed by the Six governments, and Japan, although differences in the treatment of Japanese goods have narrowed during the last few years as trade has been liberalized. The Commission has for a long time tried to persuade the member countries to move to a system of Community quotas rather than national quotas, but it has had no success.[3] The present French government will undoubtedly continue to oppose any such development. It seems probable that there will be some harmonization of national quota systems and continuing reliance on Article 115 [4] to prevent trade diversion within the Community where differences in the treatment given to goods from third countries still exist.

The purely practical difficulties arising from the failure to move to a common commercial policy can doubtless be handled in this way, since the amount of trade affected is relatively small. The main disadvantage today of not having a common policy is not the danger of trade diversion but the fact that the world's largest trading complex, the EEC, is unable to play the creative role in UNCTAD discussions and elsewhere which it could play if the Six could agree to act as one.

Similarly in the monetary field, the problems within the system that are likely to arise in the next few years can probably be handled by reaching *ad hoc* agreements among the national authorities. Very probably these agreements will be worked out within the existing committee structure of the Community: the Central Bankers' Committee and the Monetary Committee. But here again, as in the case of commercial policy, the pattern seems likely to be essentially one of intergovernmental cooperation, not, as had earlier been planned and hoped, the progressive adoption of common policies and the gradual development of an institutional infrastructure capable of sustaining a unified system. And, again, the main result of the failure to move toward a common policy will be the inability of the Community to play as large a role on the wider international stage as it could play if the Six could agree to act as one.

[3] The Commission's efforts to persuade governments to move toward a common commercial policy are discussed in more detail in Camps, *What Kind of Europe?*, cited.

[4] Article 115 permits members to take "protective measures," e.g., intra-Community quotas, when differences in policies toward third countries lead to economic difficulties.

The inability to play a collective role internationally in monetary matters may, however, have rather more serious repercussions for the long-term development of the Community than will the fact that the Six are partially paralyzed in the field of commercial policy. It seems probable that, if the French position in the Group of Ten continues to be one which is too extreme for its Common Market partners to accept, there will eventually be some agreement on monetary reform to which the Five will subscribe without the French. Depending on the pattern of reform agreed upon, this might make it extremely difficult for the Community to move toward a monetary union after a change of government in France. Perhaps here, as clearly as in any other field, the *timing* of a change in attitude on the part of France assumes great importance. Presumably effective reform of world monetary arrangements is still a few years off. If a change in the French government and the accession of the United Kingdom to the Community come *before* any agreement is reached in the Group of Ten and in the IMF, any reform of the international system might well assume that some form of "European" unit might, in time, replace sterling as a reserve currency. If, however, the present French government remains in power (or a subsequent French government maintains the uncompromising attitude of the present government), it seems probable that the reform of the system will proceed on different assumptions. This, in turn, will make more difficult the later emergence of a European monetary system or of a European reserve currency.

A similar pattern seems likely to develop in the next few years in other policy areas as well, e.g., energy, taxation, budget policy, social policy. That is, there will presumably be enough coordination or harmonization of national policies to make the customs union work, but there is unlikely to be any substantial progress toward an economic union, if that is defined as the substitution of common policies—internally and externally—for national policies. And there is unlikely to be any shift in power from national authorities to Community institutions, rather the reverse.[5]

In short, as long as General de Gaulle is in power in France, it seems reasonable to expect that French efforts will be directed toward securing the economic benefits of the Common Market at a minimum cost in terms of interference with, or limitation on, national freedom of action. There is, of course, a contradiction here, for it is becoming increasingly clear to everyone—and, not least, to French industry—that many of the economic advantages of the Common Market can be expected to come precisely from the consequences of looking at and treating six (or more) economies as a single economic unit rather than, as General de Gaulle tends to do, as six separate units which have agreed to free trade and to make certain limited agreements of other kinds with one another. However, the whole trend of Gaullist thinking and particularly the crisis in the Community in 1965 make it difficult to believe that General de Gaulle will be prepared to accept any new arrangements which significantly impair the French government's control over the French economy even though such arrangements might, in fact, be very advantageous for France.

Before the crisis, the French had shown a certain interest in extending Six-country action to two new subjects: first, they had put forward proposals for a "European" form of company law; second, they had suggested some kind of Six-country action to encourage technological and scientific research. More may well be heard of both ideas, for action on either, or both, would be perfectly consistent with Gaullist ideas of how relations between states should be organized. A "European" com-

[5] It is worth noting that since the Luxembourg settlement the French have succeeded in restricting the scope of the Commission in various small ways. For example, a fact-finding study to see whether differences in credit terms available to Eastern European countries gave rise to distortions of trade was entrusted to the permanent representatives rather than to the Commission as would have been normal. Each case of this kind is likely to be, in itself, too small to be worth making an issue of, but the cumulative effect may well be quite important.

pany law would, in a sense, be the obverse of the provisions in the Treaty of Rome which prohibit certain types of agreements among firms and guard against the abuse of a dominant position. The purpose of a standard European form of company law would be, in contrast, to encourage certain types of merger.

At the time the treaty was drafted it was widely assumed that the removal of barriers to trade and the greater freedom of movement of labor and capital foreseen by the treaty would, in themselves, encourage the emergence of large companies and that the problem would be to see that dominant positions thus acquired were not abused. One of the "failures" of the Common Market has been the fact that "Europe-sized" companies have not developed. The effect of acceptance by the Six of a standard form of company law would doubtless be to encourage mergers and, in particular, to encourage firms in Community countries to link up with firms in other Community countries rather than with American firms. To the extent that a new legal framework stimulated intra-Community links, the industrial interest in the preservation of the Common Market would obviously be strengthened. But any action resulting from this kind of essentially permissive legislation is not likely to have any very great restraining effect on national freedom, nor would it necessarily lead to the development of central institutions or new centers of decision taking. It is worth underlining that the French proposals envisaged the bringing into line of national laws. The Commission, needless to say, would prefer the substitution of a new "European" law; if anything is done in the near future, the French view seems sure to prevail.

Similarly if action is now taken either at French initiative or with French concurrence to encourage European scientific and technological research, the kind of encouragement given to European firms seems likely to be consistent with Gaullist concepts. Discussion among the national governments may well lead to a decision to encourage—perhaps by some form of joint financial assistance—certain types of research and development. But the key decisions will clearly remain firmly in the hands of the national governments and not be transferred to central institutions. The recent history of French opposition to increases in the Euratom research budget underlines, once again, their unwillingness to support any form of action which removes the effective power of decision from French hands.

"Organized cooperation" on the Gaullist model can, of course, lead to a more integrated European economy, as did the "organized cooperation" encouraged by the OEEC (Organization for European Economic Cooperation). And the existence of cooperation over a wide field obviously makes a later move to common policies easier than it would be if there were no prior experience of working together. The familiarity with each others' problems gained from cooperation in the OEEC, and the warm personal relationships formed during the early days of the OEEC, made the tasks of the Six far easier than they would otherwise have been. There is, however, a difference in kind between a number of governments deciding, on the one hand, to delegate powers to common institutions and to act in common and only in common for certain purposes, and their deciding, on the other hand, that it is to their mutual advantage to free trade and to remove various impediments to movements of manpower and capital, and to encourage research or scientific developments by national fiscal or financial measures. The first type of action is envisaged by the Treaty of Rome and is what makes the Common Market an exciting new experiment; the second type of action is eminently useful, but it is not different in kind from the organized cooperation that the EFTA, the OEEC–OECD, and other traditional intergovernmental organizations have shown themselves well suited to perform.

It is important to be clear about this point, because there is frequently a tendency in "European" circles to assume that any kind of action by the Six countries—particularly if it is formally launched by the Community institutions—is necessarily progress toward the goal of European union. If the goal is eventually reached, organized cooperation on an intergovernmental basis will doubtless have helped. But organized cooperation on a Six-country basis even when promoted by Community institutions does not lead necessarily and inescapably to the goal of European union.

On the assumption that the "Europeans" cannot hope for much more than a holding operation until there is a change of policy in Paris (or a realignment of the European countries pursuing the goal of union) then cooperation, where possible, is useful, both in itself and to lay the groundwork for later, more radical, action. But it should be recognized for what it is, and not seen as evidence of a change of heart on the part of the French government and of a new "post-Luxembourg" willingness to accept the "logic" of the Common Market. It is nothing of the sort. On the contrary, all signs point to continuing French resistance to the "logic" of the Common Market, that is the built-in propulsion toward an economic-political union. Not unlike the attitude of the British government during the OEEC period and, again, during the free trade area negotiations, the French attitude today seems to reflect a willingness to undertake a considerable measure of practical cooperation with her Common Market partners but to draw the line at any action which would effectively transfer the power of decision in matters of any significance to non-French hands or which would create a system with a dynamic of its own that would, over time, inescapably limit French freedom of action.

Despite the similarities between the French position today and the British position in the past, there is, of course, the significant difference that the Gaullists endorse the objective of a distinctively European construction—a power group with a policy of its own. The British position of the 1950s was more logical, for unlike the Gaullist position it was internally consistent in refusing both the limitations on national freedom of action and in questioning the objective of a "European Europe." General de Gaulle's position, in contrast, rests on a fundamental contradiction. But because the Gaullist objective of a "European Europe" has some features in common with the "European" objective, the kind of Six-country cooperation that may still be possible while General de Gaulle remains in power is not necessarily incompatible with European objectives and may, in the long term, assist the process.

Unless he is prepared to take France out of the Common Market, General de Gaulle cannot, of course, completely arrest the integrating process and the gradual encroachment on French independence of action that has already been set in train by the progress of the Common Market to date. The settlement of the crisis seems to show that he has concluded that the disadvantages of that course of action (not least the electoral risks [6]) are likely to be greater than the advantages. However, a government that is determined to throw sand into the gears can do a lot to slow down the *engrenage* in which the "Europeans" put their trust.

Today (May 1966) the expectation among the "Europeans" is that the present position cannot only be held until General de Gaulle relinquishes power but can be improved on a little by rounding out the agricultural policy and by completing the customs union for industrial products. Despite widespread doubts about their chances of success, the Six finally agreed (at 5 A.M. on May 11) to a settlement of the financial regulation for the Agricultural Fund, and to dates for the fixing of the remaining common agricultural prices and for the completion of the customs union for industrial goods. If these deadlines are lived up to, the Six will be a rather curious form of customs union by mid-1968, with rather more ambitious agricultural arrangements than are strictly necessary to ensure free trade and rather fewer commitments to common action in other areas than one would have expected.

The Common Market is now probably irreversible in the

[6] *The Observer,* February 20, 1966, reported that the French government had received the results of a secret poll of a sample of 2,500 people investigating why people who had previously voted for de Gaulle had voted against him in the 1965 election. The largest group (more than 40 per cent) was dissatisfied with social programs. But more than a third feared that General de Gaulle was out to destroy the Common Market.

sense that it is almost impossible to see the Six re-erecting tariffs and the other barriers to trade that have been torn down since 1958 and returning to their earlier systems of agricultural protection. But it is by no means "irreversible" in the sense in which this word is frequently used by some "Europeans." There is no iron law of "spill over" nor an irresistible internal dynamic that is bound to carry the Six to full economic union and beyond that to some form of political union. Again, recent history is instructive.

Despite the claims made in earlier days, those closest to the scene and those most accustomed to talk of irreversibility were probably rather more doubtful whether the Community would survive the 1965 crisis than were those farther from the scene and less emotionally committed to the thesis that the unification of Europe had become an inevitable development. But to some extent the two groups were talking about different things. The fear of the "Europeans" was not that the Six would go back to the pre-Community days but, rather, that the Community would be transformed into something looser with less promise of developing eventually into "Europe." This transformation might have occurred either by the Five yielding completely to the French and turning the Community into an intergovernmental organization of a more traditional kind, or by a break between the Five and the French followed by an arrangement on a broader, looser basis between the Five and the EFTA countries. Characteristically, some of the strongest "Europeans" were more alarmed at the prospect of the second than at the prospect of the first. The Community has been "saved" in the sense that neither of these things happened in January 1966, but either of them might still occur.

Even with no new decisions, the interdependence among the Six grows every day simply as the result of the steps already taken. But so, too, does the interdependence of the industrialized countries of the West. It will take something more than the simple departure of General de Gaulle from the scene to ensure that the Common Market becomes, in the end, more than a roundabout route to a Western European customs union or to an Atlantic low-tariff club.

*The longer-term outlook*

Despite the skeptics and today's unpromising signs, it seems probable that the "something more" that is needed to carry the process of European unification further does exist, and that once General de Gaulle has left the scene the process will again acquire momentum, provided the change in France is not too long delayed. As indicated above, the proviso may well be of crucial importance.

Doubts about the probability, and also the validity, of the development of something that could legitimately be called a European union have been intensified by General de Gaulle's attacks on the Community and the NATO, but they would have arisen in any case, for many of the factors that formerly pushed in this direction no longer exist, or have a greatly diminished force. There is no imminent external threat, no sense of imperative need, no dynamic leader. Many of the strongest "Europeans" are old men. Europe is prosperous. The "German problem" does not exist in the acute form it took in the fifties. The nation-state which in Western Europe, at least, was supposed to be in decline has reasserted itself. "Gaullism" will not disappear with General de Gaulle. The present French government has given a new emphasis to nationalism, but it has probably only accentuated a tendency that was bound to appear in any case as a consequence of prosperity, stability and *détente*. "Gaullism" is, in part, a sport, a phenomenon that depends on the exceptional personality of one man whose return to power in 1958 was an accident of history. But "Gaullism" is also, in part, a reaction to the process of losing sovereignty—both the "planned" loss of sovereignty that has been occurring in the Communities and the "unplanned" loss of sovereignty that has come from the shift in power from the former great powers in Western Europe to the two superpowers.

There are today few signs of the popular enthusiasm, the leadership, the sense of need, that would seem to be required if the European countries were to achieve anything like a federation within, say, the next decade. Nevertheless, the evidence of the resilience and the durability of the European idea is impressive. The differences with the French have led, at times, to near stagnation in the Community, but the Six have shown an ability and a determination to absorb differences of view that on any rational calculation should have destroyed the Community. And three years after the veto the British are far more "European" than they were when membership in the Community seemed imminent.

In the world of the sixties European union is not a necessity but a matter of choice for the governments and the peoples involved. It is probably the best road to the kind of society and the role in the world the key Western European countries seem to want. But it is difficult to make a convincing case that either their economic prosperity or their political freedom depends upon it. It is not surprising, therefore, that the enthusiasm and the emotionalism that characterized the European movement in the early postwar years when many people on the Continent quite genuinely felt that union offered the only hope of restoring an acceptable economic and political system in Europe has disappeared.

Those who talked of "making Europe" and dreamed of a federation in a decade are growing old and somewhat disillusioned. But so, too, are those who dismissed all talk of European union as unreal and Utopian. Both groups are being replaced by a new generation that accepts European unity as a long-term goal and, what is more important, sees nothing very revolutionary or controversial in the fact that it should do so. This matter-of-fact assumption that Western Europe is in the process of uniting, and that the process is both desirable and more or less inevitable, is widespread on the Continent and growing in the United Kingdom. It is not an attitude that leads to rapid or dramatic changes, but it is one that seems likely to sustain a slow but continuing process of unification.

Today the safe prediction for the future is that the Western European countries—i.e., the Six joined in a few years' time by the United Kingdom and some of the other EFTA countries—will become a customs union with an agricultural policy based broadly on the system of the Six. But, for a number of reasons, the process seems unlikely to stop there.

Although it is true that some of the arguments for a European union that appeared most persuasive in the past have lost their force, some of them are still valid and some have assumed new forms. An economic union may not today seem necessary for prosperity, but on both sides of the Channel there is a strong and growing belief that the only road to a technologically advanced economy that is indigenous in character, rather than increasingly controlled by American industry, lies in organizing industries on a European rather than a national basis. Much of the new British interest in Europe stems from this consideration. And much of the new French interest in British membership, which is detectable in some quarters, comes from their recognition that the British have a sophisticated industrial base and spend appreciably more on research and development in industries such as aircraft, electronics, and atomic energy than does any other Western European country.[7] The technological and scientific pressures for "European" action seem likely to grow as the lead the United States already has in these fields continues to lengthen. And European action will mean more than the removal of tariffs.

There are also persuasive reasons arising from the situation in Germany for continuing down the road toward union, although the "German problem" presents itself in rather different terms today than it did in the past. In the fifties the need to

[7] In 1962 research and development expenditures, per capita in U.S. dollars, were as follows:

Federal Republic, 20.1
France, 23.6
United Kingdom, 35.5
United States, 93.7

Source: *The OECD Observer*, February 1966.

put the relationship between Germany and France on a new basis seemed to many people the most compelling reason for trying to build a community within which the old nationalisms could be replaced by a new loyalty. Franco-German relations are not today as warm and harmonious as many people in both countries would like them to be, but a new relationship exists between the two countries and also between Germany and her other neighbors in Western Europe. There is inevitably, if unfortunately, some lingering mistrust of the Germans in Western Europe which shows itself in various ways, perhaps most clearly in the continuing British reluctance really to accept the Germans as equals in the defense field. But the earlier argument that European union was necessary to ensure peaceful relations between Germany and her Western neighbors now has little meaning. And the earlier argument that, for Germany, the road to equality and the end of occupation and discriminatory controls lay through participation in a European union has been so overtaken by events that, today, the willingness to treat the Germans as equals has become in the eyes of many continentals the test of whether or not the British have become "good Europeans."

Although these aspects of the question are radically changed, there is still a need to give the Germans an emotional and practical alternative to German reunification, for no acceptable basis for German reunification yet exists. Pressures in the Federal Republic for some progress toward German reunification have always been most apparent when progress toward European unity has been halting and uncertain. It is not surprising that these pressures are conspicuous today. They seem likely to become increasingly important as Germany grows stronger and as a new generation comes to power that has no personal sense of guilt for the Hitler period.[8] For the present, the German government needs the prospect of continuing progress toward a European union if these pressures are

[8] For a persuasive British statement of the importance of giving the Germans a "European alternative" to a purely national policy, see Kenneth Younger in *The Listener*, November 25, 1965.

to be contained. But, somewhat paradoxically, the Germans also need to feel that the two policies—German reunification and European unification—are complementary and not true alternatives if they are to go much further down the road toward union. Unless an acceptable connection between the two policies is clearly seen and agreed upon, both in the Federal Republic and in the other countries of the Community, the Germans will inevitably be reluctant to give up their own freedom of action.

As discussed further below, the development of the Community (expanded to include the United Kingdom) may, in the long term, offer a way to an acceptable solution to the problem of German reunification. The path ahead is not very clearly seen today, and any substantial pressure for European unification as the road to German reunification lies in the future. Nevertheless, the desire to play a more important part in the eventual settlement in Central Europe is one of the factors turning thoughts, in the United Kingdom as well as in the Six, to the advantages of collective action. With the appearance of signs of a *détente* between the United States and the Soviet Union following the settlement of the Cuban missiles crisis, the Germans became increasingly alarmed that their future might be settled by some deal between the two superpowers. General de Gaulle's attempt to exploit this fear and to induce the Germans to see in his Europe the road to reunification seems to have failed, but he has brought home the need for agreement among the Western European countries on the question of German reunification, as well as the dangers that lie in the lack of any agreed Western policy on this central issue.

The desire for a bigger voice in the settlement of this key issue is, of course, only one aspect of the general proposition that only through unity can Europe regain its proper place in the world and exercise the influence that is both its right and its duty. The desire to increase European influence, or power, has always been one of the motives for unity. Today it is by far the most compelling pressure pushing in that direction. It is the connecting thread that links together the economic, political, and military arguments that now seem most persuasive. And it has provided the common ground between the "Gaullists" and the "Europeans" that has enabled the Community to continue despite the profound differences between the member countries about the methods by which Europe is to unite and about its relationship with the United States.

If, as now seems probable, the British again seek to join the Community they will do so because—whatever Mr. Wilson may say today—they have decided that they can best maximize their power, both economic and political, by acting as a part of a European complex rather than by acting independently, or as a junior partner to the United States, or as an elder sister to the Commonwealth. If the French let the British join the Community it will be because the French have reached similar conclusions about their own role in the world, or, more accurately, because the French have rejected the Gaullist illusion that France can gain the power they want through independence and have returned to the analysis of French interests which led them to take the leadership in promoting the Communities of the Six. Put another way, if the French and British do come together within the Community framework [9] both governments will have decided that their interests lie in creating a workable, cohesive European grouping. The reasons that have led them to this decision will compel them to make the new group an effective one.

Both Britain and France are coming to the end of a long and difficult period of decolonization. Both countries have found it hard to adjust to their diminished roles in the world. Both believe that they have contributions to make to the world—cultural, intellectual, political, technological, and scientific—that entitle them to an influence that is quite disproportionate to the real influence either, alone, can now

[9] The qualification "within the Community framework" is important. Obviously what follows would not be true if the French and British governments made it their common cause to transform the EEC into a broad free-trade area.

exert. Unlike the other countries in Western Europe, they both, rightly or wrongly, think in big power terms. They feel instinctively that what happens elsewhere in the world is their concern and something for which they have a certain responsibility, although in the last few years the French view of their world role has been an eccentric and unhelpful one. And both countries in their hearts believe that the other one is the only European country with which it can fairly be classed.

The attractions of an Anglo-French partnership are so obvious that the temptation will be to give that relationship too high a priority and to repeat on an Anglo-French basis the mistakes General de Gaulle has made by treating the rest of the Five, and particularly the Germans, as a useful chorus which is expected to come in on the refrains but is not allowed to sing any of the principal parts. The consequences of any such policy, like the consequence of General de Gaulle's policy, would be to strengthen German ties with the United States and to defeat the larger purpose of establishing a European group with an identity of its own. However, if this temptation can be avoided, the underlying strong similarity of interests between the British and the French in having the Community become a group which can exercise effective influence in the world should be a powerful pressure toward union. For only a group that can find its way to common policies and common institutions can use its power effectively.

Although the pressures pushing the Six and the United Kingdom to form some kind of effective union seem likely to prove stronger in the long term than the pulls in other directions—and the inertia—that today threaten the process, the "building of Europe" seems likely to be a slower and much more pragmatic process than it has been in the past. At times the pace can probably be deliberately forced by careful contriving by the institutions at the center. But one of the lessons of the last fifteen years would seem to be that it is usually counterproductive to try to take a very big leap forward. The EDC failed, the ambitious original conception of Euratom was watered down in the negotiations (and further watered down by the French after it was established), the Commission's attempt last year to manipulate the governments into taking a giant step forward would probably have failed even had the French played by the rules of the treaty and the conventions of the Community.

A strong and imaginative Commission can use conflicting pressures to push governments to opt for a Community solution and to speed up a process that has been started, as it did in twice accelerating the pace of tariff adjustments and in pushing through the common agricultural policy. But the kind of integration by stealth that M. Monnet was able to accomplish in the halcyon days of the Schuman Plan is unlikely again to become practical politics. To an even greater extent than was true in the past, the future development of the Community seems likely to be a slow, organic one, with integration occurring partly as a consequence of past actions, partly as the product of new policy decisions which have been undertaken quite deliberately in full awareness of their consequences.

There is clearly a spill-over effect at work in the Community. But, as the Six have demonstrated, the spill-over process is much more effective when there is acceptance of the principle of moving toward further integration than it is when there is not. If spill-over were irresistible, the Six would now have a common commercial policy and a common monetary policy. Governments now know about the virtues, and the dangers, of *engrenage*. And progress in the future is not likely to result from decisions taken half blindly without adequate thought about the consequences. The strongest reason for thinking that something like a federation may one day be formed in Western Europe is not because the pressures of a customs union will force the governments irresistibly to federate, although a customs union undoubtedly sets up pressures pushing in that direction, but because it seems probable that the key governments will decide that a federation is an acceptable long-term goal. They are unlikely to give progress toward that goal a high priority, because there is unlikely to be any great need to do so. But once it is accepted that a federation, however loose or far off, is at the end of the road down which they are traveling it will become easier for governments to settle many of the problems that arise by going farther down the road toward union than by taking separate national action. The more clearly the eventual goal is accepted the more the process of integration tends to feed on itself.

The Community is today a mixed system, a construction that is *sui generis,* which cannot be equated with either a federal state or an international organization in the conventional sense, although it has some of the attributes of each. It promises to remain a mixed system for a long time, with the members acting collectively for some purposes, individually for others with the amount of coordination of policy and of common action depending on the extent to which the interests of the member countries coincide and with the advantages to be gained from common action.

Although the "Community method," the dialogue between the Council of Ministers (representing the governments and the separate national interests) and the independent Commission (representing the common interest) survived the Gaullist attack in 1965, the effect of the crisis—both the crisis itself and the settlement early in 1966—was to tip the balance of power in the Community away from the institutions at the center and toward the governments. This may well be a temporary shift. But no very radical advance toward an institutional system that is more "supranational" than the Community system was when it was working best (i.e., 1959–62) seems probable for quite a number of years. Until there is a change of attitude in Paris the problem will continue to be to preserve a system that makes it possible to give any effective expression to the common interest.

If sometime between, say, 1968 and 1972 the British join the Community, they will be followed by a number of other countries—Denmark, certainly, and probably Norway and Ireland. The Community institutions are already cumbersome and slow moving, and simply adding new members, however "European-minded" they may then be, will add to the difficulties. Perhaps the occasion can be used for some streamlining and, hopefully, for more delegation of power to the Commission. The Council of Ministers has always been far too involved in details, and, following the crisis and the Luxembourg settlement, the foreign ministers seem likely to become even more burdened with the minutiae of Community decisions. But, on the assumption that it is the present British government that finally takes the United Kingdom "into Europe," it is stretching credibility too far to believe that Mr. Wilson's known distaste for a strong Commission will change overnight into acceptance of the need for greater delegation of authority to the Commission if only to prevent the machine from seizing up.

Following British entry and a change of attitude in Paris, some improvements in the system will doubtless be made. But broadly the Community method as it has evolved during the last fifteen years seems likely to persist for some time, perhaps for another decade. With all its imperfections it is an institutional innovation that has "worked," albeit slowly. And it has now acquired a kind of sanctity simply because it has been under attack, in the early days from the British, more recently and with greater vigor from the Gaullists. Tampering with the system, even in the name of efficiency, has become suspect; it is likely to remain so until the new members have been absorbed and confidence in France has been restored.

The drafting of a new treaty to replace the three existing treaties (the Treaty of Paris establishing the ECSC and the two Treaties of Rome establishing the EEC and Euratom) is supposed to begin as soon as the institutions have been merged and to be completed within three years.[10] This may well be too soon. Perhaps British membership will have occurred before the drafting of a new treaty is completed, but this is not today assured. It would seem to be desirable to draft the new treaty after, rather than just before, the addition of new members, for then various consequential adjustments could be

[10] The fusion of the institutions seems unlikely to take place before 1967 or 1968.

taken into account and the revised treaty made responsive to the problems that an expansion of the Community from six to ten, or more, will create. Furthermore, if the revision is undertaken while General de Gaulle is still in power, there will obviously be a tug of war between the Gaullists and the "Europeans" and the result, like the result of the 1965 crisis, will tend to be a formula that patches over differences but offers no clear guide to future action. Even if the process can be dragged out until after General de Gaulle has gone, a revision in the near future is likely to be made with the assumptions of the past and the struggles of the last few years too much in mind. There is no urgent need for a revision. The opportunity should be used to look ahead to the kind of action that should be taken in the seventies, not simply to remove a few anomalies which is the best that is likely to happen if the process of revision begins too soon.

One of the unfortunate by-products of the fact that the "Europeans" have been on the defensive for so long, and also of the stagnation that the Community has suffered during the last year or two, is that there has been a sterility in "European" thought and a tendency to continue to think in the patterns of the fifties. At a time when the "Europeans" have been trying above all to save and to protect what they have built, they have, naturally enough, resisted change and experimentation for fear that any tampering with their construction would open the path to its complete destruction. Had the "Europeans" felt confident of success they would have dared to experiment, and had the Community been developing rapidly the simple fact of having to deal with new problems would have stimulated new thoughts. Inevitably there has been a tendency to look nostalgically at the plans that are gathering dust in the files and to think of returning to the previous pattern when the Gaullist road block is removed. There are, unhappily, few signs anywhere today of creative new thought and of a willingness to experiment—either with institutional or substantive questions—that were characteristic of the "Europeans" a decade ago. Similarly, in the United Kingdom the effect of having been blocked in 1963 has made some of the British "Europeans" more committed than ever to a "European doctrine" that is becoming slightly musty. They have learned their "European lessons" too well.

### *The problem of "political union"*

The defensive character and consequent sterility of thought have been most apparent in the discussions about "political union" which have gone on intermittently since 1960.[11] Thus far, the political union debate has gone around in circles or, more accurately, in a descending spiral with the expectations of all the participants declining each time talks are resumed. When General de Gaulle put forward his first proposals in 1960 for a Council of Heads of Government with specialized councils for political, economic, and defense and cultural questions, there was understandable concern among the Five that he was trying to supplant the Economic Community and to undercut the NATO, and he encountered considerable resistance. By the following spring he had, however, persuaded Dr. Adenauer that he was trying to supplement, not to weaken, existing organizations. The smaller countries were far less sure, but they agreed to participate in the Fouchet Committee (composed of representatives from the Six governments) which was to try to agree on precise proposals for consideration by the six heads of government. In July (1961) the heads of government reached agreement on the Bonn Declaration: this was the high-water mark of common understanding among the Six, a point that has not since been reached. Moreover, as soon as the Fouchet Committee sought to turn the general principles of the Bonn Declaration into a treaty, the underlying differences of view again became apparent. Negotiations were broken off in April 1962, when the Bel-

[11] Or perhaps more accurately since 1952 when the proposal for a European Political Community was included in the EDC treaty. Since 1960 the discussions among the Six have, in a sense, been one continuing, if unproductive, negotiation.

gians and the Dutch refused to go ahead with the kind of treaty then under discussion (which contained no supranational element) unless the British were invited to participate from the start. The Franco-German treaty of cooperation was then quickly negotiated during the autumn and signed in January 1963. The "political union" discussions among the Six were apparently dead.

By the end of the year (1963), however, both M. Spaak and Dr. Erhard were talking again about the possibility of resuming negotiations. During the spring of 1964 Dr. Erhard sounded out his partners, but the Dutch and the Italians were reluctant to take any new steps until after the British election. In the autumn of 1964—after the British election—both the Italians and the Germans put forward proposals, but neither has as yet been officially discussed. After the settlement of the cereals prices at the end of 1964 and the shelving of the MLF, the Germans hoped for a resumption of discussions on "political union," and, during his discussions with General de Gaulle at Rambouillet, in February 1965, Dr. Erhard apparently thought he had been given a green light by the French. Plans for a meeting of the foreign ministers of the Six in Venice were fairly far advanced when M. Couve de Murville visited Rome at the end of March (1965) and informed the Italians, very abruptly, that any such meeting would be premature. Then came the crisis among the Six. Predictably enough, with the settlement of the crisis, suggestions for a meeting of foreign ministers to consider the political union question were heard once again. The possibility of such a meeting was discussed by Dr. Erhard and General de Gaulle when they met for their semi-annual meeting under the Franco-German treaty early in February 1966, and General de Gaulle reverted to the subject in familiar terms at his press conference later in the month:

> By virtue of what evil charm will the Six find it impossible to consider between themselves political subjects of common interest —in short, to organize their political relations?
>
> It is well known that France has for a long time been pro-

posing that this should be done. It is well known that, for their part, the German Government, the Italian Government, and the Belgian Minister of Foreign Affairs have subsequently made similar proposals; and although these projects differ to some extent from one another, they are all agreed on an essential point, which is this: to lead the six Governments to meet regularly, in order to consider together political subjects of common interest. Well, since the economic organization of the Six has resumed its normal course after Luxembourg, France believes that this is more than ever the appropriate time to put these political meetings into practice.

Obviously, it is not a matter of the Six brandishing afresh absolute theories as to what should ideally be the future European edifice; of imposing a rigid framework laid down in advance for such complex and changing realities as those of our continent's life and relations with the outside world; of supposing that the problem of building Europe is solved before we have even begun to live together, politically speaking, in Europe; in short, of being bogged down once again in myths and abstractions that have always prevented the Six from undertaking together anything else than the arduous adjustment of their trade and economic production. On the contrary, what the Six must do is meet to work with the aim of cooperating. It so happens that, during the recent Franco-German meetings held on the occasion of Chancellor Erhard's visit to Paris, the two Governments agreed on this point, and this seems to me to be one of the chief results of this cordial meeting.[12]

Throughout the long negotiations in the Fouchet Committee and the spasmodic discussions since then it was clear that the French were trying to downgrade and control the Economic Community by capping it with an intergovernmental arrangement.[13] The Five tried to guard against this, and they also sought to have any new "political" construction contain

[12] From the English text issued by the French Embassy, London.

[13] The Dutch, and particularly Dr. Luns, have always been the most outspokenly critical of General de Gaulle's intentions. Until the summer of 1964, Dr. Luns was frequently felt by some "Europeans"—European and American—to be too intransigent. He was, at least, singularly free of any illusion that General de Gaulle could be coaxed or trapped into doing anything he did not want to do.

the germ of the Community principle. At times they hoped to achieve this by a revision clause ensuring that any new intergovernmental structure would take a more Community form after an agreed number of years; at other times they sought French agreement to some form of Commission, or group of wise men, or even a secretary-general with a limited power of initiative. It has, however, been clear for some time that the present French government would accept no system that would now or in the foreseeable future give any effective role to an independent body representing the common interest.

The French view of the role of any new organization in the defense field was also, of course, fundamentally different from that of the Five. The French wanted to turn the Six into a European defense base from which to force a reorganization of NATO. The Five, although willing to consider some reorganization of NATO, were not prepared to question its primacy in the defense field, or to weaken the links with the United States—both of which seemed to be part of the French plan.

Had General de Gaulle not decided a few weeks after the Luxembourg settlement to take immediate action to alter the NATO arrangements, a move foreshadowed in the February press conference quoted above, it seems probable that some new discussions among the Six on political union would have been held during 1966. With the outbreak of the NATO crisis, the prospects for discussions on political union again receded. But, in any case, the most that the Six could conceivably have agreed upon would have been to hold regular meetings of foreign ministers, and, perhaps, of heads of government, following the pattern of the Franco-German Treaty. In any meaningful sense, an agreement on a "political union," like any other major step toward a more integrated Europe, is very unlikely so long as General de Gaulle remains in power.

What are prospects after that? On the perhaps optimistic assumption made in this chapter that the key governments —France, the Federal Republic, and the United Kingdom— will eventually decide that their interests lie in forming a cohesive European group able to act as a unit externally for many purposes, the question of going beyond the Treaties of Rome and Paris will certainly arise. It would be unfortunate if before that time comes some new thought had not been given to the problem, for the argument has been a singularly sterile one and both the assumptions and prescriptions of the past are rather archaic.

Perhaps the first thing to be done is to get rid of the term "political union." Dr. Hallstein is, of course, right in maintaining that the Economic Community is a political phenomenon. The task in the future will be to decide on the areas beyond those already defined by the existing treaties in which the Community countries want to act in common and then to agree on the institutional arrangements that will make it possible for them to do so most effectively. The kind of Europe that is likely to emerge in, say, the next decade will be determined partly by the dynamics of the commitments undertaken within the framework of the existing treaties, partly by the reasons for unity that now and in the future are likely to seem important to the key governments, and partly by the developing pattern of international life into which the Community must fit.

In the past the "motor" of unification has been the pressures set up by trade liberalization. These will continue to be important. So, too, will the pressures of the common agricultural policy. But the desire for technological equality with the Soviet Union and the United States will also be a powerful factor in the future, with consequences for the way the Community approaches questions such as the organization of capital markets and economic planning. In the longer term the desire for the increase in power and influence that comes from common policies and collective action seems likely to become the most important propellant toward unity.

In the field of foreign policy, the central issue on which the European countries will want to maximize their power will presumably be the settlement in Central Europe. At present views on this issue divide rather than unite the key countries. Is it possible to conceive of a common policy emerging, in time, in this critical field? If it is not, the prospects for a union with a common foreign policy eventually developing in Western Europe are bleak. But provided the *détente* between the United States and the USSR continues, perhaps an approach on which all the countries in an enlarged Community could agree can be envisaged.

The possibility of seeking an acceptable solution to the problem of the division of Germany through the further development of the Community and a far-reaching form of association between East Germany and the Community would seem to be well worth exploring. By this means a *de facto* unification of the German people might eventually be achieved, although no single German state would be re-created.[14] The process of establishing such a relationship would obviously be a gradual one, extending, no doubt, over many years. The sequence of events might be something as follows.

First, the Community's relations with Poland, Czechoslovakia, and other Eastern European countries would be normalized. This process has, of course, already been started. Then, a gradual modification might be made in the relations between the Community and Eastern Germany. A protocol to the Treaty of Rome provides that interzonal trade is to be considered as internal German trade. By building on this protocol, the question of recognition of Eastern Germany could be sidestepped, initially at least, and very likely for the duration of the Ulbricht regime. As a first step toward the new relationship, the existing interzonal trade arrangements might become arrangements relating to the Community as a whole. Later, and by gradual steps, the arrangement between Eastern Germany and the Community might be extended to the free movement of capital and labor as well as goods. Eventually, the economic and social relationships between Eastern Ger-

[14] In this connection it should be noted that M. Monnet's Action Committee for the United States of Europe in its declaration adopted in Bonn on June 1, 1964, referred to the eventual "reuniting of the Germans in the European Community" as "an essential condition for peace." The declaration adopted by the Committee at its meeting on May 8–9, 1965, in Berlin, contained a similar reference.

many and the Community might be not too dissimilar from those existing between the members of the Community. Clearly, the Community itself would have to develop much further toward a real union before an association that would be comprehensive enough to satisfy the Germans could become a practical possibility.

Would such an arrangement be acceptable to the other interested countries—Germany's neighbors in Europe, the Soviet Union, and the United States?

The real interests of the United Kingdom, France, Italy, and the Benelux countries would seem, in the long run, to be very much the same, whatever the differences among them appear to be today. Although these countries have no strong national interest in a reunited Germany, they have a very strong interest in a stable and peaceful situation in Central Europe. And they have strong political and economic interests in having participation in the process of European unification remain the policy of the Federal Republic. An alliance-free reunited Germany would be a destabilizing factor, whether or not it was technically neutralized. A reunited Germany which was appreciably the strongest partner in a loose alliance of Western states would raise psychological and other problems. But a *de facto* unification of the German people achieved by means of a far-reaching form of association between Eastern Germany and a strong Community might well seem to be an attractive arrangement to this group of countries.

The United States' interest is essentially one of seeing that the existing balance of power does not shift against it. Such an arrangement would improve the present balance. Why, then, should it be acceptable to the Soviet Union? Presumably it would not be today. But provided the *détente* between the Soviet Union and the United States continues, provided the cohesion of the Atlantic Alliance can be maintained (with or without France), and provided the Federal Republic continues to refuse all political deals with the East, the Soviet Union may well come to regard the development of a unified Western Europe more benignly than it has in the past. Presumably the

Soviet Union would rather see the Federal Republic effectively integrated into a strong community than it would see either a weak community dominated by a strong Federal Republic, or a Federal Republic following in "Gaullist" footsteps and pursuing an independent national policy. The Soviet Union and the Eastern European countries may, therefore, come to regard British membership in the Community and a far-reaching form of integration in Western Europe as being to their advantage. This seems even more probable if as a result of the formation of an effective European union there were a change in the nature of the military links between the Federal Republic and the United States. A reorganization of NATO defense arrangements on a "two-pillar" basis, even though a strong transatlantic link remained, would doubtless be regarded by the Soviet Union as an improvement on present arrangements. If the price of a real integration of the Federal Republic in Western Europe and, consequently, of a change in some of the bilateral German–United States' defense arrangements, were, as it may well prove to be, a freer relationship between Eastern Germany and the Community, would the price always seem to the Soviet Union to be too high?

Whether or not something along these lines suggests a possible approach to the problem of German reunification, it is clear that until the relationship between German reunification and European unification is much more seriously and widely discussed and until some common agreement is reached among the members of the European Community on the nature of and the steps to an acceptable eventual settlement of the German problem, there is little prospect of a union with a common foreign policy emerging in Western Europe, no matter how often foreign secretaries may meet or what the powers of initiative vested in an independent Commission.

Defense has always tempted the "Europeans" as a short cut to political union, but there is little reason to believe that it is a short cut that will be any easier to take in the future than it has been in the past. On the contrary if, as seems probable, the result of the NATO crisis is to increase the "interdependence" between Germany and the United Kingdom, on the one hand, and the United States, on the other, the lack of symmetry between the economic organization of Europe and the defense organization of Europe seems likely to become rather more pronounced for the next few years.

It is just possible that the British might still take the opportunity provided by the NATO crisis to propose a European defense community as a first step toward the reshaping of the alliance on to a "two-pillar" basis. But it seems much more probable that the effect of General de Gaulle's attack on the NATO system will be to retard the development of a "European pillar" and hence any real reshaping of the Alliance. An integrated Atlantic defense system can be maintained without France, but an integrated European defense system without France could only be a political maneuver, although possibly quite a useful one.

On the assumption made in this chapter that the process of integration will continue, common action in the defense field will clearly develop eventually. It is not improbable that a future French government would propose turning the *force de frappe* into a "European" *force de frappe* if the British would agree to do the same with their nuclear weapons. The nuclear issue is not dead, but sleeping. But, for a number of reasons, it would seem to be a mistake to reawaken it too soon.

If the nuclear issue were forced in the near future—by the Germans, by the French, or by the United States—the effect might well be to halt, possibly even to reverse, the "Europeanization" of the Wilson government. There is obviously a problem of nuclear equality for the Germans that must, in the long term, be solved. Presumably it will eventually be solved either by putting the British and French nuclear weapons under a collective "European" control or by letting obsolescence reduce the importance of the British and French systems. The former has seemed a rather more probable development, given the European uneasiness at complete nuclear dependence on the United States. But the political organization of Europe that would make it possible to elaborate a workable control system will not exist for many years to come. Moreover, as discussed above, the kind of union that could support a nuclear weapons system only seems likely to develop if the key countries—the United Kingdom, France, and Germany—can agree on a common approach to the problem of German reunification. This, in turn, will obviously have a bearing on the nuclear role the Europe of the future will want to have. These are long-range questions that will have to be discussed and agreed; but they are not questions that will be settled quickly.

The relationship between European unification and German reunification also has a bearing on the arrangements made for the neutral countries of the EFTA, on the assumption that within the next few years the United Kingdom, Denmark, and Norway join the Community, and Portugal negotiates a "Greek-type" association with it. In the past, the "Europeans" and their supporters in the United States have tended to feel that Sweden and Switzerland, unlike Austria, were indulging in the luxury of neutrality at the expense of others, and that there was, therefore, little reason to encumber the Community with additional association arrangements on their behalf. Today these attitudes are changing, and they seem bound to continue to change. If, as seems probable, the Community completes an association arrangement with Austria it will be difficult, in fact, to maintain that what can be done for Austria cannot be done for the other two neutrals, despite the differences in the origins of their policies of neutrality.[15] Moreover, it now seems almost certain that the EFTA will have become a full free trade area before the question of British membership has been settled.[16] It is almost unthinkable

[15] A parallel agreement between the Community and the Swiss would of course strengthen the Austrian position that there is nothing inconsistent between an association with the Community and political neutrality.

[16] Under the present schedule the reduction of tariffs among the EFTA countries (except for Portugal which has a longer timetable) will be completed at the end of 1966.

that, given the history of the last few years and the affair of the surcharge, the British would agree to raise their tariffs against their EFTA partners.

Much of the "European" opposition to association arrangements under Article 238 of the treaty [17] has, in the past, stemmed from the feeling that such arrangements would be a drag on the development of the Community. To some extent this view arose because association arrangements under Article 238 were regarded as lineal descendants of the original free trade area proposal. At the time of the free trade area negotiation, the British would have been in the "outer" group and the Community was barely formed; there were, therefore, good grounds for fearing that the wider group would supplant the narrower group. Opposition to association arrangements has also stemmed from the fact that there are very real difficulties in working out satisfactory association arrangements between a highly industrialized country, such as Austria, and the Community. And the difficulties tend to be greater the closer the form of association that is sought.[18] The essential problem is, of course, how to give the associated country an adequate voice in the formulation of those policies that affect it directly (e.g., modifications in the Community's external tariffs) without creating a situation in which the tail wags the dog.

The reasons that have aroused apprehension in the past seem likely to apply with diminished force in the future. At a time when the benefits of the Community were mainly those derived from participating in a larger area of free trade it was difficult to conceive of forms of association that did not, in effect, give the advantages of membership without the disci-

[17] Article 238 provides for the association of other European countries with the Community. The African countries are associated under a special convention, and a special section (Part IV) of the treaty.

[18] "European" thinking on the problem of association has, in the past, tended to assume the opposite, that is that an association arrangement with other European countries should be as nearly as possible a replica of the Treaty of Rome. This line of reasoning is probably faulty and another legacy of the free trade area negotiations.

plines and restraints of membership.[19] In the future, as the benefits from participation in the Community tend to come increasingly from common policies, the trade benefits will lose some of their special significance. The more cohesive the Community itself becomes the easier it should be to find meaningful forms of association with it. And once the British are in the "core group" there will be little force of attraction in the "outer group."

Apart from these reasons for thinking that some form of association with the neutrals is probable, it seems likely that the political advantages of having a category of relationship which has many of the economic advantages but none of the political-defense overtones of the Community will become increasingly attractive to a number of the Community countries as a way of extending the Community's contacts with the Eastern European countries, with Finland and Yugoslavia in the near future, later, perhaps, with Poland and Czechoslovakia, and probably in a somewhat different form with Eastern Germany. This seems particularly likely to be true if it is a Labour government which finally takes the United Kingdom into the Community, for one of the most pervasive arguments against membership that is found particularly, but not only, in Labour circles is that the unification of Western Europe will harden the dividing line between East and West in Europe.

In the early sixties the Community of the Six might have developed quite rapidly into a federal union had General de Gaulle chosen to make common cause with the "Europeans" and had he seen his destiny, and that of France, as the creator of a new federal Europe. He chose another course, and the "Europe" of Schuman, de Gasperi, and Adenauer is no longer the possibility it once seemed. The "Europe" of tomorrow will almost certainly include the British, the Norwegians, the Danes, and the Irish. It is likely to be rather blurred at the

[19] Much of the "European" coolness to the provision for an elimination of tariffs in Title I of the Trade Expansion Act derived, of course, from the fact that tariff discrimination was the cement that held the Common Market together.

edges with various kinds of special arrangements, south to the Mediterranean countries and Africa, east to the neutrals and perhaps some of the smaller countries of Eastern Europe. It is unlikely for many years to become a system that can fairly be described as a federal union. Perhaps what is happening in Western Europe is the pioneering of a new form of relationship among states, perhaps it is the building of an infrastructure of a European federation. It is much too soon to tell. However, if the enlarged Community is to be an effective force in the world, it must have a high degree of cohesion and the will and institutions to enable collective action to be taken. These seem likely to develop, in time; for the essential reason that is impelling the key countries in Western Europe to come together is, at bottom, the desire to play a larger and more effective role in the world.

CHAPTER SEVEN

# *The American Interest in European Integration*

From the time the United States decided to support the Schuman Plan it has shown a remarkable consistency in encouraging the Six in their efforts to become more united economically, politically, and militarily. In 1950–51, when the Schuman Plan was being negotiated, the United States was, of course, still deeply involved in assisting Europe to recover from the war and it was still an occupying power in Germany. It was inevitable, therefore, that American officials should have been closely concerned with the negotiations leading to the establishment of the first of the Communities of the Six, the European Coal and Steel Community. However, the very close rapport and the mutual confidence that were established in those early days between key Americans and key "Europeans," and in particular with M. Monnet and his group, were deeper and more enduring than the relationship of trust and confidence that commonly results from working together in difficult and ambitious international projects. The personal relationships that were then established could not alone have sustained the American policy of warm support for the Six, but it is no exaggeration to say that the quality and intensity of American support for the ventures of the Six during the last fifteen years would have been different and our support would probably have been rather less consistent had exceptional personal relationships not existed throughout the period.

There is no need to review here the reasons why in the late forties and early fifties a strong Western Europe was a prime and unchallenged objective of United States' policy. But before turning to the question of where the American interest would seem to lie in the future, it may be useful to recall briefly the main reasons why at a time when the European countries were themselves divided about how best to organize their economic and political relationships the American government consistently favored "deep" integration among a few European countries rather than a shallower, less committing form of relationship among a larger group of countries. As indicated above, no account of American policy during this period can ignore the fact that M. Monnet greatly affected the thinking of key individuals. However, there were important substantive reasons why the Community doctrine, particularly as expounded by M. Monnet, was attractive to the U.S. government; it would doubtless have commanded American support at this time even had it not had so compelling an advocate.

Probably the principal reason for the strong and continuing American support for the "deep" integration of the Six was the judgment that it offered the best available answer to the problems posed by a truncated but dynamic Germany. The integration of Western Germany with its neighbors made the elimination of discriminatory controls and rearmament easier for its European allies, particularly France, to accept; it made possible a new relationship between France and Germany which, in the words of M. Schuman's statement on May 9, 1950, made war not only "unthinkable, but materially impossible," and it incidentally made manageable the thorny problem of the Saar; it offered to the Germans, in the short to medium term at least, a practical and emotional alternative to reunification, an alternative which has, in fact, proved to be acceptable. At a time when reunification was clearly impossible on any terms remotely acceptable to the West, the possible conflict between unity in Western Europe and German reunification seemed to German and American policy makers alike to be too academic a concern to be relevant. The assertion that the first was a precondition of the second was frequently made; but only relatively recently has the assertion come to be examined in any very serious way either in Germany or in the United States. The importance of now coming to a clearer understanding with our European allies about the way the future development of the Community and German reunification might be linked is stressed below. The point to be made here is that given the nature of Soviet policy during the fifties the case for involving Germany as fully, as equitably, and as indissolubly as possible with its Western neighbors was a very strong one. This was the promise the Community approach held much more clearly than any other.

On economic grounds, too, the Common Market approach was bound to be more attractive to American policy makers than was the wider, looser free trade area approach, partly because the more radical approach seemed a better response to the economic needs of the countries concerned, partly because it was a good deal easier to reconcile with other aspects of American policy. Thus, the formation of a new economic unit, which the Six proclaimed as their objective, could be reconciled far more easily with the pattern of nondiscriminatory relationships laid down at Bretton Woods, and elsewhere, than could broader, less far-reaching arrangements which aimed at the freeing of trade but not, as the Six did, at an economic system which could be thought of as analogous to that existing within a single state. There was also the obvious commercial fact that a wider area of free trade meant a larger area within which American exports competed at a disadvantage, a consideration which gained in importance as the U.S. balance-of-payments position deteriorated in the late fifties.

There was undoubtedly a strong emotional factor, as well,

in the American support for the Six. It would have been very surprising, indeed, had this not been the case, for the Community idea was bold, imaginative, and creative. And it accorded with what most Americans felt in their bones was right, sensible, and long overdue.

There was, too, among those most closely concerned with these developments, fairly widespread appreciation of, and acceptance of, the argument that only by uniting could Europe again exercise an effective role in the world and also of the corollary, that an increase in the European voice in world affairs was in the American interest as well as responsive to European desires.

The criticism is frequently heard today that the United States has unwittingly and foolishly encouraged the growth of a rival power bloc. Perhaps there was some underestimation of the potential strength of the new center of power that the United States was encouraging, but the encouragement was not given blindly. On the contrary, support for the Six rested squarely on the assumption that the Six were in the process of forming a new entity so that they could exert more influence collectively than they could do individually. It was an essential part of the basic assumption on which American policy rested that this growth of European self-confidence and increase in European power would lead to a more stable and more fruitful relationship with the United States. It is fair to say that this was recognized to be an assumption, not a certainty. Any policy involves risks; perhaps the risks were underestimated. There was certainly an underestimation of the strength of France: most doubts centered on the ability of the Community to contain a renascent Germany. But it seems probable that even with the advantage of hindsight the same broad policy would again be followed as was pursued in the fifties.

Nevertheless, even though the main thrust of our European policy was responsive to the problems of the day, there are criticisms that can legitimately be made of the way it was at times pursued. Before turning to the central issue in this chapter—the nature of the continuing American interest in a uniting Europe—it is perhaps worth looking briefly at some of these mistakes or, more precisely, errors in emphasis and in tone that were made in the past.

Perhaps the most important criticism to be made of American policy over the past fifteen years is that there was too uncritical an acceptance of the assumption that the American interest always coincided with the "European" interest. There was a large measure of overlap, to be sure, but not as complete an identity of interest as seems, at times, to have been assumed. In particular, there seems to have been too little recognition of the fact that even where our objectives coincided, our priorities were almost bound to be different. In consequence, there was too sweeping an assumption that the American interest always lay in having the European countries adopt those measures that would carry the process of integration furthest down the road toward federation, and too much reliance on this rather *simpliste* rule of thumb in day-to-day decision making. This tendency to accept as our own the criteria applied by the "Europeans" was, perhaps, most conspicuous in the American attitudes toward the repeated British efforts to find a way to come to terms with the Six. Despite the continental belief in the potency of the "special relationship" between the "Anglo-Saxons," the American government has tended to look at the British relationship with Europe through a "European" prism.

It was true enough that the kinds of relationship the British sought to establish with the Community, before they decided in 1961 to negotiate to join it, threatened to weaken the Community, either by making the commercial advantages of membership available on less exacting terms and thus attractive to some of the existing members of the Community, particularly the Germans, or by creating a cumbersome double-tier institutional structure, or by doing both. It is understandable, therefore, that many of the "Europeans" took an uncompromising line in the last stages of the free trade area negotiations and, later, strongly opposed various British ideas for "bridge building." It was clearly better—both from a "European" standpoint and from an American standpoint—that the British should, in the end, come to feel that it was in their own interest to become full members of the Community rather than simply associated with it. And it is doubtless true that the fact that no other options were open to it—that there was no middle way—helped the Macmillan government to decide to try to join. It can, therefore, be argued that the United States was right to give the British no help in salvaging the free trade area negotiations in 1958 and that we were also right to back the "Europeans" in fending off various British attempts at "bridge building" after the collapse of the Maudling negotiations. But if, as hindsight would suggest, the United States was right to have taken these positions, it was at the time far more concerned with preserving the integrity of the Community than with inducing the British to reach the conclusion that they must join the Community.

Slower progress toward union was a price the United States should have been more willing than were the "Europeans" to pay to have the British in the main stream of the process of European unification. American efforts were, however, never directed at trying to see whether there was any acceptable way of bringing the Six and the United Kingdom together, but, rather, at keeping the pressures toward union among the Six from being diminished in any way. Because the British eventually came to see their role as a member of the Community our hard line was in the end justified by events. But this was not foreseeable. Perhaps no satisfactory arrangement could have been found; but we never really tried to play the role of imaginative broker.

The tendency to equate American priorities with the priorities of the "Europeans" was also noticeable during the negotiations for British accession to the Community. Wholly apart from the particular difficulties the common agricultural policy of the Six—in the form devised by the Commission and supported by the French—would pose for our own agricultural exports, the United States should have supported the British in urging the Six to delay the formulation of their common agricultural policy until after the problem of British accession had been settled.

The fact that the lines of the common agricultural policy had not yet been finally settled and that they could reasonably expect to participate in shaping the policy in a way that would take account of their own special needs was one of the strongest reasons impelling the British to decide to open negotiations in 1961, rather than waiting, as some within the British government had advocated, until after the departure of General de Gaulle. However, the Commission, M. Monnet, and other strong "Europeans" backed the French in urging that the main lines of the common agricultural policy be settled by the Six before they began negotiating with the British on agricultural questions. Not only was valuable time lost at the start of the negotiations as a result,[1] but the problem of accession was made considerably more difficult for the British than it would have been had the main lines of the agricultural policy still been negotiable. The Commission, quite deliberately, used the British negotiations as a device for driving through the common agricultural policy. Looked at solely from the standpoint of advancing the unity of the Six this was understandable, perhaps even defensible, for the agreement on a common agricultural policy was the biggest step toward union the Six have taken since signing the Treaty of Rome. It was not, however, so important from an American standpoint that this forward step should be taken at that time as it was that the negotiations with the United Kingdom should succeed. Again, perhaps an American intervention would not have succeeded, but on this

[1] The British have been accused of negotiating too slowly. Probably they did, but one important reason for their slowness was their desire to avoid making the mistakes they made during the free trade area negotiations when the Six felt they were inventing false deadlines. During the first months of the accession negotiations the British deliberately let the Six set the pace. And it was a very slow one.

particular issue a strong case can be made that we should have urged the "Europeans" to give British membership priority over the consolidation of the Community.

It is too crude to argue, as General de Gaulle did in 1963, that the American interest in British membership in the Community arises from the belief that the United Kingdom would be an American Trojan horse. The British inside the Community are likely to be more "independent" of the United States than they will be if they remain outside, and a Community that includes the British will be a stronger force in the world with greater bargaining power vis-à-vis the United States. But it is, of course, true that the American interest in seeing the United Kingdom become a member of the Community derives partly from the assumption that a community that included the British would be more likely to pursue policies compatible with our own. This assumption is perhaps open to question when it comes to a number of particular policies, e.g., trade with Cuba. But it seems likely to be true in so far as major questions of basic orientation and democratic structure are concerned.[2]

Partly because of the tendency to assume rather too much identity between American interests and those of the "Monnet Europeans," partly because of the loyalties that were formed and the struggles that were shared in the early fifties when the United States had, in fact, no choice but to be an active participant in the process of European integration, there has also been a tendency for American officials to become too involved in the details of the European construction and to regard the unification of Europe as "our policy." This involvement and

[2] There are, of course, other reasons for the American interest in British membership: the judgement that the British economy needs the competitive stimulus of the Common Market; the fact that until the relationship with the United Kingdom is settled it is a source of tension inhibiting the development of the Community; the belief that a relationship with a community that included the United Kingdom would be closer and more fruitful for all concerned than the uneasy triangular relationship that exists today.

identification with the "makers of Europe" has always been exciting and exhilarating, and it has frequently been very exhausting. But it has also, at times, been counterproductive.

American officials have tended to become too involved in the sometimes submerged, sometimes all too obvious struggle in the Community over the distribution of power. Looked at from a "European" standpoint, it was clear that the way to accelerate progress toward union was to build up the power at the center and, in particular, to safeguard and gradually to enhance the role of the Commission. Although we cannot help but share the anxieties and aspirations of the "Europeans," this is the kind of problem which we mix in at their peril. The price paid for Dr. Hallstein's night at Blair House in the spring of 1965 was a high one.

By becoming overidentified with the "Europeans" we have made them vulnerable to Gaullist taunts that they are simply stooges for the American "federator." By letting American support for the Community of the Six acquire emotional overtones and, at times, an almost religious fervor, we have made it an easy target for the "new realism" that has become fashionable in the last few years on both sides of the Atlantic. The unique nature of the American involvement with the European venture has led both those most closely concerned and some of their harshest critics to talk rather dramatically of a "failure" of American policy whenever the process of integration suffers a setback. And the confusion of priorities that, as indicated above, has occasionally resulted from the closeness of the relationship between American "Europeans" and European "Europeans" has given a little ammunition (although not very much or very powerful ammunition) to those who today question whether continuing support for the European Community is in the best interest of the United States.

On the other side of the scale must, of course, be put the fact that the closeness of the American contacts with some of the leading "Europeans" has had an important reverse effect.

As a result, the "Europeans" have unquestionably been stauncher in their support for durable Atlantic ties than would otherwise have been the case. At a time when General de Gaulle was attacking the European process itself as well as the Atlantic connection the temptation to seek to buy his support for "Europe" by sacrificing the Atlantic link might otherwise have been irresistible. This is too often overlooked by those who have felt the relationship has tended to be too close and too charged with emotion.

The situation in Europe and in the world today is radically different from that in the early fifties when the American policy of warm support for the Six first took shape. It is also very different from that in the early sixties when the rapid progress made by the Community and the prospect of early British membership gave substance to the two-pillar image and a sense of immediacy to the concept of an Atlantic partnership. What of the future? Where does the American interest now lie and what, if anything, can we do or should we do to encourage or discourage any particular pattern of European organization?

The conclusion reached in previous chapters about the probable development of the Community was that the process of creating an integrated Western Europe would continue, although it would probably be slow. The legacy of the latest crisis in the Community is a bundle of contradictions: a customs union for industrial goods and a common agricultural market among the Six still seem assured, but what had previously been widely assumed to be the logical and necessary concomitants in terms of common policies—both in the related economic fields and in the foreign policy field—seem to be firmly ruled out as long as General de Gaulle is in charge of French policy.[3] Instead of the progressive strengthening of the roles of the Commission and of the Parliament and the gradual

[3] This seemed fairly clear before the crisis. See Camps, *What Kind of Europe?*, cited, pp. 118 ff. The crisis has underlined and made explicit a number of trends that then seemed to be probable.

accretion of power at the center which had been foreshadowed in the treaty and widely anticipated during the early years of the Community, the crisis brought to a halt the already very slow transfer of power from the national governments to common institutions, and both the nature of the settlement and the fear of further crises will put substantial difficulties in the way of a resumption of the process in the future. As discussed in Chapter Six, it now seems probable that there will be very little further progress toward union—beyond the implementation of the decisions already taken—until after General de Gaulle has retired from political life and the British have become members of the Community. It is impossible today to put a date to either, and it may make considerable difference to the kind of European Community that develops how soon they happen.

Nevertheless, although it is impossible today to foresee with any precision either the rate of progress or the form a "united Europe" might eventually take, it seems probable that the process that has been going on fitfully but steadily since the war will continue and that the states now joined in the European Community plus, at a minimum, the United Kingdom, Denmark, Norway, and Ireland will progressively integrate their economies and tend increasingly to conduct their external affairs in concert.

It is an illusion to suppose that the United States now has or is likely to have in the future much influence over these developments. It is an even greater illusion to suppose that the option of establishing an effective American hegemony in Western Europe today exists, despite our preponderant nuclear power. Hegemony was an option the United States was right to reject in the days when it was a possibility. Our continuing influence in Europe despite the insistent anti-Americanism of General de Gaulle has owed a great deal to the fact that most Europeans recognize that the United States had that option and did reject it when we might, in fact, have chosen it. Today, somewhat paradoxically, strong American opposition to European union would, in all likelihood, prove the catalyst the "Europeans" need to take a major step forward. Fortunately, not even the most dedicated American "Europeans" are quixotic enough to recommend it on those grounds.

In the future, as in the past, the American ability to influence developments will be greater if we continue to support the consolidation of Europe than if we seek to slow it down. But, at best, our influence on the pace and nature of the future organization of Europe will be marginal. This, coupled with the fact that the American interest has shifted away from Western Europe as other areas of the world have become centers of conflict, suggests that the errors of the past are not likely to be repeated in the future. On the contrary, the danger today is that the pendulum will swing too far in the other direction, and that instead of becoming rather too involved in arguments which are of peripheral concern to us and might better be left to the Europeans, the United States may become too little concerned with the nature of the continuing process of integration and too indifferent to the patterns that are forming in Western Europe.

Although our power directly to affect the shape of the emerging Europe is limited, we can do much to affect the environment in which a uniting Europe grows and this will have a certain impact on its form. By our own actions and by our willingness to accept parallel restraints on our own freedom of action we can encourage close and harmonious relationships between ourselves and a uniting Europe. Conversely, we can do a great deal to antagonize the European countries, individually and collectively, and to encourage them to shape their policies not only in isolation but in conscious opposition to our own. In short, whether the uniting Europe is "Gaullist" in its external policies or prepared for "partnership" with the United States is a decision which we can affect to a significant extent. How "Europe" builds its institutions is something we can do much less about.

This is not a book about defense policy, but, as the events

of the last few years have shown, it is not possible to keep the economic-political aspects of European integration and the organization of Western defense in separate, watertight compartments. And it is, of course, through our dominant role in the organization of the defense of the West that the United States now and in the future will primarily affect the shape of Europe, whether or not we consciously choose to do so.

It is far easier to point out the contradictions in American policy than it is to see how they are to be overcome, for to a large extent the contradictions are inherent in the fact that there is a lack of parallelism between the West's defense arrangements and its political structure. The "Gaullist" answer to the American hegemony they see in this lack of parallelism is the simple destructive one of breaking out of the system. The "European" answer to the lack of parallelism is the more constructive one of trying to create a better balance within the system. But the "European" approach comes up against two obstacles: first, the political substructure capable of providing the greater "European" voice they seek does not today exist, and it cannot be made to exist until the British and French governments have decided they want it to exist. Both governments seem likely to come to this conclusion eventually, but neither one has a coherent "European" policy today.

The second obstacle is the fact that the organization of a collective defense system involving nuclear weapons raises questions that are different in kind, not just in degree, from the organization of a collective defense system involving conventional weapons only. The unwillingness of many "British Europeans" to accept the conclusion that is widespread on the Continent that "Europe" must eventually be a nuclear power has been seen on the Continent, and sometimes in Washington as well, as evidence of the shallowness of the British commitment to Europe. This is true, in part, but it is not the whole explanation of the British attitude, any more than the hesitations and the seeming contradictions in American policy on the question of a European nuclear deterrent can be simply equated with being "for" or "against" the development of a new center of power in Europe.

Although the United States cannot in any real sense share power with a "Europe" that does not today exist, it can do something to make the present imbalance in the alliance more acceptable and to encourage the emergence of a "Europe" with which the difficult process of sharing power might later become feasible. If the McNamara Committee can become a place where the assumptions underlying American strategic policy are really discussed and if, through this and other means, the European countries come to feel that they are in the main stream of the process of planning there will be fewer temptations to follow the Gaullist example. There will also, presumably, be less "European" and German pressure for an immediate "hardware" solution to the problem of nuclear sharing, although the later development of a nuclear "Europe" would not be foreclosed.

Beyond that, in the reorganization of the NATO that General de Gaulle has precipitated, we can deliberately leave room for the development of a European defense community comprising a common command structure and a common procurement and supply system. As indicated in Chapter Six, military integration on a European basis without the French makes little sense. But there is enough evidence to suggest that both a post de Gaulle France and a Britain that had become a member of the Common Market would be ready to accept an integrated European defense system to make it desirable to have this possibility in mind when dealing with the current NATO problem.

Our attitude toward "Europe's" and toward Britain's extra-European commitments will also have a considerable impact on the way Europe unites. It is understandable, and basically healthy, that the United States should look to other like-minded countries to share its responsibilities and should not want to police the world alone. But effective sharing assumes a common, or at least a similar, appreciation of the dangers to be counteracted or contained. At the present time, rightly or wrongly, the British support for American policy in Vietnam and the continuation of a British presence east of Suez is widely assumed—in the United Kingdom and on the Continent—to stem less from a genuine sharing of objective than it does from financial dependence on the United States, on the one hand, and nostalgia, on the other.

At a time when we are ourselves deeply involved in Southeast Asia it is probably too much to expect the United States to urge the British to hasten their withdrawal from the area. But we should recognize that our attitude tends to nourish the contradictions in British policy and to complicate their relations with the Continent. In the longer term it is to "Europe" not to the United Kingdom alone that we should look to share our responsibilities. Provided we make that plain, and provided, too, that we recognize that shared responsibilities are only acceptable when objectives as well are shared, there need be no real ambiguity in American policy about Britain's continuing a role east of Suez, not as a hold-over from an imperial past but as the forerunner of a "European" responsibility.

It was argued in Chapter Six that European union is today not a clear imperative for any of the countries directly concerned, but a matter of choice. It is a choice they seem likely to make and if they do choose to unite we should welcome it. But it is for them, not us, to decide what kind of society they want to live in and what kind of role in the world they want to play. Their choice should not become a central concern of American policy, partly because there is not a great deal that we can do to affect the choice, more importantly because although we have an interest in the choice they make our interest is not of anything like the same order as theirs.

What is the nature of our interest? Many of those who believe most strongly that continuing American support and encouragement for European unification is a self-evident proposition seem at times to be reasoning from the suppressed premise that the alternative to further integration is chaos. It is not hard to demonstrate that the solution of the major problems confronting the world, whether they be the attainment of decent standards of living or the maintenance of peace, requires a harmony of view and close cooperation in many fields among the major countries of Western Europe and between them and the United States. But it is difficult to demonstrate that the necessary level of agreement and cooperation can only be attained by the unification of Europe. Further progress toward unity is obviously not of the same overriding importance to us, or to the Europeans, as was the re-establishment of a prosperous, politically stable, reasonably cohesive Western Europe in the immediate postwar period. Nevertheless, there are persuasive reasons why continuing progress toward a more effective union in Western Europe is in the American interest and in the wider interest of a better organized international society.

As discussed above, the strongest reason for American support for European unification in the past was the need to give the Federal Republic an alternative to reunification at a time when the only kind of reunification that was possible would have pushed the boundary of the cold war to the Rhine. How necessary—from an American standpoint—one believes further progress toward European union to be depends, in part, on how one views the probable development of German policy. The Federal Republic today is strongly committed to the Western alliance; its commercial and financial interests run, for the most part, to the West rather than to the East. Whether or not the Community becomes more than a customs union, the links among the Common Market countries are likely to become stronger simply as a consequence of the customs union. Moreover, the Federal Republic is, today, an important participant in the network of political-economic arrangements—the OECD, the GATT, the Group of Ten, the BIS, the IMF—that knit together the economies of the industrialized West. It is now far less persuasive than it was in the fifties to argue that further progress toward a European union is necessary to remove from the Germans the temptation to make dangerous deals with the East.

Although the continuation of the Federal Republic's commitment to the West would not now seem to require the development of a far-reaching form of unity in Western Europe, continuing progress toward this goal nevertheless still seems to offer the West Germans the best framework within which to shape their current policies. The feeling that they have been working toward a wholly new form of relationship with their traditional enemy, France, and with the Low Countries has proved to be psychologically satisfying to the Germans in making the difficult postwar adjustments. And the larger economic space of the Common Market has played its part in restoring self-confidence and optimism to German industry.

Today, however, a more compelling reason for encouraging the continuation of the movement toward union lies in the probability that a Western European group that had moved a long way down the road toward union might open the way to an arrangement with Eastern Europe that satisfied the many conflicting criteria any stable settlement in Central Europe will have to meet.

American policy on the interrelationship between European union and German reunification, like American policy on a number of other issues, is in some danger of being pushed on to the defensive by General de Gaulle. Although his prescriptions are old fashioned and nostalgic, much of his diagnosis of today's problems is not, and it finds an echo throughout Western Europe. The German question cannot be settled as General de Gaulle seems to expect without the participation and agreement of the United States. But he is undoubtedly right in stressing that a precondition for a settlement is a new equilibrium between "Europe" and the United States.

A Western Europe that had attained a high degree of coherence and had realized and organized its own internal strength could establish a new relationship with the United States that, although still very close, was not one that either the Western European countries or the countries to the east felt to be one of dependence or subservience. Except in the very long term, it is difficult to see how a settlement that the United States would find satisfactory could be reached in Central Europe unless the Western European countries are capable of acting together as a coherent group and unless their relationship with the United States, although different from that which exists today, is one that breeds confidence on both sides of the Atlantic.

General de Gaulle's way of seeking to achieve a new equilibrium with the United States and a settlement with the Soviet Union is unlikely to succeed. Nor is the "European" way unless the United States and the Western European countries can together reach a real meeting of minds on the nature of the two central, and interconnected, relationships of a European Community, that with Eastern Europe and that with the United States. These large questions of direction and long-term strategy are the kind of issue with which American policy toward the European Community should now be primarily concerned, rather than with short-term, essentially tactical questions that are better left to the Europeans to work out among themselves.

Although the problems arising from the division of Germany still provide the most persuasive reasons for continuing American support for a uniting Europe, there are other reasons for believing that further progress toward unity in Western Europe is in the American interest.

The Community for all its weaknesses and anomalies is an important experiment in trying to create gradually and within the framework of law a new relationship among states. M. Monnet is clearly right when he argues that the way to a better international order lies in finding means to maximize and to institutionalize the common interest. The Community in the days when it was working well provided a new technique for doing this.[4] The interplay between the Commission, representing the common interest, and the Council of Ministers, representing the separate national interest, that had evolved in the EEC proved to be a more fruitful, if less radical, institutional innovation than the outright delegation of power to an independent supranational authority which M. Monnet and others had felt to be required in the more ambitious days of the Schuman Plan.

M. Monnet and some of those closest to him have seen the construction of "Europe" not as an end in itself but as part of a larger process of organizing international relationships. In the process of pooling sovereignty for particular purposes—first in the Coal and Steel Community and, later, in Euratom and in the Economic Community—nationalist feelings would, it was argued, become attenuated. Moreover, by changing the nature of the relationships among the European states a wider process would be set in train. An organized Europe would lead to a change in relationships with other countries, starting with the United States, and this process would lead, eventually, to a new and more disciplined international system.[5]

The emphasis given by M. Monnet to the importance of the process and his insistence—which has become more pro-

[4] Many "Europeans" tend, however, to attach rather too much significance to the difference between the institutional aspects of the Community system and those of other international institutions and rather too little to the difference in objective. Although the Community system goes further to institutionalize the common interest than do traditional international organizations, the sharpest break with the traditional pattern lies in the fact that the objective of the Treaty of Rome is the formation of a Community which would act as a unit externally for certain agreed purposes and increasingly replace national policies with common policies internally.

[5] Although M. Monnet has emphasized the importance of the Community "method" and has always had something more in mind than simply replacing six states by one, he has, nevertheless, consistently described the process of unification of Europe in terms of forming the United States of Europe and, like the vast majority of continental "Europeans," he has consciously used the model of a federal state in planning, thinking, and talking about the European Community.

nounced of late as the threat of a Gaullist Europe has become more apparent—that he is not interested in encouraging a new European nationalism do not, unfortunately, correspond to the attitudes that now give the main impetus toward union. And they seem unlikely to do so in the future. Nevertheless, although the strongest pressure toward union seems likely to come from those—in the United Kingdom and on the Continent—who consciously think and act with the ultimate goal of something very like a new European federal state in mind, the fact that the European countries are caught up in a new process that blurs national divisions and transmutes national objectives will be important. And the process of thinking in a larger frame of reference is not likely to stop at the frontiers of "Europe," if only because those frontiers seem likely to be rather fuzzy.

It is much too soon to tell how far the process of unification will go or what institutional form a "united" Western Europe will eventually assume. It would not be surprising if, in fact, the unification of Western Europe turned out to be a "process" after all and not the road to a new superstate. It seems probable that the United Kingdom and the Six will find a way to act in common for many purposes and that the role of the nation-states in the new European complex will be progressively diminished. But for a great many years the system seems likely to be a hybrid one with no very clear or very logical division of power between the European center and the existing national governments. This will have advantages as well as disadvantages. As suggested in the last chapter it may well offer the possibility of a more flexible and growing relationship with the countries of Eastern Europe than would be possible if the Western European group were more firmly set in a pre-federal mold. But, as experience with the EEC has shown, as long as its external relations are handled in a variety of ways the European Community will be an awkward complex for third countries to deal with.

Despite the fact that a "uniting Europe" is likely to be a

cumbersome group with which to deal, the development of a new center of power in Western Europe could, nevertheless, help lift the process of international organization to a new level. The process of organizing relations among states can only succeed if governments are convinced that it is in their own interest to accept restraints on their freedom of action. Any country is obviously more willing and more able (in terms of gaining domestic support) to accept restraints on its own freedom of action if the advantages of so doing seem to outweigh the disadvantages of losing freedom of action. And it is, of course, the biggest states that have the least incentive to give up freedom of action. The existence of the Common Market made the massive tariff cutting envisaged for the Kennedy Round commercially attractive to the United States and politically possible. Parallels for the future suggest themselves in other fields, e.g., monetary policy, agricultural policy, the organization of defense. Similarly, in the West's relationship with the developing world it should be easier to approach the level of generosity we all know to be necessary by a process of mutual prodding than it is alone. Legislatures balk at unilateral altruism, but they are usually ready enough to match, or better, a standard set by someone else.

The United States has been groping for something—not simply turning phrases—when it calls the Kennedy Round a symbol of Atlantic partnership. To many people a hard-fought tariff bargain seems a curious symbol of partnership. But in some ways the symbol suggests the right relationship more accurately than does the concept of partnership, for a partnership implies too exclusive and too diarchic an arrangement. The days when two powers, however large, can run the world are over. The concept of partnership must find its main expression in providing the solid core of mutual understanding and of commitment to common objectives which the wider process of international organization needs if it is to prosper.

The United States as the dominant power in the non-Communist world has, on the whole, used its power prudently.

It has shown a desire to work with other countries that is, perhaps, unique in the world's history: the initiative, the planning, and the money for most of the world's international organizations, both global and regional, has come preponderantly from the United States. Nevertheless, although the American belief in the advantages of collective action is plain, we have frequently lacked the incentives that would make it possible for us to give the collective approach as large a role as we profess to believe it should have. We complain about the "burden" of leadership, yet it is not a burden any country willingly shares unless it clearly gains by doing so. Today these gains—the incentives for sharing power—can really only come from Western Europe, for only those countries, collectively, both possess comparable economic power and, broadly, share our concepts and our goals.

The countries of Western Europe already seek to play this role of friendly critic and partners in progress, but they cannot do so effectively as long as they speak with several voices and dissipate their strength by acting separately, and sometimes at cross-purposes. The gap in power terms is too wide. The result is frustration and resentment on both sides of the Atlantic. We resent criticisms that are not based on a willingness, or the means, to provide an alternative. They feel the frustrations of their impotence.

If General de Gaulle succeeds in reversing the European tide and sets it flowing again toward "independence" and unfettered nationalism the result will not be the better equilibrium he purports to seek but fewer effective restraints on American power. To some, this may be an attractive prospect. It is not likely to lead to catastrophe. But it is not the road to an international order that matches the needs of today's world.

# Index

COUNCIL ON FOREIGN RELATIONS

## PUBLICATIONS

FOREIGN AFFAIRS (quarterly), edited by Hamilton Fish Armstrong.

THE UNITED STATES IN WORLD AFFAIRS (annual). Volumes for 1931, 1932 and 1933, by Walter Lippmann and William O. Scroggs; for 1934–1935, 1936, 1937, 1938, 1939 and 1940, by Whitney H. Shepardson and William O. Scroggs; for 1945–1947, 1947–1948 and 1948–1949, by John C. Campbell; for 1949, 1950, 1951, 1952, 1953 and 1954, by Richard P. Stebbins; for 1955, by Hollis W. Barber; for 1956, 1957, 1958, 1959, 1960, 1961, 1962 and 1963, by Richard P. Stebbins; for 1964, by Jules Davids; for 1965 by Richard P. Stebbins.

DOCUMENTS ON AMERICAN FOREIGN RELATIONS (annual). Volume for 1952 edited by Clarence W. Baier and Richard P. Stebbins; for 1953 and 1954 edited by Peter V. Curl; for 1955, 1956, 1957, 1958 and 1959 edited by Paul E. Zinner; for 1960, 1961, 1962 and 1963 edited by Richard P. Stebbins; for 1964 by Jules Davids; for 1965 by Richard P. Stebbins.

POLITICAL HANDBOOK AND ATLAS OF THE WORLD (annual), edited by Walter H. Mallory.

ATLANTIC AGRICULTURAL UNITY: Is it Possible?, by John O. Coppock (1966).

TEST BAN AND DISARMAMENT: The Path of Negotiation, by Arthur H. Dean (1966).

COMMUNIST CHINA'S ECONOMIC GROWTH AND FOREIGN TRADE, by Alexander Eckstein (1966).

POLICIES TOWARD CHINA: Views from Six Continents, edited by A. M. Halpern (1966).

THE AMERICAN PEOPLE AND CHINA, by A. T. Steele (1966).

INTERNATIONAL POLITICAL COMMUNICATION, by W. Phillips Davison (1965).

MONETARY REFORM FOR THE WORLD ECONOMY, by Robert V. Roosa (1965).

AFRICAN BATTLELINE: American Policy Choices in Southern Africa, by Waldemar A. Nielsen (1965).

NATO IN TRANSITION: The Future of the Atlantic Alliance, by Timothy W. Stanley (1965).

ALTERNATVE TO PARTITION: For a Broader Conception of America's Role in Europe, by Zbigniew Brzezinski (1965).

THE TROUBLED PARTNERSHIP: A Re-Appraisal of the Atlantic Alliance, by Henry A. Kissinger (1965).

REMNANTS OF EMPIRE: The United Nations and the End of Colonialism, by David W. Wainhouse (1965).

THE EUROPEAN COMMUNITY AND AMERICAN TRADE: A Study in Atlantic Economics and Policy, by Randall Hinshaw (1964).

THE FOURTH DIMENSION OF FOREIGN POLICY: Educational and Cultural Affairs, by Phillip H. Coombs (1964).

AMERICAN AGENCIES INTERESTED IN INTERNATIONAL AFFAIRS (Fifth Edition), compiled by Donald Wasson (1964).

JAPAN AND THE UNITED STATES IN WORLD TRADE, by Warren S. Hunsberger (1964).

FOREIGN AFFAIRS BIBLIOGRAPHY, 1952–1962, by Henry L. Roberts (1964).

THE DOLLAR IN WORLD AFFAIRS: An Essay in International Financial Policy, by Henry G. Aubrey (1964).

ON DEALING WITH THE COMMUNIST WORLD, by George F. Kennan (1964).

FOREIGN AID AND FOREIGN POLICY, by Edward S. Mason (1964).

THE SCIENTIFIC REVOLUTION AND WORLD POLITICS, by Caryl P. Haskins (1964).

AFRICA: A Foreign Affairs Reader, edited by Philip W. Quigg (1964).

THE PHILIPPINES AND THE UNITED STATES: Problems of Partnership, by George E. Taylor (1964).

SOUTHEAST ASIA IN UNITED STATES POLICY, by Russell H. Fifield (1963).

UNESCO: ASSESSMENT AND PROMISE, by George N. Shuster (1963).

THE PEACEFUL ATOM IN FOREIGN POLICY, by Arnold Kramish (1963).

THE ARABS AND THE WORLD: Nasser's Arab Nationalist Policy, by Charles D. Cremeans (1963).

TOWARD AN ATLANTIC COMMUNITY, by Christian A. Herter (1963).

THE SOVIET UNION, 1922–1962: A Foreign Affairs Reader, edited by Philip E. Mosley (1963).

THE POLITICS OF FOREIGN AID: American Experience in Southeast Asia, by John D. Montgomery (1962).

SPEARHEADS OF DEMOCRACY: Labor in the Developing Countries, by George C. Lodge (1962).

LATIN AMERICA: Diplomacy and Reality, by Adolf A. Berle (1962).

THE ORGANIZATION OF AMERICAN STATES AND THE HEMISPHERE CRISIS, by John C. Dreier (1962).

THE UNITED NATIONS: Structure for Peace, by Ernest A. Gross (1962).

THE LONG POLAR WATCH: Canada and the Defense of North America, by Melvin Conant (1962).

ARMS AND POLITICS IN LATIN AMERICA (Revised Edition), by Edwin Lieuwen (1961).

THE FUTURE OF UNDERDEVELOPED COUNTRIES: Political Implications of Economic Development (Revised Edition), by Eugene Staley (1961).

SPAIN AND DEFENSE OF THE WEST: Ally and Liability, by Arthur P. Whitaker (1961).

SOCIAL CHANGE IN LATIN AMERICA TODAY: Its Implications for United States Policy, by Richard N. Adams, John P.

Gillin, Allan R. Holmberg, Oscar Lewis, Richard W. Patch, and Charles W. Wagley (1961).

FOREIGN POLICY: THE NEXT PHASE: The 1960s (Revised Edition), by Thomas K. Finletter (1960).

DEFENSE OF THE MIDDLE EAST: Problems of American Policy (Revised Edition), by John C. Campbell (1960).

COMMUNIST CHINA AND ASIA: Challenge to American Policy, by A. Doak Barnett (1960).

FRANCE, TROUBLED ALLY: De Gaulle's Heritage and Prospects, by Edgar S. Furniss, Jr. (1960).

THE SCHUMAN PLAN: A Study in Economic Cooperation, 1950–1959, by William Diebold, Jr. (1959).

SOVIET ECONOMIC AID: The New Aid and Trade Policy in Underdeveloped Countries, by Joseph S. Berliner (1958).

NATO AND THE FUTURE OF EUROPE, by Ben T. Moore (1958).

INDIA AND AMERICA: A Study of Their Relations, by Phillips Talbot and S. L. Poplai (1958).

NUCLEAR WEAPONS AND FOREIGN POLICY, by Henry A. Kissinger (1957).

MOSCOW-PEKING AXIS: Strength and Strains, by Howard L. Boorman, Alexander Eckstein, Philip E. Mosley, and Benjamin Schwartz (1957).

RUSSIA AND AMERICA: Dangers and Prospects, by Henry L. Roberts (1956).

## ABOUT THE AUTHOR

Mrs. Miriam Camps is a research fellow working on European-Atlantic affairs for the Royal Institute of International Affairs, in London, and the Council on Foreign Relations, in New York. Born and educated in the United States, she worked for the Department of State on European problems for several years during and after the war. Since 1954 she has lived in England. Her previously published books are *Britain and the European Community, 1955–1963*, and *What Kind of Europe? The Community Since De Gaulle's Veto.*